ANATOLE FRANCE, THE PARISIAN

ANATOLE FRANCE

THE PARISIAN

By

HERBERT LESLIE STEWART
PROFESSOR OF PHILOSOPHY, DALHOUSIE UNIVERSITY

New York
DODD, MEAD & COMPANY
1927

PRINTED IN U. S. A.

MANUFACTURED IN THE UNITED STATES OF AMERICA
BY THE VAIL-BALLOU PRESS, INC., BINGHAMTON, N. Y.

PREFACE

Much light is cast upon the personality of Anatole France in those numerous volumes of memoirs which have been written by his more or less intimate friends. Of these, M. Gsell's book, translated by Mr. Ernest Boyd under the title *Opinions of Anatole France*, is freely cited in the following pages, and I have made like constant use of M. Brousson's *Anatole France en Pantoufles*, translated by Mr. John Pollock. Three other collections of memoirs appeared while my manuscript was passing through the press, but not too late for me to avail myself of much interesting detail published for the first time by M. Corday, M. Le Goff, and Madame Bölöni.

No other foreign writer of recent years has had his works so successfully introduced to the English-speaking world by the medium of translation. Herein is the most significant tribute to one who, as Mr. H. G. Wells has remarked, "wrote for all mankind." Though all translations are at best inadequate, it has seemed to me right in the interests of the general reader to quote for the most part in an English rendering, and I have constantly used the admirable English version executed under the general editorship of the late Frederic Chapman, Mr. J. Lewis May, and Mr. Bernard Miall. It has preserved with wonderful closeness the felicity and charm of the original.

I am indebted to the kindness of several colleagues in Dalhousie University for painstaking care in the revision of my proof-sheets. These have been read by Professors C. L. Bennet, A. K. Griffin, E. W. Nichols, R. W. Scott, and

G. E. Wilson. While for the views expressed I am, of course, solely responsible, I have profited by much suggestive criticism they have offered, and I trust that the margin of sheer error in the text has thus been so far as possible reduced. I have further to thank the *Weekly Review Corporation* and the *Chicago University Press* for leave to reprint here certain paragraphs which had previously appeared in their magazines.

H. L. S.

Dalhousie University,
Halifax, Nova Scotia
May, 1927

CONTENTS

PART I

CHILDHOOD AND YOUTH

CHAPTER I

AN ENIGMATIC PERSONALITY

CHAPTER II

THE CHILD OF PARIS

(*Le Livre de Mon Ami, Pierre Nozière, Le Petit Pierre, La Vie en Fleur*)

CHAPTER III

YOUTHFUL FATALISM

(*Les Noces Corinthiennes, Jocaste, Les Désirs de Jean Servien*)

PART II

THE MIDDLE YEARS (1893–1905)

CHAPTER VI

SATIRIST AND SCEPTIC UNDER THE THIRD REPUBLIC

CHAPTER VII

THE SCEPTIC AS SOCIAL REFORMER

CHAPTER X

CHRISTIANITY OR HUMANISM?

(*Thaïs, Sur la Pierre Blanche, L'Étui de Nacre, Le Puits de Sainte-Claire, L'Ile des Pingouins, La Révolte des Anges*)

CHAPTER XI

CLERICALISM AND CHASTITY

(M. Brousson's *Anatole France en Pantoufles, La Rôtisserie de la Reine Pédauque, Les Opinions de M. Jérôme Coignard, Thaïs, Les Contes de Jacques Tournebroche, Le Lys Rouge, Histoire Comique*)

PART IV

IN THE SHADOW OF THE GREAT WAR

CHAPTER XII

PAMPHLETEERING FOR THE ENTENTE POWERS

(*Sur la Voie Glorieuse*)

CHAPTER XIII

A REVERSION TO TYPE

(Conversations as recorded by M. Gsell—Interview with Mr. Pitts Sanborn—*La Vie en Fleur*)

CHAPTER XIV

ANATOLE FRANCE IN PRIVATE LIFE

CHAPTER XV

ANATOLE FRANCE AND HIS LITERARY KINSMEN

PART I

CHILDHOOD AND YOUTH

CHAPTER I

AN ENIGMATIC PERSONALITY

One that hangs in the balance with all sorts of opinions, whereof not one but stirs him and none sways him; a man guiltier of credulity than he is taken to be, for it is out of his belief of everything that he fully believes nothing.

BISHOP EARLE

Two years ago, the tribute of a world's admiration was paid with singular unanimity to Anatole France. How far that cynical observer of human estimates would have been gratified by the unanimity, we are free to guess. One remembers how he wrote in *Coignard* that it is mediocrity which receives a general honour; that in the success of a commonplace person all the nobodies feel a proud joy of kinship; that even good luck is not envied so long as it is unmerited; while talent really exceptional is sure to rouse a certain dumb hate and "calumnies not loud but deep." [1] In his own judgment, it was his two best books that had been comparative failures, his two worst that were universally praised, and the most insipid of all that had been "crowned." [2] Thus contemptuous of his readers, yet amusing himself with facile conquest when he deigned to seek it, Anatole France spent a literary life of defiant originality, and his popular ovation at the close was its marvellous climax. The vast assemblage that lined the route of his funeral cortège was not unlike the procession which a century and a half before had escorted the

[1] *Les Opinions de M. Jérôme Coignard,* Introduction.

[2] J. J. Brousson: *Anatole France en Pantoufles,* p. 335.

aged Voltaire. If he had been present in the flesh, he might have said, too, with Voltaire, on the day when that admiring throng was stopped by Customs officials at the barrier of Paris: "On my word, gentlemen, I believe there is nothing contraband here except myself."

For two generations Anatole France had been studiously and impartially provocative. He had chosen dangerous subjects, writing about government and religion and social morals with a deliberate purpose to exasperate. Yet in that strange tumult of acclaim in November, 1924, one heard the voices of royalist and republican, radical and reactionary, enthusiast for the Treaty of Versailles and enthusiast for the Third International, prophet of the superstate and sentimentalist of the small nationality. The reason is, perhaps, not far to seek. Out of some volume in the vast series of his works almost every kind of zealot can borrow a suggestive text or a moving appeal. Preachers have delivered memorial sermons, rich with telling quotation, to demonstrate his "unconscious Christianity"; freethinkers, with quotation yet more copious, have extolled his fearless atheism. Most of all have his works proved a treasury for another class different from either of these,—that familiar group to whom all opinions are tolerable except such as are suffused with zeal, and who can appropriate in myriad forms the very epigram they have long needed but somehow could never coin. What oft was thought, by men of the most diverse types, but ne'er so well expressed,—this is what every kind of seeker can find there, to suit every kind of taste.

Anatole France espoused different causes in turn, making himself the champion of each at the moment when it was especially in disgrace. Perhaps it was just because he thus courted a combination of perils that he so wonderfully escaped them all, for he could usually thank his adverse critics for answering one another's criticisms. Men of various schools forgave him for castigating themselves, just because—with an effectiveness so much more piercing than their own—he castigated others whom they disliked more than they disliked him. There was at least general agreement that in his death the greatest contemporary man of letters had passed away. And herein lies a problem—the problem of determining precedence among great contemporary men of letters. It cannot be fully discussed until we have escaped alike from the indiscriminate superlatives of the biographer and the kindly restraint of the writer of obituaries.

A number of admirers have written his *Life*, as well as could be expected from men suffering under a severe visitation of what Macaulay has called *lues Boswelliana*.[3] The apparently ceaseless need for panegyric, together with the circumstance that in our dull English language the stock of adulatory adjectives, while quite considerable, is by no means inexhaustible, has affected the biographer's pen almost as a stammer affects one's speech. Anatole France must have lived for some eighty years an actual life in the flesh, whose story we should wish to have presented, besides that life of the spirit which his biographers have described mainly in epithets of profuse compliment. To discover the stages and events of this career, we have to disregard those innumerable asides in which the narrator stops his story to re-stimulate admiration and abash once again those who would depreciate. Such pauses and readjustments of interest are both provoking to the reader and injurious to the record.

One can picture the shade of Anatole France contemplating this miscellaneous homage—as Gibbon said clergymen might contemplate a copy of the *Articles*—with a sigh or a smile. Yet it was in the nature of things that an incon-

[3] Essay on William Pitt.

sistent genius should be rewarded with an inconsistent recognition. That he was a man of many and various moods, the most dexterous re-interpreter will struggle in vain to disprove. He denounced war in language that would have appealed to Tolstoy, and applauded it in terms that Clausewitz might have thought extreme. In the spirit of an aristocrat and an artist, he found the French Revolution too vulgar for sympathy, but the Russian Revolution not too violent for praise. His admirers remind us that he was a silver-tongued apostle of the movement for university extension among the masses; how he idealized the school as the great hope for mankind, admonished the teacher in glowing rhapsody about the responsibilities of his great calling, and bade his audience look ever forward *vers les temps meilleurs*. But his admirers conveniently forget how he likewise declared that only on the firm basis of an undisturbed stupidity can the happiness of most people repose, that the great safeguard of goodwill is an attitude of mutual contempt, that "Pecus" is fed fat with ancient lies and can progress in no other sense than that of contriving some novel deformity in the traditions he imitates, that human nature is unchangeably jealous, sensual and cruel, that growth in knowledge can yield only an ever clearer recognition of this world of ours for "the drop of mud that it is", that man is predestined for ever to illusion, and that on the whole it is best to keep such long-worn illusions as have lost their sparkle.

If it be objected that most of these are mere explosions of pessimism on the part of some character in a Francian novel, one must point out that they are often the views of those with whom the author so fully identified himself as to reprint their aphoristic wit as his own considered judgments. That the writer of *Le Lys Rouge* or *La Rôtisserie de la*

Reine Pédauque should have reproved Zola for the impropriety of his works, is enough to make one wonder whether Mr. Bernard Shaw may not yet deplore the satiric note which has somehow corrupted the English drama. That the satirist of *L'Ile des Pingouins* or *La Révolte des Anges* should have thrilled French soldiers with a trumpet call to the defence of church, cathedral and village belfry, may well cause an amazement like that of those who once asked "What is this that has come to the son of Kish? Is Saul also among the prophets?" Let any passage be produced in which Anatole France has advocated some project as worthy and practicable; it will not be hard to match it with some other passage in which he has mocked a like project as either base or visionary.

He would have regarded it as sheer waste of time to attempt a reconciliation of his different opinions. Whether he had opinions at all, is a matter about which there may be quite reasonable doubt. To an importunate admirer telling him that the English were wondering at the apparent decisiveness of his mind in old age, he replied that such people should open again their *Don Quixote*.[4] One can understand the zest with which he drew the figure of the philosopher in *Thaïs*, who was by no means a denier of "appearances", just because it was in appearances alone that he really believed [5]—and appearances at least are contradictory. Here one recognizes a central element in the charm of Anatole France. He appeals to the mood of disillusionment, of intellectual weariness, and in these days—when so many are disillusioned—he strikes the one chord that is still not too exhausted to vibrate.

[4] J. L. May: *Anatole France, the Man and his Work,* p. 248.

[5] *Thaïs,* p. 36.

Such mood belongs to an old civilization, and Anatole France was first and foremost a child of Paris. If he cultivated "the international mind", he cultivated this as an exotic, for it was his immediate surroundings which not only constituted his material but in great measure formed his temperament. So enthusiastic a devotee of the creed of Hippolyte Taine could scarcely have quarrelled with such an initial assumption about himself. And if I have not wholly failed to understand the tenor of Anatole France's own writings, this is the critical spirit and method which he would have bidden an interpreter to adopt.

CHAPTER II

THE CHILD OF PARIS

The Revolution swept away all this, and new Paris has sprung to life out of the Revolution, like Athene from the head of the Thunderer. Out of extreme confusion, symmetry; out of ancient privilege, absolute democracy; out of paralysis of rival authorities, intense concentration of authority; out of squalor, splendour; out of barbarism, the latest devices of civilization. Yet, for all these changes, Paris is not Chicago or Washington; it is no fine city built on an open plain. Her nineteen hundred years of history are still there; the gay boulevards stand on the foundation-stone of a thousand structures of the past; the placards on each omnibus recall the names of mighty centres of faith, wisdom, devotion, purity, love.

FREDERIC HARRISON

For the early life of Anatole France, our source of knowledge is in four reminiscent volumes written by himself. When he was forty years old, and remembering—as he humorously suggests—the precedent of Dante, he decided that he too would give the world an account of his spiritual past, *nel mezzo del cammin di nostra vita.* Whether he then resembled Dante in any respect other than that of his age, must be left to the reader of *Le Livre de Mon Ami* to determine.[1] Fourteen years afterwards he resumed the thread of autobiographic narrative in the little volume called *Pierre Nozière*, and ten years later still in *Le Petit Pierre.* In 1922 he completed all that he desired to say about himself in the fourth of the series, *La Vie en Fleur.* But apparently fol-

[1] It is of some interest to recall how Goethe too, in *Dichtung und Wahrheit,* fixed the age of forty as a suitable time for autobiographic work.

lowing Renan, whose example ever haunted him and so often prescribed his method, he limited his account to recollections of childhood and youth. For later events and further spiritual evolution we must depend upon his novels, his speeches, and his pamphlets.

We are fortunate in having such autobiographic records, not so much perhaps because of their authoritativeness for the stages of his mental growth, as because they are composed with such literary charm, and express directly so many opinions at which we should otherwise have to guess from the indirect evidence of novels. The autobiography, with all its apparent value for first-hand knowledge, is subject to perils of its own. When Richter said that he knew more about his own life than any other man could possibly know of it, one had to accept the statement with important qualifications. Especially the autobiographer who writes in old age, if he has had a significant life at all, has changed far more than he is aware, and it is natural that he should attempt to show a symmetry which did not exist. He may be quite sincere when he disbelieves in many a change of himself which others—not concerned to prove him consistent—can see perfectly well. He is less sincere, but very human, when he takes care not to acknowledge in print even those personal changes that he may at least suspect. What a reflective old man discerns in his own youth has been fitly described as just the shadow of his subsequent self cast upon the coloured and distorting mists of memory.[2] Thus the real sequence is easily misrepresented because it is first misunderstood. Anatole France was well aware of the risks he ran. "Memories of divers times", he said, "have a habit of changing places in the mind, of dissolving into one another and

[2] Leslie Stephen: *Hours in a Library,* p. 237.

forming themselves into a single picture. That is what I am afraid of in these tales of mine, which if they have not the merit of truthfulness have no merit at all."[3] But, observing such precautions as are here indicated, it is to the four volumes of his autobiography that we must in the first instance turn.

Always and everywhere he was mindful of what he owed in temperamental direction to the place of his birth and the scenes amid which he had grown up. No man, he once remarked, can have a wholly commonplace habit of mind if he has spent his early years on the quays of Paris, opposite the Louvre and the Tuileries, looking out upon the glorious Seine as it runs amid the belfries, towers and spires of the historic city.[4] It was there that he studied and played as a boy during the first years of Napoleon III. Compared with the Paris of to-day, the city of that time would seem not much more than a country town upon which the manifold and often doubtful blessings of steam and machinery had yet to be bestowed. Changes of this sort were then just in sight. The frightful influx of population from the rural districts was indeed already in full tide, though its menace was still but faintly conjectured. Baron Haussmann, with his zeal for hygiene and town-planning, was as yet little recognized as either a reformer or a destroyer. "The vulgar rattle of the tramcar had not yet ruffled the majesty of the quays."[5] Not yet had sentimental Parisians begun to borrow the rhetoric of Ruskin or William Morris, asking whether the symmetrical and obtrusive cleanliness of a new city is worth all the price that must be paid in sacrifice of

[3] *Le Petit Pierre,* chap. xvi.
[4] *Le Livre de Mon Ami,* chap. vi.
[5] *La Vie en Fleur,* chap. xvii.

the begrimed but touching memorials of a remote past. Still unprofaned by the hand of the modernizer was many an old tower or church that stood even in the Paris of Gambetta as a symbol of thirteenth or fourteenth century devotion. A *faubourg* was still a *faubourg*, not yet just a street. The countless picturesque alleys had not been so straightened as to make room for business traffic at the expense of shadowy tradition. New boulevards and strategical avenues had yet to obliterate memories more precious than any civic enterprise they could promote.

In this respect the boyhood of Anatole France was spent amid transitions. Three-quarters of a century had elapsed since the downfall of the monarchic *régime*, and the fierce demolition of so many feudal emblems. Much of the oldest Parisian scenery was represented by more or less mutilated remains. The era of "reform", though it had still far to go, was substantially advanced, while the era of "restoration" had not yet begun. It was the sort of period which impresses itself very differently upon different types of mind. One remembers how to the unimaginative radical a city of historic traditions has often borne its message in vain. If Paris was to the revolutionary Anatole France what London was to Charles Lamb, one can mention another lifelong Londoner who cared nothing for the antique suggestiveness of a mouldering capital. Absorbed in the future and reckless of the past, Jeremy Bentham once proposed to drive a public thoroughfare through the site on which Milton's house had stood, and to remove the memorial tablet which had been set there by unscientific piety. But Anatole France was of another temperament. That wonderful blend of the new and the old which constitutes the very soul of Paris was so faithfully mirrored in his mind that his historic sense was ever standing in the way of his eager radicalism. Like the late

Mr. Frederic Harrison, he loved to escape from the roar of the boulevards and "the modern screen of Haussmannic Paris" [6] to those spots upon which the spirit of bygone centuries still seemed to hover. He would turn away from the triumphs of contemporary engineering and architecture, to seek out in a back street above the Sorbonne that old inn where Rousseau first met his wife, to stand by the tomb of Richelieu or retrace the familiar haunts of Pascal, to examine some Gothic arch which the fury of a reformer had somehow been prevented from destroying, or to look wistfully down some old lane in which he could still recognize the very features as Boileau or even as Dante had observed them.

Childhood and youth are not very sensitive to such ancient remains. In this respect these reminiscent volumes tell us more of what the writer afterwards became than of what he is at all likely to have been at the period described. There is indeed no doubt about the Parisian enthusiasms of the later Anatole France. On such spots the vehemence of the satirist was hushed in the brooding calm of the historian and the poet. A note of pessimism was there too. Thinking of the Present as arid and restless, while the Future was hidden from sight, the Past he once declared is "our only Pleasaunce", wherein are stored the richness, the splendour and the grace of the world.[7] The same imagination that has placed such unforgettable figures upon the canvas of his creative work would never allow him to forget the history of those winding corridors and stately buildings and romantic vistas amid which he moved—Notre Dame and the Madeleine, the Palais Mazarin and the Palais Bourbon, the banks of the Seine and the Garden of the Tuileries—places of

[6] F. Harrison: *The Meaning of History,* p. 375.

[7] *La Vie en Fleur,* chap. iii.

which he has said that the very stones are still eloquent of glorious adventure by the human spirit. In truth, for a mind of such quality, there can be few sights better fitted to stir the imagination than the ancient landmarks of the city of Paris. One can fancy Anatole France passing in turn from the Conciergerie, where the Cordelier Club was roused by the clarion call of Danton, to the dingy structure—now a hospital—which two and a half centuries ago sheltered the persecuted Jansenists; from the gilt statue of the Grand Monarque to the house where Coligny was murdered in the St. Bartholemew; from the cenotaph of Voltaire to the scene of illicit love between Abelard and Héloïse; or exploring with pagan joy the remains of Roman baths, aqueducts and cemeteries that carry one back to the Paris of Julian, Clovis and Hugh Capet.

* * *

He was born in 1844, when the tempest which surrounded the last years of Louis Philippe was just gathering force. It was the time when the adroitness of Guizot was being driven to more and more desperate expedients. Before long the "political banquet" was to resound with protests against oligarchic rule, and the conception of the *pays légal* was to become harder and harder to maintain against an ominous demand for universal suffrage. Anatole France must have been too young to understand anything of that strange drama through which the Orleanist monarchy was passing first into the Second Republic and next into the Second Empire. But as a child he would hear much gossip, for his father—an old guardsman of Charles X—was of that notoriously gossiping class, the bookseller who reads his own books. In those days of political convulsion, it was a reflective and reminiscent group that used to meet of an afternoon

[8] Cf. *La Vie Littéraire,* I, p. 218.

in that little *librairie* on the Quai Voltaire.[8] Anatole France never lost his memories of it, and it was clearly the original of many a scene he has described in his novels.

It was a rendezvous, as bookstores have so often been for the politically-minded,—like Allan Ramsay's shop in Edinburgh, for instance, which a hundred years earlier had been such a haunt of Jacobites awaiting news of Bonnie Prince Charlie in the Forty-Five. There too men would talk of their favourite pretenders. Many a Legitimist might have been heard, and many an Orleanist, but they weighed their words, for under the *régime* of the Second Empire the very walls had ears. One can imagine a good deal of the desultory conversation. Much would be said about current events in Parisian literature and life, about Victor Hugo's latest tirade against Napoléon le Petit, about Lamartine's *Restoration of Monarchy in France,* about the prosecution of Flaubert for his "immoral" novels, about the moving eloquence of Lacordaire last Sunday in the pulpit of Notre Dame, about the Socialist escapades of Pierre Proudhon, about Renan's tireless campaign for Freethought in the *Revue des Deux Mondes,* perhaps about the new religion recently invented for mankind, whose canonical scriptures were even then in process of composition by the pen of Auguste Comte.

Those were days when old generals and old soldiers of the first Napoleon might still be heard quarrelling with one another about great military events in which they had borne a part long, long ago.[9] But as Anatole France reached early manhood, such memories were growing faint and dim. By birth quite outside the higher social circles, he was once a guest at a "very exclusive salon" of the Faubourg St. Germain, to which through clerical influence a youth of the pro-

[9] *La Vie en Fleur,* chap. v.

letariat was sometimes admitted on the chance that "another Veuillot" might be found. There he met former peers of France, ex-deputies of the National Assembly, *grands seigneurs* of a bygone time—with those graciously condescending manners which belong to the champion of a lost cause. He never forgot how on that particular afternoon one old gentleman inveighed so vehemently against Jacobins and Bonapartists that he spilled his tea into his hat! [10] On the whole, those high-descended folk impressed him much with the distinction of the old *noblesse*. For the most part, however, his own social opportunities were limited to the bourgeois family where the hostess welcomed any young man who could dance, where the ostentation of wealth was in unfavourable contrast with the simple ways of the Faubourg St. Germain, and where the women obviously competed to imitate the dress and deportment of the Empress Eugénie. There were many Jews and Jewesses at such gatherings. It remained for the Third Republic to develop the rage of anti-Semitism.

* * *

He went to school at the Collège Stanislas, the place where Ernest Renan ten years before had found temporary employment when he abandoned the seminary, until he had to leave it because all masters were required to wear the soutane. It was a Jesuit institution, and the boy there had his first taste of Greek and Latin. If we may trust his own memoirs, he quickly saw that classical literature had depths of meaning which those Jesuit minds were unfit either to unfold or to understand.

In those old Imperial days the French aristocracy resorted to such schools as the Stanislas, whose moral tone was

[10] *ibid.,* chap. xxv.

known to be of the very highest. It was too expensive an institution for the poor, and the sons of professional men were kept distinctly in that place to which it had pleased Providence to call them. The annual list of school honours, for example, bore witness to a remarkable coincidence between God's distribution of talent and the State's assignment of rank. Anatole France was generally sure of returning home from a "Prize Day" with no trophies except the prize-list and a copy of the printed speech delivered by some eloquent visitor. He used to point out to his friends how the names of leaders of the school from year to year constituted a regular book of armorial families.[11] He remembered, too, the conventional speech of the orator on such an occasion, with its inevitable parallel and contrast between Corneille and Racine, its exhortation to model citizenship, its closing passage about the legitimacy of holidays based on the divine example of rest on the Seventh Day, and its advice that the bright summer should be used in contact with natural beauties, while a time of dull or stormy skies might be improved in studious company with Pascal or Massillon.[12] After such painful experience in the Great Hall, young Anatole had always to expect that his teachers would pay a visit at his parents' house, to discourage them by emphasizing how slow he was in his studies, how it was obvious that he would never justify much expenditure on his education, and how it would be best to apprentice him quickly to some trade. It was arranged that he should take lunch each day at the school, where a devotional book—such as Rollin's *Lives of the Saints*—was read aloud as the meal proceeded.

How far this account, which he gave long afterwards to

[11] J. J. Brousson: *Anatole France en Pantoufles*, p. 177.
[12] *ibid.*, p. 180.

M. Brousson, is quite fair to the authorities of the Collège Stanislas, may be open to doubt. It was but natural that he should revenge himself for his childhood's disappointments by recounting the names of those who had outshone him at school, but had won no fame in the conflicts of the wider world. His scorn for the competitive system in education, like nearly every other youthful trait he records, has thrown biographers into a transport of delight. But we may doubt whether it was sheer favouritism on the part of his examiners that kept him in the background. G. H. Lewes once drew an admirable distinction between the receptive intellect that is talented and the productive intellect that is genius.[13] Unfortunately, it is the receptive sort alone which school tests can appraise, but the appraisal is worth making. At all events, this case is as futile as many others constantly quoted to commend the view that boys rather dull at school are for that reason more likely to succeed afterwards. It is a doctrine naturally popular with parents of dull children, and invariably proclaimed—in defiance of statistics—by some genial visitor on Speech Day. The exceptional instances which seem to favour it are about as significant as those lucky escapes of a daring speed-maniac on the roads to prove that other aphorism: "It is generally the careful motorist who has accidents."

But although young Anatole was negligent of prescribed studies, his mind was not inactive. He knew that good literature was no monopoly of writers on his school course, that some notable fiction was being produced, for example, by Jules Sandeau, whom he used to meet many a day on the quays and contemplate with a boy's wonder at a magician of

13 G. H. Lewes: *Life of Goethe,* I, ii.

the pen. Many an hour of illicit delight was spent in the Greek classroom over the pages of *Marianna*, cunningly interposed between the leaves of a Greek lexicon, while his teacher was expounding Thucydides or showing the intricacies of the verbs in μι.[14] He had his own love, too, for the classical texts he read. His parsing might be poor, and he might be weak in the mystery of the particles; yet as he made his way through some passage of Livy about Roman soldiers in retreat, he would imagine he saw them—as he saw Sandeau's Madame Belnave—those broken legions "passing silently in the moonlight, over the naked plain and the long road flanked with tombs, foul with blood and dust, battered helmets, wrenched and tarnished breast-plates, shattered swords." [15] He would stumble over many an unfamiliar word, make very objectionable use of optatives and subjunctives, or get hopelessly mixed about aorists and gerunds; but as he read Vergil or Homer, there would rise before him in imagination the plaintive Dido or the palm-tree of Delos, and for six months together he was far from the Quai Voltaire—journeying with Odysseus on the wine-dark sea. When he reached the tragic poets, bending over a torn Teubner text and an ink-bespattered desk, his thought might commit many a grammatical blunder about relative clauses, and his scansion of iambics might be dreadful, but he had the picture of Alcestis and Antigone; could "see divine figures, arms of ivory drooping over white tunics, and hear voices sweeter than the sweetest music, lamenting in harmony." [16] We cannot do without our prosaic grammarians. But one feels how true may have been Anatole France's judgment

[14] *La Vie Littéraire,* I, p. 21.

[15] *Le Livre de Mon Ami,* chap. ix.

[16] *ibid.,* chap. x.

that when escape had been effected from the teachers who tried to explain, there was nothing to mar or obscure for him the charm of ancient poets any more.[17]

* * *

One experience of childhood left a terrific impression upon his mind. His father had been induced to invest some savings in a project for exploiting mineral springs in the Hautes-Pyrénées. As in so many other cases that we know, the inducement was offered by a promoter "with a voice like a silver flute."

What, exactly, the company was to do, how far the old bookseller had accepted responsibility for its fortunes, or what happened to the whole business, Anatole France never understood, and he disclaimed the task of describing the thing as one fit for Balzac but not for him. What he did remember was that the Saint Firmin Mineral Water Company came to grief, and that he often heard his mother speak bitterly about the association of an evil heart with a flute-like voice. He remembered in particular how lawyers had finished what the promoter began. Whoever else might lose, they at least had to be paid.[18] As a child, he grieved over the pawning of his mother's little bits of jewellery, odds and ends of family plate, a massive soup-ladle, a sugar-basin with swan handles, the coffee-pot with his grandfather's crest. Last of all, because there was nothing else left to be sacrificed, a little farm near Chartres had to come under the auctioneer's hammer. Anatole France watched, as Ibsen at eight years old had watched a like scene, and acquired, like Ibsen, what Thackeray has called "the dismal precocity of poverty." [19] To the end he could forgive all others who

17 *La Vie en Fleur,* chap. xxiii.

18 *Le Petit Pierre,* chap. xx.

19 *Vanity Fair,* Book II.

had shared in the business, but not the lawyers, and upon them as a class, when he was approaching eighty years of age, he still poured the vials of his wrath. These, he said, constitute the one race of men who amid all the changes of the world remain true to type. As Rabelais had portrayed them, so they are to-day—the same to their beak and claws, and even to their unintelligible jargon. When he went back to school, out of the wreckage of his family, and his teacher told him about the Harpies in Vergil, who snatched meat from tables and defiled the food and spread around a loathsome stench, he felt that he knew those Harpies as his more fortunate fellow-pupils could not know them. Throughout later life he used to reflect how that cave in the *Æneid* must have been a wholesome and pleasant place compared with the offices and green-cardboard files of a man of law. This feeling, he conjectured, may have been the reason why he could never endure to have any files or filing cases about him, and why in consequence he used to mislay his own manuscripts.[20]

It is a very human picture. Dickens would have revelled in it.

* * *

Anatole France's boyhood in Paris may be likened to the life of an Italian boy to-day in the Rome of Mussolini. Louis Bonaparte had won his place as the champion of order in a city wearied of Revolutions. In the Paris of 1848, not less than in the Florence of 1919, were to be seen the unmistakable portents of a Red Terror. Just as the proletariat of Italian cities seven years ago was inflamed by the speeches of Lenin and Trotsky, the Paris workman of the "Year of Revolutions" had been fed daily on reprints of the wisdom

20 *Le Petit Pierre,* chap. xx.

that had flowed half a century earlier from the lips of Robespierre and Marat. And though the workman of the capital might feel, as before, the intoxication of this, it seemed very different to the French peasant and to the French capitalist even on a small scale. They felt that escape from Orleanism had been bought dear. So in terror of worse things, the office of President was conferred on Louis Bonaparte by a popular majority of over four million votes. Men of every political colour save "Red" flocked to the polls for another Napoleon who would at least be less dangerous than another group of *Sansculottes*.

Like Mussolini, he had himself dabbled in Revolutions. He was well and favourably known in those obscure committee rooms of many a European centre where men, admitted by a password, were hatching behind closed doors some project of "liberty." Like Mussolini too, he had combined such zeal for the poor with a profession of intense national patriotism. Conjuring with his uncle's name, he would set forth his plans for the regeneration of France under the title *Idées Napoléoniennes*, just as his Italian counterpart traces his own spiritual descent to Julius Caesar, whose *Life* Louis Napoleon so enthusiastically wrote. To both alike the ways of mere Liberalism were anathema, as feeble in the cause of the proletariat as they were disloyal to the cause of the country. Neither was, like Macbeth, "too full o' the milk of human kindness to catch the nearest way." To each it seemed not short of providential that the country's need for a resolute commander was just the need he knew how to supply. No one can miss the true Mussolini touch on noticing how the Emperor dwelt alternately on the two great subjects, *extinction du paupérisme* and *gloire*. The Socialist editor in Florence evolved into the leader of Fascismo. The alien co-conspirator of the Carbonari graduated through the preliminary stage of special constable in London against the Chartists into the office of Prince President to suppress the disorders of French Communism. "I am here", wrote Louis Bonaparte, "to put an end to Revolutions."

He was at work, very openly and very alarmingly, putting an end to them and to all that might lead to them, in the Paris of Anatole France's schoolboy years. Leading agitators were exiled; the common sort of dangerous people were crowded into prison, so that half the military barracks in the country had to serve as receptacles for the overflow from ordinary jails. Ten thousand suspects were shipped to Algeria. But in truth the judgments passed were almost wholly on suspicion, for the tiresome process of trial by the courts was given up. A commission, consisting of one general, one lawyer, and one official, disposed of such matters summarily. Again it was a scene to make Mussolini's heart rejoice.

Constitution-making was next on the order of business, and Rouher, the *fidus Achates* of the Dictator, got through that job single-handed in twenty-four hours. The new Constitution, not passed but "proclaimed", provided for a presidency which should last for ten years. There was to be a Chamber of Deputies, occupying itself with the concerns of a futile debating society, powerless to initiate legislation or to remove ministers, but invited to suggest amendments to such decrees as might be sent down to it. The amendments were subject to acceptance, change, or rejection by the autocrat in a *Conseil d'État* of his personal nominees. Ministers, so-called, were to have no relations with anyone, except the President to whom they owed their appointment. The speeches of deputies were not to be reported in any organ of the press, but an official "Minute" would be supplied. Of republican opposition in the Chamber there was but a group of five persons, and *les cinq* in a House of over two hundred might as well have held their peace even if the House itself had wielded real power. Anatole France was a boy of fourteen when Orsini threw his bomb in vain, and this was followed by an immediate tightening of the repressive machinery.

The ex-pamphleteer for freedom and for the cure of unemployment had not scrupled to dissolve the trade-unions and to subject all newspapers to a rigorous censorship, passing through various stages from "warning" to "suppression." With a gesture of defiance, the time-honoured inscription *Liberté, Égalité, Fraternité* was officially erased from all public buildings. It was announced that offending newspapers would be prosecuted before a tribunal that had no jury, and that no report would be given of the trial, the decision only being intimated,—and the sentence. In picturesque imagery the President set forth how he reconciled such measures with the democratic ideal he had so often advocated, and had found in those sacred scriptures written by the martyr in exile. Not from the isle that is called Patmos, but from the isle that is called St. Helena, had come the charter of the new world-redemption. Its keynote was universal suffrage, instead of the *pays légal* of the Orleanists, and had not the President been thus duly elected? But he had been elected to *rule*, to give direction, not to seek it. "My desire", he said, "is to be baptized in the waters of universal suffrage, but by that I do not understand that from those waters my feet shall never be withdrawn." It was clear enough.

The *régime* was accepted, not with reluctance, but rather with delight. Paris had ceased to care for parliaments, and the material prosperity of those Napoleonic years soon stifled almost every lingering protest of discontent. Here and there, in a drawing-room of very elderly people, there was a whisper about the Comte de Chambord; here and there some survivor of the court of Louis Philippe spoke regretfully about the Comte de Paris. But the Legitimists hated the Orleanists far more than they hated Bonapartism, and of the Orleanists themselves a large majority had hastened to pay worship and celebrate ritual before the rising sun. Such as cherished genuine republican sentiments used to speak in apocalyptic figure, not against Napoleon, but against "Tiberius" or "Caligula", in veiled phrase like that of the author of the Book of Revelation when he wrote in the days of Nero about "the Beast", feeling sure that his readers would understand. After the disordered years of provisional government there was satisfaction in a rule that was at least effective. And though at first all hope of effectiveness lay in the prestige of Napoleon's name, it was soon found that his personal vigour had been under-rated.

For the upper ranks, too, there was a glow and a sparkle about the revived splendour of the Tuileries, the restoration of titles of nobility, the sight of the Imperial Eagles glittering once again. It seemed good to be done with the dowdiness of the court of Louis Philippe,—that strange compromise between king and democrat, the puritanic but ungainly figure that even the cunning of a Guizot could never popularize with those Parisians who had cried out against Louis XVIII: "We want a king that can ride." The July monarch had turned out a sorry horseman, unable to keep his cocked hat in its place, as he rode through the streets stooping down—like a ward politician—to shake hands with "citizens." Heinrich Heine had watched him one memorable day at this exercise, and had thought how different had been the figure of Napoleon I, "with his statuesque, Caesar-like countenance, his fixed gaze, and his unapproachable ruler's hands." Young Anatole France must have been quick to appreciate Thiers's jest that the prayer of the Citizen-King was "Give us this day our daily platitude", and the withering phrase of the Prince President: *dix ans de mensonge, d'usurpation et d'ignominie.* Whatever else the defects of Louis Napoleon, his horsemanship was perfect, and Parisians loved a spectacular king.

Merchants, too, found it hard to be disloyal to a sovereign under whom trade had so notably revived, especially the trade in articles of luxury, whilst in the workmen there was such enthusiasm as always attends a government that keeps the factories running on full time. Vast schemes of public building promised continuous employment. Of course there were more or less inarticulate growls on the spot, and shrill notes from exiles abroad. Away in Jersey the voice of Victor Hugo kept up its fruitless plaint, and the literary men in general were peevish. Prosper Mérimée had been won over, and Sainte-Beuve was unblushingly Bonapartist, but the other men of letters spoke out as strongly as they dared,—which was by no means strong.

On the whole, too, there was comparatively little corruption. It remained for the Third Republic to have a Panama scandal, with two hundred deputies steeped in financial disgrace. Louis Napoleon, like Mussolini, restored confidence. The Paris of Anatole France's boyhood was one in which the slovenliness of the past was disappearing under the touch of builders, roadmakers, tram companies and electricians. No doubt it was an accident that the new Bonapartism coincided in time with the developments of mechanical power, but it was no accident that the Prince showed a will and a talent for turning scientific discovery to the national advantage. He delighted to call his government *paternel;* and if he interfered by official "nomination" with the free choice of electors, he took care to nominate men of business capacity rather than men dexterous in political intrigue. Sentimentalists might mourn over the reshaping of narrow and crooked lanes with many a memory attached to them, and over the demolition of picturesque but unsanitary houses to make way for the spacious boulevard and the more modern dwelling. It was suspected, too, that all this blasting and plumbing and new masonry in the Faubourg St. Antoine was intended less to make life more wholesome than to make riots and barricade fighting more difficult. The suspicion was probably well grounded, for it is only an old and practised revolutionary who knows how to defeat the revolutionaries yet to come. But whatever its motive, the effect of the policy of Napoleon III was to promote municipal progress. His name has been covered with obloquy by doctrinaire republicans like Hugo and Swinburne, who could bring home to him things that were personally disgraceful. After Sedan he had the fate of all despots who have lost,—the fate indicated by Bismarck when he said that if the Franco-Prussian War had ended in the opposite way he would himself have been pelted with dish-clouts by the women of Berlin. But it is for the later historian to rise above the vindictive reproaches of Daudet and of Erckmann-Chatrian, no less than to discount the hysteria of *Les Châtiments.* It is to the judgment of a late posterity that Louis Napoleon, like Mussolini, must appeal.[21]

For at least ten years, too, there was the intoxicating atmosphere of *gloire.* At Alma and Sebastopol the sons of

21 Since this paragraph was written, I have noticed that Mr. Lloyd George in a press article has emphasized the same similitude. And such a critic is in a position to judge.

Frenchmen who had fallen on the retreat from Moscow felt the thrill of a great *revanche*, and though they had comrades —both British and Turkish—they knew, or thought they knew, that once more it was French arms and French skill which had been decisive. On the fields of Magenta and Solferino the traditions of Jena and Austerlitz had been prolonged and expanded. Nor had the glories of land and sea been limited to Central Europe and the nearer fringe of Asia. To the sound of the old Imperial anthem, *Partant pour la Syrie*, the pioneers of French civilization had hewn their way through disorderly Eastern tribesmen. In far distant China—never reached, as they proudly reminded themselves, even by Julius Caesar at the height of his power—they had stormed the Taku Forts, leading their docile British allies to the capture of Peking. And if the enterprise of founding a new Latin empire in Mexico had turned out less successful than for a few exultant months seemed likely, it had at all events been in the old Napoleonic spirit, and the great days of half a century before seemed to have come back. In the sphere of European diplomacy at least, the nephew was playing again the uncle's part, for no other voice was comparable to his in the re-defining of territories, pulling down the lofty from their seats, and exalting those who, if not humble and meek, were at all events forced to wait upon his nod. By him an exiled pope had been restored to the Eternal City, and by him the same pope had been awed into submission whilst his patrimony was divided among his rivals.

What matter, then, if from the old shopkeeping nation there was many a murmur of impotent protest,—a Queen writing indignant letters, or a Foreign Secretary venturing more or less indiscreet complaints to a haughty Ambassador? It but added to the French pride to know that the enraged satirist of a disappointed people should find vent in such lines as these:

O Death, a little more, and then the worm;
  A little longer, O Death, a little yet,
  Before the grave gape and the grave-worm fret;
Before the sanguine-spotted hand infirm
Be rottenness, and that foul brain—the germ
  Of all ill things and thoughts—be stopped and set.[22]

Such bards had sung just so in the old days of Napoleon I. Had not English caricaturists depicted the great Emperor being pitchforked by devils into a burning lake, and haunted by the ghost of the Duc d'Enghien? Such had been the fortune of all those who had changed the world. Let the spiteful and the jealous shriek as they would. It was enough for Paris to know that after a melancholy interlude of Bourbons or Orleanists the note of *gloire* had returned.

For a people so traditionally imperialistic, such thoughts mounted to the brain. Young Anatole France was not of military age while all this whirl of conquest was proceeding. But his mother used to reflect with alarm how near he was to a time at which he might be made a conscript, and she used to talk in tones of subdued anxiety with a friend of the household named Dubois.[23] They would discuss together how wars are contrived for the personal purposes of one man

[22] A. C. Swinburne: *A Saviour of Society.* These savage lines were written in Paris in the year before the outbreak of the Franco-Prussian War. Contrast Walter Bagehot's very different estimate of Napoleon III: "He has one excellent advantage over other French statesmen; he has never been a professor, nor a journalist, nor a promising barrister, nor by taste a *littérateur*. He has not confused himself with history. He does not think in leading articles, in long speeches, or in agreeable essays. But he is capable of observing facts rightly, of reflecting on them simply, and acting on them discreetly." (*Letters on the French coup d'état.*) But much had happened between 1851 and 1869.

[23] *Le Petit Pierre,* chap. xxiii.

or of a few men, how financiers and munition-makers are very careless of the human sacrifice, how there is a fatal facility in playing upon patriotism and national spirit, how at the beating of a drum or the waving of a flag the masses will move even with enthusiasm to slaughter and death. But there was a feminine vanity mingling with a mother's solicitude. She liked to think of French bayonets bringing "freedom" to the world, and rather encouraged young Anatole's godfather when he spoke of the glorious fate of one who dies for "his country."

One element in this pious lady's thoughts was the remembrance that Napoleon III had at least revived the tradition of the "Most Christian" kings. Under his rule there was a transformation in the attitude of the French government to the ancient Church. The Voltaireans had been dominant at court in the days of Louis Philippe; but Louis Napoleon was of a different mind, or at least of a different policy. Those pious parents must have pointed out to their boy how the Pantheon was once more in the right hands, how army chaplains had been reappointed, how Cardinals had official seats in the Senate, how Sunday was proclaimed a day of rest in government dockyards, how a press censorship was enforced against the profane, and how the hated *philosophie* could no longer be taught in schools. They seemed, in some degree, to be living again in the great age of Charles X and Polignac. And the Emperor had memories of a personal kind which, for at least the first half of his reign, kept the alliance sure. Away back in the twenties, as a young exile in Rome, he had often served Mass when the celebrant was one Canon Mastaï-Ferretti—and now that canon was Pope Pius IX. The churchman had once sheltered his Mass-boy, during the 1831 Revolution, from the hot pursuit of Austrian troops; and the Mass-boy in turn, clothed with the purple eighteen years afterwards, had lent French bayonets to bring back the pope to his own again. Napoleon III, with all his faults, had a dash of sentiment and of gratitude. For the first eight years of his reign there was perfect accord between Vatican and Tuileries. During the years that followed, Anatole France's mother—like the Empress Eugénie herself—could but watch with dismay how *la haute politique* was leading in a very different direction.

How the various wars were arranged was doubtless very obscure to those common folk of Paris who were allowed to know little of European affairs beyond the decisions issued by a *Conseil d'État*. That there had been a meeting in a country-house at Plombières between Napoleon and Cavour, at which, before a map of Europe stretched on the table, it had been decided that the King of Piedmont should have Lombardy and Venetia while the French should take Nice and Savoy, and that the necessary quarrels to bring about this shifting of territory had been all planned in advance by two men,—this is matter of later history, and it cannot have been even suspected until long after its outcome was known. But one remembers such things when one reads a passage like this in *Les Opinions de M. Jérôme Coignard:*

> The ministers of good man Demos, unceasingly kicked, hustled, humiliated, thrown down and assailed with more rotten eggs and apples than the worst harlequin in a booth at a fair, will have no leisure to prepare carnage politely, in the secrecy and peace of the Cabinet, on the board of green cloth, at conferences in regard to what is called the balance of Europe, which is but the happy hunting-ground of the diplomat. There will be no more foreign policy, and that will be a great thing for unhappy humanity.

* * *

The devout Catholic household in which he was brought up may well have had still further determining influence upon our author's future. It is known that in the late forties of the last century pious people in Paris had reverted in an extraordinary degree to the very spirit of mediævalism. Mark Pattison was a visitor to the city about the time when Anatole France must have been trundling his hoop at the feet of the statues on the Pont d'Iéna,[24] or taking those daily walks with his nurse and asking those questions recorded in *Le Petit Pierre.* He was amazed by the surroundings in which he found himself. It seemed to him that all critical sense had vanished before the inrush of a renewed credulity. Every reported miracle, every saintly interference with laws of Nature, was at once believed, just because it was miraculous or supernatural. Whatever tended to the Church's glory required no further evidence, and all whose suggestiveness was different met with scornful dismissal as "a fiction of the Voltaireans." [25] This was not just a mark of uneducated Catholics, for it was not with such that Pattison chose to associate. Minds of fine endowment and high training among the Catholic laity seemed to have reopened to all sorts of ecclesiastical myth with a readiness like that of the Channel Islanders in Hugo's *Travailleurs de la Mer.* There was none of Newman's "wise and gentle minimism"; rather a diabetic thirst for the supernatural as such. In such environment young Anatole France was trained. Perhaps its results for him are not hard to discern. We may well accept his statement that a certain unusual disposition to doubt was among his own childhood characteristics.[26] Long afterwards, when he wrote *Les Sept Femmes de Barbe-Bleue*, he remarked that there was so great a desire to make men believe

24 *La Vie Littéraire,* III, p. 37.

25 M. Pattison: *Memoirs,* chap. vi.

26 *Le Petit Pierre,* chap. viii.

in Bluebeard's cruelty as could not fail to make him personally question it.[27]

But his young imagination was well fed with such nourishment as was intended to make him devout. His mother told him countless stories from *The Lives of the Saints*, and his first nursery book was a huge Picture-Bible, with gorgeous illustrations of the sacred narrative. It was about the coloured figures of Abraham and David and Daniel that his inquisitiveness was first aroused, and his dreams by night were of patriarchs, angels, holy men of old. He was, of course, taken regularly to Mass, and as a child he was much distressed because he could not bethink himself of enough sins to acknowledge at Confession.[28] He felt ashamed of such apparent unfitness to fulfil his religious obligations, and even in the manual provided as a help for the inadequately introspective he found it hard to identify his own peculiar case. So he often borrowed from the catalogue of others who, at ten years old, knew how to accuse themselves with greater efficiency. How far this was a fault, I must leave to persons more skilled in the penitential discipline to decide. One notes, however, that as a growing boy Anatole soon began to question the opinions of his royalist and Catholic father. His grandmother appealed to him more than either of his parents, for a reason we can well understand:

> Grandmamma was frivolous. Yes, grandmamma had no more piety in her composition than a bird. You ought to have seen the little quizzical grimace she would make when mother and I were setting out for church.[29]

* * *

[27] *Les Sept Femmes de Barbe-Bleue,* chap. i.

[28] *Le Livre de Mon Ami,* p. 144, sq.

[29] *ibid.,* pp. 84, 85.

There was yet another significant feature of those childhood years. If that was a golden age of superstition, it was likewise a golden age of caricature. In the forties, says Anatole France, the French people had a sense of the ludicrous which they have since lost. In picture, pamphlet, and song, the mocking spirit constantly expressed itself, and he believed he had thus caught up much of this mood when a boy.[30] Cartoons of *Le Charivari* gave him his first notions about national life. As his godfather cracked irreverent jokes about public leaders, it seemed to him that even the riots and Revolutions were predominantly comic. In that circle the nickname for the new Emperor was "the moping parrot." Such family habits are infectious, and upon this particular child the infection worked with power. John Bunyan does not seem to have regarded life more persistently *sub specie aeternitatis* than Anatole France to have regarded it *sub specie ludibrii.* Nor are the superstitious and the mocking spirits wholly incompatible. They were once seen in contemporary effulgence in the Dionysiac Theatre at Athens. And, as a witty Irish writer has reminded us, qualities inconsistent with each other may not be inconsistent with that human nature in which they both reside.

But if such volatility was characteristic of the French people as a whole, it was doubly characteristic of life in the capital. Sensitive to breezes from every quarter, Paris responded like Coleridge's Æolian harp. And in no man was there more of such *Parisianisme* than in Anatole France. *Fluctuat, nec mergitur* is the ancient motto of his city. It might well have been his own.

[30] *Le Petit Pierre,* chap. xi.

CHAPTER III

YOUTHFUL FATALISM

By thy name that in hell-fire was written,
  and burned at the point of thy sword,
Thou art smitten, thou God, thou art smitten;
  thy death is upon thee, O Lord.
And the love-song of earth as thou diest
  resounds through the wind of her wings—
Glory to Man in the highest! for Man is Master of Things.

SWINBURNE

The truth seems to be that a long line of disillusive centuries has permanently displaced the Hellenic idea of life, or whatever it may be called. What the Greeks only suspected, we know well; what their Æschylus imagined, our nursery children feel. That old-fashioned revelling in the general situation grows less and less possible as we uncover the defects of natural laws, and see the quandary that man is in by their operation.

THOMAS HARDY

Anatole France emerged from school with the general impression that he had made a poor figure there. He knew that he must earn his living before long, and his father's unwillingness to suggest a suitable career seemed due to the fact that no special aptitude had yet been shown. So, with a depressed feeling about his future, the lad began to debate with himself the usual possibilities: Law, Medicine, Engineering, the Army, Commerce, even Agriculture. The priesthood alone seems to have been dismissed without a hearing.

He decided against Law, on various grounds. That childhood recollection of a family experience among lawyers was in itself repellent. Moreover, with a judgment surprisingly sagacious for his years, he realized that he had no gift of speech, and that any sort of "eloquence" could never be achieved by him.[1] Those who afterwards listened to Anatole France on a platform know that he made no mistake in this analysis of his powers. Medicine attracted him for a time, but he suspected that his dreamy temperament gave no promise of the precision so indispensable for that kind of work, and his later judgments about science are indeed very far from suggesting the skilled craftsman with either scalpel or microscope. Sometimes he thought he would enjoy the diplomatic service, at least if he had a chance to become an ambassador! With some sort of "government position" vaguely in his mind, he employed a coach who professed to prepare youths for official life, but quickly abandoned this because he saw that recommendations from influential people had more to do with such appointment than any proof of suitability for the duties.[2] A school friend, who must have been something of a humorist, advised him to go back to the land and take up farming! But to this child of the historic city, where "the very stones seemed to sing", there was no lure in the fields. In desperation he seized a directory, examined the various businesses and trades in alphabetical order, but could see no reason why he should select any one of them in preference to the rest. What about his father's bookselling business, or that shadowy occupation called "literature"? Probably among those who advise their sons to take up the literary life a bookseller is not often to be found. He knows too much about the vicissitudes of the trade.

Yet the atmosphere of the *librairie* had wrought its spell.

[1] *La Vie en Fleur,* chap. xv.
[2] *loc. cit.*

As a child, Anatole used to carry copy to the printer, and as a youth he used to correct proofs.[3] But it was not copy or proofs of contemporary writing that interested him first. Whether his Jesuit teachers inspired or obstructed his early love of classical studies, it is certain that the charm of the ancient world fell both quickly and powerfully upon young Anatole France. He became a bibliophile. The true friends of his youth, he says, were the vendors of old books, notably those Jews whose barrows and stalls he used to frequent on the quays of the Seine.[4] His classical teachers in the Collège Stanislas had at least introduced him to ancient texts, and thus all too effectively into that world of Greek and Roman humanism whose influence was ere long to supersede their own. He had little money to spend, but by some old barrow—preferably in the one-franc box—he would toss aside the reprints of Rollin's devotional *History*, collections of religious verse by the younger Racine, or laborious and edifying pamphlets by Victor Hugo, to seek out the great masterpieces that have descended to us from an age as yet unvexed by mediaeval faith or romantic sentimentality. Such enthusiasm for the great pagans remained with him throughout life. When he was forced, an unwilling conscript, to the front in the Franco-Prussian War of 1870, he carried with him a copy of Vergil in his knapsack, for surreptitious reading in such intervals as the German guns on the Marne would permit. More than half a century afterwards, to an English visitor at his country home in Touraine, he would repeat in his garden long passages from the *Æneid* as a quasi-sacred scripture that was the staff of his old age.[5]

But he had a living to earn, and enthusiasm for the

[3] *Vers les Temps Meilleurs,* I, p. 54.
[4] *Le Livre de Mon Ami,* X.
[5] J. L. May: *Anatole France, the Man and his Work,* p. 246.

ancients was not by itself a way of earning this. A chance meeting on the street with Louis de Ronchard solved his immediate and most disagreeable problem. It happened that de Ronchard was going to bring out a series of *Lives of the Painters,* for which he needed some clerical assistance,—someone to read proofs and act as a sort of sub-editor. By what divination of fitness he offered the job to young Anatole France, is a point on which we may speculate at will. But the occasion was remembered as Carlyle remembered that decisive hour on Leith Walk. Within three days the boy—for he was little more—was installed in a room at a big bookseller's in the Faubourg St. Germain, with proofs to revise and a salary to expect. Half a century afterwards, Anatole France could recall how "it was at twenty minutes past four, one Saturday afternoon, that the event came to pass." [6]

I

To a youth of artistic sensitiveness, brought up within a stone's throw of the Louvre, it would have been a joy to be engaged on *Lives of the Painters,* even if there had been no remuneration for the work. But to Anatole France in particular, at this time, it provided a way of escape from some surrounding influences that he intensely disliked. Herein he was the child of his Age. He grew to manhood during a period of literary reaction in his own country. Romanticism, that great parenthesis between the French literature of the eighteenth century and the literature of the later nineteenth, had collapsed in 1848, with a suddenness like that of the downfall of the House of Orleans itself. Remote indeed from the spirit of Chateaubriand's *Le Génie du Christianisme,*

[6] *La Vie en Fleur,* chap. xv.

Lamartine's *Meditations*, or Hugo's *Les Vierges de Verdun* was to be the work of men like Gustave Flaubert, Prosper Mérimée, or Leconte de Lisle. To the poet of Throne and Altar was to succeed Sainte-Beuve, "bishop over the diocese of Freethought."

But in the household of Anatole France's father the neo-pagan poets and the modernist critic had not begun to reign. Apart from Picture-Bible and visiting priest, the oracle of family instruction was the *Works of Chateaubriand.* They were thick strewn through every room, duplicate and triplicate copies of nearly all the viscount ever wrote. Herein was declared to lie the priceless wisdom which the country, to its undoing, had neglected. Incessantly was young Anatole compelled to hear long recitations from *Les Martyrs* or from *Itinéraires de Paris à Jérusalem*, until he came to hate the very mention of Chateaubriand's name, as a boy is sure to hate some venerable authority who is too often quoted "at" him. Memorials of the great man, clippings of his hair, the walking-stick with which he had climbed Mount Sinai, were treasured in the house like relics of a saint.[7] In later days Anatole France believed that his father's curiously pompous style of speech had been acquired through too constant poring over *Le Génie du Christianisme*,[8] much as a Scottish Cameronian came to talk scripturally, often to the stimulation of impious thoughts in his children. It chanced that the viscount himself, in extreme old age, lived near the Quai Malaquais, and the young devotee of Greek classics remembered with no filial reverence how in company with his nursemaid he had often seen that tedious saint tottering round the streets.

[7] J. J. Brousson: *Anatole France en Pantoufles,* p. 109.
[8] *ibid.,* p. 253.

Nor could he abide Victor Hugo.[9] There was spice and sparkle in *Les Châtiments* or *L'Histoire d'un Crime*, especially as such manifestos had to be more or less furtively devoured. But it required a great deal to atone for that extraordinary ode to Louis XVIII,—the ode in which God calls upon seraphim, prophets and archangels to do homage before the heir to the French throne: *Courbez-vous. C'est un Roi.* A young pagan, enraptured with Euripides, had his patience sorely tried by royalist piety.

Before long he found spiritual companionship more to his mind. Among the distractions of the capital in the late sixties was the rise of a new poetic school which aimed at making Paris the site of a new Helicon. They would bring back the finely chiselled poetic art of those pagan masters whom the Renaissance had for a time promised to enthrone again, but whose spell had been so coarsely dissipated by fresh religious fanaticisms from the East. They were mostly quite young versifiers, exulting in a financial poverty that was known to be the true mate of the riches of the soul, "long-haired poets and little journalists",[10] as Anatole France afterwards described them. Prisoners at an office desk six days of the week, they rambled on Sundays in the country for lyric inspiration. Paul Verlaine was there, with his *Poèmes Saturniens* written on the office stationery of the Prefecture in which he was employed. Frédéric Plessis was of the circle, defying the motto that the Law is a jealous mistress, as he alternated the study of legal textbooks with intervals in the singular company of Vergil, Ovid and Lucan.[11] There too—a curious exception to the rule—was

[9] Cf., e.g., his judgment that Edmond Rostand had written "the worst verse of the century after Victor Hugo" (*ibid.*, p. 279).

[10] *La Vie Littéraire,* III, p. 310.

[11] *ibid.,* I, p. 142.

the wealthy and fashionable Herédia, whose neckties had as much distinction as his sonnets.[12] Coryphæus of the whole band was Leconte de Lisle, whose graceful *Poèmes Barbares* set a notable pattern for all the rest. Adopting the title *Parnassiens,* they used to meet for mutual encouragement in a room whose walls were adorned with pictures from classical antiquity, and round a table on which a cask of beer festooned with branches of fir served to recall, if not the Theatre of Dionysus, at least some convivial scene from the frescoes of Herculaneum or Pompeii. In such surroundings they hymned the praises of Earth, repudiating every trace of "other-worldliness", with just that dash of Promethean fatalism that is so congenial to the ardent and rebellious young. The *Parnassiens* rejoiced in every Æschylean drama of ineluctable Destiny, as in every Horatian ode that bade man gather rosebuds while he may. Under such inspiration, Anatole France made his first effort as a writer of verse.

He was having his revenge on Chateaubriand. If the old viscount had celebrated the martyrs of Christianity, why should not a new bard celebrate the martyrs of paganism? So in *Les Noces Corinthiennes* one watches the tragedy of a virgin vowed to celibate life by a mother whose Christian zeal has extinguished the natural feelings of parenthood. It is a scene from the first century, drawn as a period when grace and beauty were being put to flight,—a period when the grim and loveless Hebraism was making the smile to fade from the face of pagan Hellas, and the heavens were lowering overhead. Here are verses glorifying the flesh, pouring scorn on priestly denials of human nature, mocking the illusions of a fanatic East that had displaced the gladsome rites of the *pagani,* yet conceding with precocious charity that there is no harm in the most groundless dream provided

[12] *loc. cit.*

the dream be fair. Suppose however, that the dream be not fair? The motto prefixed to the piece is Antigone's exclamation: ὦ τύμβος, ὦ νυμφεῖον.

Most readers will pass very hurriedly over these early verses by Anatole France. The idea underlying them was fresh and striking at first, but it has long been thoroughly hackneyed, and others have presented it incomparably better. One recalls Walter Pater's *Marius*, or the passage in Swinburne about Earth growing gray from the breath of the pale Galilean,[13] or the works of Nietzsche and Oscar Wilde *passim*. It is impossible to think of *Les Noces Corinthiennes* as a rival to any of these. But the piece was meant to be a dramatic and sensational manifesto of neo-paganism. Bohemian youth generally begins in some such strain, and this experiment may be placed in the same class with such dainty volumes as *Six Harvard Poets*. That there should be six young "poets" contemporaneously at any seat of learning is remarkable enough, but wonder is abated for those who have read the work. It suggests Newman's paragraph about a youth in ecstasies over Vergil or Horace, and imitating the *Georgics* or the *Odes*—"as he thinks, successfully" [14]—in his own flowing versification.

But Anatole France did not pretend that the *motif* of his drama had originated in his own mind. He quoted its source. Goethe had depicted a like situation, more than sixty years before. In *Die Braut von Korinth* he had shown the ruthless parting of two plighted lovers, at the behest of that new Faith for which the impulses of nature and the loyalties of the heart were alike crushed under a fanatic cult of virginity. From that silent Corinthian house the kindly Olympians had been driven,—those gay and genial gods that were con-

13 A. C. Swinburne: *Hymn to Proserpine.*

14 J. H. Newman: *Grammar of Assent,* p. 78.

tent with an offering of ox or lamb, and had never demanded the atrocities of human sacrifice. But the new god was more exacting—not to be satiated by aught less than an immolation of humanity itself.

One cannot help feeling that the scene for this alleged outrage by the new Faith on the sweet domesticities of life was chosen with less than Goethe's usual skill. Such idealizing of paganism is indeed always an agreeable exercise for the learned, and they can interpret ancient texts so as to elicit the required moral with a freedom which no Biblical exegete could surpass. As George Meredith said about the dreams of an Age of Chivalry, and "the bewitching silken shepherdesses who live though they never were", this is justified by the pleasure it gives to the imagination.[15] But Corinth was the wrong background. Its authentic records are so copious and so definite that "fancy strikes fact and explodes in full." Those habits which ancient writers associated with the Acrocorinthus and the temple of Aphrodite that crowned it are quite dissimilar to all that is suggested in Goethe's play. It is safe, too, to guess that the *Noces Corinthiennes* would have puzzled Strabo[16] and Horace[17] as an account of the ideals of the city on the isthmus in the last century of the Roman republic, just as it would have puzzled Pindar,[18] Plato[19] and Aristophanes[20] at an earlier time. Rightly or wrongly, the verb κορινθιάζεσθαι[21] had a sinister significance, and one needs be no mediævalist to think that the worship of the Virgin, like that of 'Αθήνη Πάρθενος at

15 G. Meredith: *The Egoist,* II.

16 *Geog.,* VIII, vi, 20; cf. Gellius, I, viii, 4.

17 *Epistles,* I, xvii, 36.

18 *Fr.* 122.

19 *Rep.,* III, 404.

20 *Fr.,* 133

21 *loc. cit.*

Athens, might have been a change for the better. We have the witness too of another document, which in the light of so much pagan corroboration can hardly be dismissed as a product of Christian bias. It is the *First Epistle to the Corinthians*, written by a zealot of Hebrew birth, who had been more than once to the city, with observant eyes.

II

There was little bread and butter in the enterprise of a Parnassian, and for his daily living young Anatole France had to turn to a more prosaic task. So he helped his father with short bibliographical papers about authors of general appeal, and wrote pieces of dramatic criticism upon contemporary French plays that had "made a hit" without being in the least degree Sophoclean. In 1874, when he was just thirty, he was fortunate enough to get a post on the staff of the Senate Library, but he soon lost this through a difference of opinion with his official chief, who happened to be his former poetic friend, Leconte de Lisle. To share a life of Bohemian protest against the superstitions of the Age was one thing; to work in subordination at the humble job of making book catalogues and registering the issue of books to readers was quite another. And it seems a mistake for a library to employ officials who are "creative." That group consisted of men who were such artists as to "hate one another like poison." His inconsiderate superior in business hours insisted upon turning young Anatole into "a mere scribe"—which was of course more than a Parnassian could bear.

So he resigned his post, and turned to writing biographical introductions to French classical texts for a publisher who was issuing popular editions of Racine, Molière, La Fontaine. Like Mr. Bernard Shaw, who complains that his present popularity makes it impossible for him to stop the re-issue of his own worst books, Anatole France disapproved in vain of the later publication of these youthful studies under the title *Le Génie Latin*. They are, in truth, just what they profess to be, short introductions to school texts. The boyhood ambition of "having my own proofs to correct" never left his mind, and he aimed at having proofs not of a preface to someone else's work, but of an independent masterpiece. In 1879 appeared his first short tales, *Jocaste* and *Le Chat Maigre*. Intrinsically, these books are of no great importance. Admirers of Anatole France's later work read such products of his nonage as admirers of *Rob Roy* read such "dotages" as *Count Robert of Paris* or *Castle Dangerous*.

But *Jocaste*, at least, has a certain interest of its own, for it reflects that mood of Determinism by which the author had at this time become possessed. Darwin's great work had crossed the Straits of Dover, and its message to this youthful pagan was to confirm by modern science the fatalistic outlook of Greek tragedy. As Mr. Hardy would say, what the Greeks had only suspected, modern science had made certain.[22] Free will seemed to have been driven from its last asylum when every trait of developed mankind was seen as but the result of minute modifications of structure, stretching back over unimaginable time, until they find their first beginnings in some quality of the amoeba. A process which man did not choose had made man what he was. For his so-called virtues he could no longer be praised, and for his so-called vices it had become idle to blame him. All was the

22 T. Hardy: *The Return of the Native*, iii, 1.

effect of his heredity and surroundings. "We are born so old." [23]

It was not indeed Darwin alone among modern writers who had pressed this fact on Anatole France's notice. Biological evolution had but supplied the climax, or the experimental proof, of that theory of things which he had already seen in Benjamin Constant's account of the development of the religious idea,[24] or in François Mignet's view of the genesis of the revolutionary spirit.[25] Almost contemporaneously with the *Origin of Species*, the great work of Hippolyte Taine had proceeded on the assumption that even imaginative and poetical masterpieces are no more than a necessary product of the race, environment and period in which they appear. In vain were men like Carlyle protesting that it is not the Age which makes the Hero, but the Hero who makes the Age. Two years before Darwin's monograph had startled the world, it had been argued by Buckle that the really significant things, which explain the very character of a people, are the soil on which it dwells, the food it eats, the climate and natural influences amid which it is nurtured.

Thrilled by such ideas, Anatole France wrote the story of a luckless woman upon whom inherited temperament and the blows of circumstance acted no less fatally than the curse in the House of Œdipus upon the Jocasta of Sophocles. The Greek original of this piece is indicated by its name. In the *Œdipus Rex,* Jocasta hangs herself, and so does the ill-mated wife in Anatole France's novel. But the Erinyes that bring doom on Hélène Fellaire are not drawn from ancient legend. It is biological fate that has taken the

[23] *La Vie Littéraire,* II, p. 7.

[24] B. Constant: *De la Religion.*

[25] F. Mignet: *Histoire de la Revolution Française.*

place of the Fates of old mythology. The victim is cursed, not by being made an unwitting sinner, but by being born an epileptic. Her wretched alliance is chosen for her, not by decree of the Olympians, but by the compulsions of a sordid parent. Slowly but inexorably, the web is woven though the hands are unseen, and the determining force is just a march of natural incident as inscrutable to Hélène as to Œdipus. When in wistful regret she becomes party to her husband's murder, she is driven by those impulses of thwarted love that she can no more control than she can guide the pulsations of her heart. To her suicide she is hurried by those hauntings of remorse that are the modern equivalent of the ancient Furies. It is thus in form and language alone that life's perplexities have changed. There still remains a Sphinx, putting to man those problems which he must answer or perish—and, as of old, man cannot answer.

Here is a blend of Darwin's "Natural Selection" and the ancient doctrine of "Fate." Anatole France in his earliest philosophic mood used to reflect how close was Vergil's cosmogonic dream in the *Sixth Eclogue* to the actual findings of modern science. The old poet had sung of primeval chaos, of the slowly hardening Earth's crust, of the first living things that began to wander over unfamiliar peaks: *Rara per ignotos errant animalia montes.* Was it not indeed a true world-scheme that was there half revealed "beneath the damask wings of poesy"? Was it not far nearer to genuine fact than those barbarous Eastern fables that Western peoples had come to believe? [26] For to Anatole France it showed how at the very beginning of things lay that Destiny which was to unfold in the world as men had come to know it. Therein lay the conception of Man as like in kind to the

[26] *La Vie en Fleur,* chap. xxiii.

animal species whose very life depends upon killing. Therein too, for our young pessimist, was the hideous key to that future which alone could be expected, that ceaseless course of mutual conflict in which Man will surpass other animal types only by his increased skill in fashioning a murderous machine that will continue to be used until life shall be no more.[27]

It sounds terrifically saddening, but not to youth, and Anatole France in describing such boyish reveries has spoken of the "deliciousness of despair." [28] At his open window, gazing into the vault of a starlit sky, he did not feel —like Mr. Hardy's young astronomer—that the stellar universe as seen through a telescope is a ghastly sight.[29] He was no theist, no believer in Providence, with Addisonian raptures over the spacious firmament whose music sounds in Reason's ear and proclaims its great Original. But he felt indescribably exalted by the appreciation of cosmic vastness, as well as by his own subtle insight into the puny insignificance of Man.

For him, this mood became tempered with time. Eighteen years after he published *Jocaste*, Anatole France sketched in rapid outline, and with a tinge of humorous contempt, those fatalistic fancies of his for which Darwin had been his Bible and the Zoological Museum a place to frequent as the devout frequent a sanctuary. He recalled how he had once stood in reverential spirit, contemplating the fossil crinoids, the long jaws of the saurian, the bent backbone of the elephant and the curiously shaped head of the gorilla.[30] In

[27] *ibid.*, p. 218.

[28] *La Vie Littéraire,* I, p. 22: "When one is fifteen, one is eager for suffering."

[29] T. Hardy: *Two on a Tower,* IV.

[30] *La Vie Littéraire,* III, p. 55.

the middle of the hall was to be seen a marble Venus, "symbol of the sweet invincible power by which all animate races are multiplied." Amid the uneasiness of some youthful neo-Catholic friends, he had extolled the *Origin of Species* as a true Holy Writ of the modern Age, and had dwelt with serene confidence on this final disclosure of the secret of things. But time had passed, and this dream had faded like its predecessors. "To-day we know full well that this romance of the universe is as full of disappointments as the rest." Despair had become no longer delicious. But melancholy brooding was as foolish as sanguine exaltation. To the mood of fatalism was to succeed the mood of humour.

CHAPTER IV

FROM FATALISM TO HUMOUR

Aristotle saith, there are certaine litle beasts alongst the river Hyspanis that live but one day. She which dies at 8. a clocke in the morning dies in her youth, and she that dies at 5. in the afternoon dies in her decrepitude; who of us doth not laugh when we shall see this short moment of continuance to be had in consideration of good or ill fortune? The most and the least in ours, if we compare it with eternitie or equall it to the lasting of mountaines, rivers, stars and trees, or any other living creature is no lesse ridiculous.

MONTAIGNE

In Anatole France's next novel there are no murders, no victims of remorseless Fate, no epileptoid or alcoholic ancestries, no vain strugglings of high purpose against the constraint of passion and environment. There is rather a tranquil joy in life, a fine composure of spirit in fulfilling the day's task, keen aesthetic appreciation of the wonder and beauty of the world, genial sympathy with everyone, and a readiness to believe that *tout comprendre, c'est tout pardonner*. If the grosser realism was to be pursued in French fiction, it was left for such as Zola to pursue it. Anatole France had come under the spell of a very different guide. For him, Darwin and Taine had given place to Ernest Renan,—the Renan of the late seventies and the early eighties, whose magic wand was to chase the dusky gnome of ennui from many a theoretic pessimist.

It was in 1879 that the author of the *Vie de Jésus*, after much resistance from the more orthodox Academicians, was at length elected to the French Academy. His inaugural address, when he took his seat for the first time among the Immortals, was very characteristic of the mood he was destined to inspire. It was not, he said, until somewhat late in life that he had been so honoured, but he had come to see that there was justification for the delay:

> One arrives in your Assembly at the age of Ecclesiastes, a charming age, most proper to serene cheerfulness, when after laborious youth one begins to perceive that all is vanity, but that many a vain thing ought to be thoroughly enjoyed.

This is the prevailing tone of the next heroes in Anatole France's literary work, so remote from the indignant iconoclasm of *Les Noces Corinthiennes*, the dreary fatalism of *Jocaste*, or the hopeless disillusionment of *Jean Servien.*

I

It was just two years after the inaugural address by Renan that Anatole France published *Le Crime de Sylvestre Bonnard.* There is nothing sensational about the book, except its title, which many critics have found it hard to justify or even to understand. It has no plot that is worth mentioning. We are introduced to an old scholar, who keeps a diary of his quite secluded life in the days of Napoleon III. He has no care save his literary work, remaining aloof from the tumultuous excitements outside, a little sensitive to what is said about his authorship, but on the whole raised above both the hopes and the fears which younger men entertain, and praying that when his time comes to leave the world it may please God to take him as he stands on his step-ladder before his book-laden shelves. Here and there he is gently ironical in his talk, but in general he is guileless, obedient to his housekeeper who exercises a despotic care over him, very generous to the poor, interested in children and in cats, surprised that tradesmen should swindle him, but never really irritated except with the cruel. This elderly bachelor lives in a flat on the Quai Malaquais, where the industrious Thérèse cooks his meals, finds him his neckties, and endeavours to protect him against cunning imposture.

Bonnard is not worried about the Italian question, or about the Taku Forts, or about the Mexican enterprise of the Archduke Maximilian, or indeed about any of the public problems which in those middle years of the Second Empire so agitated the Parisian mind. He is not even concerned about the speculations of Darwin and Taine. His one great hobby is the collecting and collating of old manuscripts which may cast light upon monastic life in the France of four or five centuries ago, and he is proud to think that he is among the ten or twelve men who have really added to knowledge in that historical field. When the diary opens, he is hard at work upon the special case of the Abbey of Saint-Germain-des-Près, whence issued those king-monks who founded the national dynasty of France. And he discovers with a thrill of delight, in a book-catalogue, that an antique shop in a Sicilian town has the original fourteenth century manuscript called *The Golden Legend*, by Jacques de Voragine. What are the noisy "public events" compared with this? It is the very manuscript of the Clerk Alexander, that will clear up a dozen mysteries about the Abbey of Saint-Germain-des-Près! "Perspiration moistened my forehead, and a veil seemed to come over my eyes." [1] He starts at once for Sicily.

There is no "march of incident" in the book, for there were no incidents in the old scholar's life, except one love-affair in which he had lost. Sometimes he thinks about that

[1] *Le Crime de Sylvestre Bonnard,* chap. i.

still. By sheer accident he discovers the daughter of his old sweetheart in a boarding-school of the harsher type. Moved by the thought of his old flame, he rescues her, with lawless disregard both for her school and for her appointed guardian. Was this his "crime"? Perhaps. Or perhaps, say the bibliophiles, his real crime was the selling of his beloved books to provide the girl with a marriage portion! Incidentally he talks a great deal on all sorts of subjects, sometimes to the harsh schoolmistress about a gentler method of education, sometimes to a sympathetic friend about his early love experience, often to his cat Hamilcar about things in general.

Why does this plotless tale so hold the reader's interest? Why do those entries in the diary of an inactive life lure one on with such unfailing enchantment? To explain this is to penetrate far into the secret of Anatole France's literary art. Perhaps the nearest parallel one can quote for a like elusive charm is George Gissing's book, *The Private Papers of Henry Ryecroft*. One reads that book, declares there is nothing in it, and then reads it again.

Le Crime de Sylvestre Bonnard was crowned by the Institut. It well deserved this honour, for it was the creation of a new figure in the French novel, a distinct temperament so vivid to the reader that—as Lafcadio Hearn said—it is impossible to think Bonnard unreal.[2] We know him as we know Dr. Samuel Johnson, and love him for reasons not very dissimilar. To have created this reflective personality, endowing it with life, despite the absence of all vigorous action, was consummate art. Here Anatole France enlisted our affections for a pattern of virtue. His humour was next to

2 Preface by Lafcadio Hearn to the English translation of *Le Crime de Sylvestre Bonnard.*

make us enthusiastic over one equally human, but not equally virtuous. The mood alike of polemic and of despair is definitely dropped.

II

Bonnard was but a preliminary study for that diverting figure in which the spirit of our novelist found more characteristic expression: the figure of abbé Jérôme Coignard, of *La Rôtisserie de la Reine Pédauque*.

The abbé is an eighteenth century ecclesiastic, with the eighteenth century distrust of "enthusiasm", an insatiable bookworm, jovial in his cups, not averse to a tavern brawl, disgraceful for his amours, but with a tender human sympathy that atones for much. In an impecunious and thirsty moment he will raid another man's cellar; and when chance puts some fine diamonds in his way, his nimble fingers are at the service of a collector's aesthetic taste. Melancholy experience of the ups and downs of life has shown him that even for a man of learning cash is not to be contemned, for this he has found difficult to procure honestly "or even otherwise." [3] But, like the rogues so beloved of Fielding and Sterne, he is always good-hearted, responsive to a delicate distress, wise enough to be indulgent towards every amiable weakness of poor human nature. Coignard is sure to be on the side of "the bottom dog", convinced that in this hard world the best course is always a course of mercy, and that those who persecute others for the sake of an "ideal" are but ministering to their own conceit. He was an orthodox priest, withal, never failing to check his intellectual curiosity where dogma barred the way, and quite certain that in matters of faith the more blindly one believes, the better.

[3] *La Rôtisserie de la Reine Pédauque,* chap. v.

Lapsing often into fornication, but never into Jansenism, he recalled as the chief sin to his account how he had once let himself be hired as secretary to a Huguenot who had dictated pamphlets "against religion." [4]

According to George Meredith, it is the classical scholar whose blood is "most nuptial to the webbed bottle." [5] So Coignard translates Zosimus between drinks, and carries with him to his favourite alehouse a copy of the *De Consolatione Philosophiae.* Not much troubled by peccadillos in practice, he has searched in vain for a satisfying theoretic account of the moral nature. Those endless variations in the dicta of conscience from Age to Age and from clime to clime have quite baffled him, and he can find little help in the "utilitarian" principle, for who can ever decide what is in the end useful in conduct? [6] Yet he is too good a churchman to accept the facile formula (good enough for Anatole France himself) that "morality is just the custom of the greatest number." [7] So he flees for refuge to theological prescription,—those divine laws whose absurdity indeed is apparent, but which must be accepted as enshrining a wisdom that man cannot grasp.[8] He was all the surer that they were divine just because they were incomprehensible, and what he liked best about them was the emphasis they laid upon "repentance." Herein, for the reflective, was something that approached explanation. Scripture taught that the highest sainthood is possible only for such as have had a chance to repent thoroughly, and none but great wrongdoers are capable of this. For example, if the blessed Pelagia

4 *ibid.,* ii.
5 *The Egoist,* chap. xx.
6 *La Rôtisserie,* xiv.
7 Preface to *La Vie Littéraire,* First Series.
8 *La Rôtisserie,* XIV.

had not sinned so deeply in her youth, she would in later years have been no more than "a matron of average and commonplace goodness." [9] There lay a theological solution of the ancient mystery about evil. All things, including sin, must find their final cause in the inscrutable purposes of God.

This may sound remarkable as Apologetic. But it is perhaps not more absurd than many an argument, for example, from the *Bridgewater Treatises.*

* * *

Despite his rascality, which, as Mr. W. J. Locke says, would be bad enough in a layman but is beyond words in a priest,[10] the abbé Coignard delights the reader by his unfailing humanitarianism. He will have nothing to do with the advocates of war,[11] or with those who shriek for savage penalties against the criminal.[12] If he is ever stern in judgment, it is towards those who want to shed blood. And in his view such men are persecutors for a very simple reason, —they are far too sure of themselves. Mankind must be taught to rely less on what passes for knowledge, and on what has become sacred as traditional usage, for it is a sort of vanity about what we have discovered or established that nerves one's arm to be cruel. Human nature is kind enough in itself; but when it puts trust beyond itself in some ancient prejudice that has hardened into a dogma, it will perpetrate frightful injustice with an easy conscience and even with a sense of duty well done. So the foundations of conventional law and practice ought to be dusted from time to time, that men may see upon what they were orig-

[9] *loc. cit.*

[10] Preface to English translation of *La Rôtisserie.*

[11] *Les Opinions de M. Jérôme Coignard,* X, XI, XII.

[12] *ibid.,* XIX–XXII.

inally laid.[13] Spiders and scorpions have their habitat in the gloom of cellars and the damp of back-gardens, over which the broom should be passed occasionally. In like manner, the philosophic and historical broom should cleanse those dark places of the mind. Perhaps there should sometimes be even the touch of a pick here and there on the walls of cellar and garden,—to scare away the vermin.[14]

III

Les Opinions de M. Jérôme Coignard appeared in 1893. Beneath the thinnest veneer of eighteenth century colouring, it is the French politics of the preceding years that one can see shining through, and it is upon French politicians of the present that the reflective abbé has his comments to make. They are thus Anatole France's own comments upon the public life of his time.

It had been a time rich in incident, including the two presidential periods of Jules Grévy and Sadi Carnot. The older men, whose thoughts went back to the Second Empire, were wondering how far there had been an improvement. They recalled manifestos and promises of all kinds. There had been the proclamations of Napoleon III, showing what a true democrat he was in substituting the real democracy of an elected Emperor for the false democracy of the Orleanists. War after war had been initiated under the most diverse pretexts, as the Emperor fought Russia in defence of Catholic ideals and fought Austria for their overthrow, as he supported nationality in Piedmont and suppressed it in China, made himself the champion of imperialism in Mexico and the guardian of local autonomies across the

13 *ibid.*, Preface.
14 *loc. cit.*

Rhine. Frenchmen had seen how this "son of the Revolution" had always and everywhere combined a militarism like that of Louis XIV with a fluency of abstract formulas which might have come from Robespierre. Always and everywhere it was an *idée Napoléonienne* that he affected to serve. Next, there had been the horrors of the Commune, the birth travail of the Third Republic, the struggles of Thiers and Gambetta against ceaseless machinations by Legitimists, Orleanists, Bonapartists. There had been the comedy of Frohsdorf, and the breakdown over the question of "the flag." At length the Republic had been equipped with its "Constitution", and there had followed those years during which, with incessant denouncing of the corrupt *régime* that had preceded, one leader of democracy after another had entered politics in the poverty of a Diogenes and had emerged with the wealth of a Crœsus.[15] But whatever else had been wanting, they had one and all had their plentiful supply of phrases, principles, and ideals.

For the fourteen years immediately preceding the issue of *Les Opinions de M. Jérôme Coignard* there had been a strange public life both at home and abroad. Colonial expansion had proceeded apace—the conquest of Tunis, Tonquin, Madagascar, the Ivory Coast and Dahomey—whilst England had kept a watchful and somewhat suspicious eye. There had been an odd *rapprochement*, too, between French democracy and Russian despotism, contrived as a counterstroke to the Triple Alliance. Fundamental changes had taken place in the French educational system. There had been ceaseless intrigue by royalists, culminating in the ludicrous adventure of General Boulanger with his plan for a republic on the American instead of the French model,

[15] Cf. A. D. Vandam, *Men and Manners under the third Republic*, p. 168. But Mr. Vandam's partiality for the Second Empire is well known.

supported alike by survivors of the old *régime*, because it meant a dictatorship, and by radicals like Henri Rochefort because the dictator was to be chosen by universal suffrage. And there had been one administrative scandal after another: the Daniel Wilson episode in which the President's son-in-law had been found trafficking in badges of the Legion of Honour, and the Panama episode in which deputies by the hundred had been bribed by a great corporation, fifty millions of francs had somehow "disappeared", and a Cabinet minister had been sent to penal servitude for fraud.

* * *

It is on subjects such as these that the genial abbé is lured to speak his mind. He talks, not about the Panama scandal, but about "the affair of the Mississippi";[16] not about Henri Rochefort, but about a revolutionary named "Rockstrong."[17] A question, or a provocative opinion expressed in his hearing, will suffice to open his lips,—at the counter of a bookstore or at the table of a tavern. What does he think, for example, about colonies? About political reform and the change of ministry? About city magistrates, and financial corruption in high places, and the development of a citizen army?

The abbé wants his listeners to understand that the sort of thing now happening has always happened before and will continue to happen again, no matter what change may be made in the Constitution, and no matter how the personnel of ministries may come and go. Coignard is not much impressed by "great statesmen." He explains them, with a rather startling anticipation of Taine. The movements they seem to have caused were in truth, he says, determined by that unseen force of which their personality was rather the

16 *Les Opinions de M. Jérôme Coignard,* IV.
17 *ibid.*, XIV, XV.

superficial token. One remembers here the merry tale in *Les Sept Femmes de Barbe-Bleue* about the two doctors who were attending a patient. They hoped that Nature would effect a cure during the period of their visitation, and that "the coincidence would be noted to their advantage." [18]

Colonizing, too, the abbé points out, is by no means a specially modern enterprise. It was well known, for example, as far back as the days of Cadmus and the Phœnicians. Its chief mark of late had been that such missionaries of civilization always thought it necessary to exterminate native tribes in Asia or Africa—which seemed hardly fair.[19] But this was just a tendency of the time, and those who apparently led it deserved as little personal glory for its success as they deserved personal shame for its frequent failure. Look at yonder recruiting sergeant on the Pont Neuf! He is calling for volunteers to go to some colony in the Far East, telling them about roads strewn with diamonds and the luscious fruits that grow without cultivation. Five or six unhappy beings are lured in this way to die of yellow fever in some distant swamp.[20]

From the top of a step-ladder in a bookshop, and with his nose buried in a volume of Seneca, the abbé discourses about "government reform." Politicians in his day were, he acknowledged, a bad lot, but for his own part he would never be a revolutionary, for he was convinced that a new group of rulers would bring nothing new—except their inexperience—to the task of governing. There was special risk, he thought, in those who came to power as reformers, for a reformer was likely to meddle with freedom far more than an old administration which, like old wine, has become

[18] *Les Sept Femmes de Barbe-Bleue,* "La Chemise", I.
[19] *Les Opinions de M. Jérôme Coignard,* I.
[20] *ibid.,* X.

more mellow with the years.[21] Sure that in any event the country must be governed ill, he would take his chance with princes or statesmen in whom the first ardour had cooled off. That was a wise old crone in Syracuse long ago who used to pray that the tyrant Dionysius might have long life. She explained that she did this, not because she admired him, but because she had generally observed that a bad ruler was succeeded by a worse.[22]

Interrogated about the "affair of the Mississippi", in which certain company directors were supposed to have bribed the ministers of State, but in which the truth was that those ministers had stripped the company bare "with the greed usual to people in office under weak governments", the abbé said it was a bad business, and that he would favour a change of ministers. It was shocking that they had tried to roll the chief blame upon the Jansenists, and even offered to buy evidence which would lead to the conviction of that evil sect. But he is quickly reminded of the old woman of Syracuse, who thought a change would more probably be for the worse than for the better. "Tournebroche, my son", he replied, "I acknowledge with a good grace that I have fallen into a contradiction. . . . My reason always sides with the old woman of Syracuse. I think to-day what I thought yesterday. Only I have let my feelings run away with me, and have yielded to passion as do the vulgar."

Rockstrong, the exiled English revolutionary, gets little comfort from Coignard. He is called a rebel, and the abbé explains this as the name for a revolutionary who has failed. It was useless to point out how honest men are often conquered by rogues. Such a distinction in the characters of contestants was applicable, he is told, to the war in Heaven

21 *Les Opinions de M. Jérôme Coignard,* I.
22 *loc. cit.*

of which John Milton wrote, while on this terraqueous globe the only difference is between those who have won and those who have lost. That, at least, is the abbé's opinion, but he has no idea that his opinions will ever be shared by any large number of people. Most men, and especially most political agitators, will continue to contrast themselves as virtuous with their adversaries as wicked, though in truth they are all made of much the same material. In State matters the greatest advance of thought was achieved by Machiavelli, who was "the first to remove from political action the legendary foundation of justice." [23]

IV

In 1894, the year following the publication of his two Coignard books, Anatole France issued a little volume of general reflections about life and destiny. He called it *Le Jardin d'Epicure.* It contains a considerable number of very short and quite miscellaneous pieces, not unlike the *Essays* of Bacon. There are grim sections of it which surpass even the gloom of *Jocaste,* but they must be read in connection with those other parts through which runs that spirit half dismal but half humorous which marked the abbé Coignard when he was at his sober best. And the book was well named, for it has indeed the Epicurean temper of ἀταραξία, the temper of many a Roman noble of the first century who looked back to him of "the Garden" as his philosophic high priest, and who felt toward the gods of old Rome as Anatole France felt toward *l'Église.*

There is indeed little to suggest ἀταραξία in the sections on science. We hear much about the lowering of human pride by modern discovery, much about the insignificance of

[23] *Les Opinions de M. Jérôme Coignard,* X.

Earth amid the stellar immensities, much about the evitable destiny that awaits mankind when this globe shall have become physically and chemically uninhabitable.[24] Whether it is at present the worst of all possible worlds, Anatole France is not prepared to say, for he knows little of the others, and would hesitate to claim any pre-eminence for the one he knows directly. But on analogical grounds he infers that other planets resembling ours in structure will resemble it also in evil, and that the whole solar system may well be one vast Gehenna whose animal life is born only to suffer and to die.[25] It is a picture like the one Lord Balfour has drawn of cosmic majesties as science by itself can disclose them, culminating in the vision of a time when the energies of the Sun shall have been dimmed, and the Earth—tideless and inert—shall no longer tolerate the race which has for a moment disturbed its solitude.[26]

But Anatole France, like Lord Balfour, reminds himself how it is not so wonderful that the universe should be vast as that the intellect of man should have measured it.[27] He exults in that "regal intelligence." The heavens show forth, if not the glory of God, at least the glory of Newton and Laplace. It is such as they who have computed the half century which the luminous ray from the pole star has occupied in reaching us, and who have revealed to us those other stars whose light went out perhaps three thousand years ago. Disheartening as it may be to realize that a luminary so unimaginably distant is "our nearest neighbour", or that countless worlds have been born and have died even as ours was born and will die, which of us is not thrilled at the

[24] *Le Jardin d'Epicure,* pp. 1–4, 16–18.
[25] *ibid.,* pp. 60, 61.
[26] *ibid.,* p. 16 sq.; cf. A. J. Balfour: *Foundations of Belief,* p. 29, sqq.
[27] *Le Jardin d'Epicure,* p. 6.

thought that men of our race have so widened the bounds of knowledge? And though we have learned that in the infinitude of systems our Sun is relatively but a bubble of gas and our Earth a drop of mud, what bearing has this upon the real values of life? Not less than in the sweet days of mediæval ignorance, when the universe was thought to exist for man alone, can the kindly charities be maintained. The tender affections of parenthood, sensitiveness to beauty and charm, the courage and enterprise of the hero, all that ever made the grandeur of life through suffering and endurance, can remain just as they were, no matter what the astronomers may say to affright us.[28] It was by his instincts and his feelings, far more than by his reason, that man lived in the past; and thus he will continue to live. No book on philosophy will ever make our universe uninhabitable. For in truth philosopher and ignoramus are in the dark together, differing only in this: that one keeps vainly knocking on the wall, while the other stays quietly in the middle of the room. Exploding popular fallacies is a poor occupation. For each error that departs, another—perhaps more dangerous—will be entertained instead. And life is ever more than logic.

Yet in another mood, in the same volume, Anatole France feels that this kind of reassurance is not quite satisfactory.[29] Scientific men, he said, were prone to insist that from their science they shall be able to extract a system of morals. Even Renan had been subject to that illusion, but he later came to know its disappointment. The best analogy for life is with a vast pottery-works, where all sorts of vessels are manufactured for purposes unknown, many being broken and tossed aside as they are made, and others used for only

28 *ibid.*, p. 40.
29 *ibid.*, p. 48.

ridiculous or degrading ends. But it is best not to know this truth. Few people do know it. And no service is rendered by him who would dispel those illusions under which alone life can be endured. It is not horses only that need blinkers to keep them from shying.

But on the whole, says our humorous sceptic, life is in many ways by no means bad. Everything depends on how one becomes accustomed to view it. At all events, mankind shows no sign of decay. "I have heard talk about decadence, but I do not believe a word of it." We are going forward instead of backward, slowly, but surely, and the climax of civilization is yet to be reached.[30] All progress must be slow in order to be tranquil.[31] But the evolution forward has the certainty of Fate, and we may well expect that our Earth will yet have forms of life as much higher than ours as ours is higher than that of the brute. Let, then, love of the race and of its future warm every heart. In pain and travail all high achievement must be wrought, and with that condition the nobler natures are content. Intense hope and distressing alarm over social changes are alike foolish. For such changes are at once extremely gradual and wholly inevitable,—like the continuous changes of the physical order. They are to be accepted, as one accepts cosmic evolution, making no futile schemes to block its way. On the other hand, the impatient revolutionary who would hasten change is as far wrong as the terrified conservative who would prevent it.

It is worth noticing that such a book, with problems as subtle as the inferences are disquieting, reached its 114th edition. One could not think of it as a "best seller" in England.

30 *ibid.*, p. 86.
31 *ibid.*, p. 101.

V

From his writings of this period we can collect a fairly clear and consistent picture of Anatole France's attitude to life at the age of fifty. The moods of Bonnard and Coignard were his own, and they reappear in many another character he has sketched: in Trublet of *Histoire Comique,* in Brotteaux of *Les Dieux ont Soif,* in Bergeret of *Histoire Contemporaine.* These are so many aliases for the author, as truly as Conrad, Lara, Harold, Juan are aliases for Byron. We get again and again the same features of critical temperament,—a tone of detached mockery, a welcome half scornful and half sympathetic for all sorts of opinions as partly false and partly true. The model was perhaps some literary noble under the *ancien régime,* a man amused at human credulity, moved by all genuine distress, zealous for knowledge though this should lead only to sardonic mirth at the discovery that nothing can be known save "the sequence and continuity of our ignorance" [32]—one long emancipated from illusions about the prospect of intellectualizing the herd, and perfectly certain that the herd, for whose happiness he has a real concern, is best left to cherish those innocent errors to which it has become accustomed.

He is at war with no one, except the man who is harsh and without feeling for his fellows. Like Burns, Anatole France has a good word to say even for the Devil, who is at least a great artist, creator of one-half the world, and whose workmanship is so cunningly interwoven with the other half that with every vice destroyed there must perish a corresponding virtue.[33] The thought seems often to recur to our humorist's mind that there is an intensely comic element in

[32] *L'Anneau d'Améthyste,* p. 144.

[33] *Le Jardin d'Epicure,* p. 66.

diatribes against evil, because they involve the pathetic illusion that it is possible to improve. Where nothing can ever be made better, where one can but exchange some form of human failure that has already been exposed for some other whose inevitable breakdown is not at the moment visible, why work one's self into a frenzy of rage? It is so unpleasant, and so ineffective.

The central figure in book after book is thus one who has seen, like Ecclesiastes, that there is nothing new under the sun, and that the real simpleton is the zealot. He feels that prophets of amelioration mean well, but that they are a futile group, to be treated with that radiant humour which they unfortunately fail to show towards those whom they would reform. The Francian hero is no democrat, but commonly some *roué* man of letters, straitened in purse, dividing his time between the cabarets of the Latin Quarter and the bookshops of the Quai Voltaire,—some one like the Marquis Tudesco who had often breakfasted on a page of Tacitus and supped on a satire of Juvenal, but for whom such artistic substitutes, though they might take the place of food, could in no wise do duty for drink.[34] In many of his books we are made to think of that sympathetic touch with which Balzac used to depict revived aristocracy in the Legitimist period of fifteen years between the fall of Napoleon I and the rise of Louis Philippe. They suggest the same unmistakable friendliness with which the frail but fair successors of Ninon de Lenclos were drawn, and the far coarser workmanship in Balzac's picture of the bourgeois semi-Puritanism prevalent at the court of the Citizen King. Not readily could Anatole France forgive that great Revolution which had "guillotined the lighter graces and proscribed

[34] *Les Désirs de Jean Servien.*

the easy smile." [35] Yet he lived to ally himself with Jaurès and his friends, to preside at Socialist dinners, inaugurate Communist printing-presses, and vaticinate with enthusiasm for *les temps meilleurs!* Things had changed, and he changed with them. Macaulay once remarked that a person is not to be called an Oriental traveller because he goes round from west to east with the earth and all things that are thereon. Nor is he necessarily to be blamed for changing his mind. As the Hibernian aphorism has it, there is a deal of human nature in man.

But the time for Anatole France's transformation was not yet. The genial Epicurean temper was to be shown in another field. And it was seldom shown with greater attractiveness than when, about 1884, he became literary critic for *Le Temps.*

[35] *La Vie Littéraire,* I, p. 54.

CHAPTER V

THE HUMORIST AS LITERARY CRITIC

The surest test of a man's critical power is the judgment he passes upon his contemporaries.

LA BRUYÈRE

Here is the most intensely French of all writers, one who in his guardianship of our speech never stumbles and is never misled, one whose lightest casual phrase is charged with witchery and spell. Anatole France, if any man in the world, was the child of that civilization we call "Mediterranean", for his work reflects as in a mirror those sunlit seas and those fair lands where Latin thought had its birth. Yet—marvellous to tell—he is at the same time that writer of our century who has so transcended all local differences of language and of culture as to wield a controlling influence over the thought and feelings of all mankind.

PAUL PAINLEVÉ.

In the appraisal of new books there is constant need for the spirit of the humorist. All degrees of foolishness are possible, from that of him who rages because what the publishing firm has sent him is not the just book made perfect, to that of him who glows with excited eulogy because he has found a reproduction not wholly inaccurate of truths that had often been stated before. Nowhere is the lack of humour more likely to mislead into a judgment that is worthless, either through the prejudice of mere traditionalism or through the impetuosity of censorious youth. And in few critics of any country has there been so much as in Anatole France of that temper at once tolerant and watchful which seeks to understand and explain rather than to extol or upbraid.

The task of literary reviewing is commonly committed to a scholar, not to an artist. But here, as elsewhere, limitations are set far less by the nature of the work than by the talent of the workman. If one approaches the book-notices collected in *Causeries du Lundi* or in *La Vie Littéraire*, looking for the sort of thing he has come to know so well in the products of Professor Saintsbury or Sir Edmund Gosse, he will miss with regret a good deal that he expected, but will find with delight much that he never expected in such a quarter at all. And the difference, while it is partly one of men, is also in part one of racial type.

I

Anatole France as a journalist was far more akin to the writers of the Second Empire than to the writers of the Third Republic. It has often been said that the press in order to be brilliant must be free, and that censorship is here fatal to art. But this is an airy generalization which cannot survive the evidence of particular cases. Those French journalists who learned their trade under the tyranny of Napoleon III had a far truer polish and a far keener wit than the men who have revelled in the freedom of republican days. They wielded the rapier, where their successors have brandished the bludgeon. Constrained by circumstance to be ironical rather than abusive, they developed that gift of irony which makes mere abuse seem foolish. The style even of the same writer, who was subtle when the censorship made him choose his words with care, became coarse and consequently ineffective when this restraint had been removed. Henri Rochefort of *La Lanterne* under Napoleon III had a far finer journalistic touch than Henri Rochefort of *L'Intransigeant* under Jules Grévy. There are many ways, Anatole France once remarked, of saying the same thing, and the roughest way is not always the best.[1] Speaking of Armand Carrel as a journalist, he appealed to "those who still remember what good writing is" for appreciation of the robust simplicity of Carrel's style.[2] The prose writers of the Third Republic have indeed too often passed through unregulated thought to unregulated diction, while the poets have expressed those ideals of *liberté* which the man of letters so much approves in the *vers libres* which all men of letters must abhor.

It was from the practice of Sainte-Beuve that Anatole France learned his own critical art. From him he learned how one duty of the critic is to discover all he can about the genesis of a book, that he may explain why the author was determined by temperament, by surroundings, by intellectual preparation, to write as he did. Carlyle had laid down the golden rule that he who has not first appreciated the degree of truth in an author's work is thereby disqualified from pointing out the degree of his error; but Carlyle was not more notable for the emphasis he set upon this in theory than for the neglect with which he treated it in practical execution. Sainte-Beuve, on the other hand, practised what he preached, and the critics who have learned from him have uniformly approached their author with what Coleridge once called a certain "initial and experimentative faith." They have tried to see their subject as the author saw it, before arguing that the subject may be seen more fully, more

1 *La Vie Littéraire,* III, p. 182.

2 *ibid.,* I, p. 213.

wisely, more deeply. In his immortal *Causeries du Lundi*, Sainte-Beuve showed, too, how the brief appraisal of a book of the hour may be itself a work of literary art.

Anatole France followed him faithfully, though sometimes afar off. He once described Sainte-Beuve as the St. Thomas Aquinas of the nineteenth century,[3]—the great architectonic mind which absorbed and synthesized the learning of that time as St. Thomas had arranged the learning of six centuries earlier. One cannot indeed pretend that the disciple had his master's invariable catholicity and sympathy of interpretation, for he had the failings of that satiric gift which, for good as well as for ill, Sainte-Beuve never possessed. But he had in a measure the same power of self-detachment, and he had in incomparable degree the same power of making criticism artistic. His weekly column of literary gossip, written to order for *Le Temps*, had just that lightness of touch so characteristic of his predecessor who had raised literary journalism to a new level.

II

As literary critic, he had the advantage of being himself a master of expression. If he had to find fault with an author for obscurity, one did not need to read the accusing sentence a second time in order to see that this was what it meant. When he disparaged another as pedantic, garrulous, or uncouth in style, his complaint was phrased tersely and elegantly. No doubt a man may write excellent criticism of music or art though he cannot pretend to be either a musician or an artist. Among our historians of literature, too, there are some whose judgment about authors is well worth the trouble of excavating it from the jumble of words in

[3] *La Vie Littéraire,* Preface to First Series.

which it is buried. Yet the habit of writing ungraceful prose must surely in time dull the edge of one's critical sense for literary form.

Herein Anatole France set a pattern which will not readily be surpassed. In his style one observes a remarkable union of those fascinating qualities which are perhaps distinctively, and are without doubt conspicuously, French. Lafcadio Hearn thought that only in the intellectual climate of Paris could such an artist in words have been disciplined for his task.[4] That style at its best may be likened to the limpid atmosphere of the Riviera. We look *through* it, never *at* it. Rare indeed in the writings of Anatole France is the "purple patch." For him language was but the clothing of thought, and the well-dressed thought—like the well-dressed man—attracts no notice to externals. Its perfection is like that of a glove, adapting itself to every movement, while it apparently never calls for either adjustment or attention. One understands how, in a mordant review of a poor workman in language, Anatole France exclaims with disgust: "We are always conscious of the composition."[5]

Yet that which may well be a secret to others was no secret to himself. The art is nowhere obtruded, but those sentences were polished with the patience of a lapidary, and the words were chosen with the finest sensitiveness to shades of meaning or effect. In one of his intimate talks with M. Brousson, the wizard explained his method of working. Quite frankly he repudiated the suggestion that he had an intuitive or inexplicable genius for style. His pen, he said, had no lyric powers, and his apparent felicities were the outcome of hard labour. Writing was like joinery. The first

[4] Cf. Lafcadio Hearn's Preface to the English translation of *Le Crime de Sylvestre Bonnard.*

[5] *La Vie Littéraire,* I, p. 74.

draft should be rough, and the sentences should be carefully "planed down", like blocks of wood. Other things being equal, or nearly equal, the short sentence was always best, and there should be no semicolons—"That bastard which is neither full stop nor comma! It gives the best style a crick in the neck." Not the goose-quill, but rather the scissors should figure on the heraldic device of an author. Let the material in its first rude form be set in type, and let proof after proof be submitted to rearrangement, in which sentences could be divorced and reunited again and again until the true mosaic was complete. In the final result, often the last in the original paragraph should be made first, and the first should be made last.[6]

The relative clause, he used to say, should be excluded so far as possible from a sentence, for it was generally cumbrous and disturbing to the flow of thought. Choice of adjectives gave room for the most exquisite art, because they could suggest so much by cunning juxtaposition or contrast. And while it was tiresome to encounter repetition of a single word, let no writer try to avoid this by the commonplace expedient of synonyms, for true synonyms did not exist. "Respect the word. Cut up the sentence. Bring the scissors into play." If a word seemed tedious because it recurred, this was due to its being badly placed. And avoid like the plague those factitious, adventitious words that resemble almond icing in pastry, which serves only to hide the poorness of a cake.

The more one reflects upon such advice, the more truth and value one sees in it. Doubtless there are nowhere two literary artists whose methods are the same, but it is a rare privilege to be taken behind the scenes by one such craftsman, and shown how—in his own opinion, at least—he so

[6] *Anatole France en Pantoufles,* pp. 79 sqq.

contrived his work that the elements of an arresting paragraph seem to fall into place with the inevitableness of nature. Nor need such revelation of his secret destroy the wonder of what he has done. It was in a moment of unusual dullness that Keats blamed Newton's account of the prismatic colours for having taken all the beauty out of the rainbow.

Such fastidiousness of form is very French. On the other side of the Rhine it is rather despised as a frivolity to which Germans are superior, and for which it is a distinction to have no gift.[7] One observes, too, in Frenchmen whom scholarly research has doomed to long residence in Berlin or Jena, that they often come back conspicuous for their Teutonic learning, but not less conspicuous for a Teutonic clumsiness of speech. Edmond Schérer noticed it in Amiel, who by such contact with the German mind had "developed certain strangenesses of style of which he had afterwards to rid himself." In a very interesting passage, Anatole France has explained this by the racial affinities of language.

It was Latin, he said, that was the true mother-tongue of Frenchmen, and the milk of the Roman wolf had formed the best part of their blood.[8] In comparison with Latin, all other languages were obscure, and those who elected to be without knowledge of it could never appreciate "sovereign clearness of speech." Compare Goethe with Livy. The most luminous genius among the Germans had no such linguistic clarities as that old Roman in whom there was no profound genius at all.[9] For this reason an ancient people, relatively poor in thought, had been educationally supreme, giving the modern world those "humanities" which were so fitted to form men, and for which the craze of to-day about exact sci-

[7] There are exceptions, of course, e. g., Schopenhauer and Nietzsche.

[8] *La Vie Littéraire,* I, p. 287.

[9] *ibid.,* pp. 288, 289.

ence in our schools had so questionable a substitute to offer.

On the other hand, a curious legend has grown up among British Germanophiles that the profound are necessarily obscure, and the late Professor Cook Wilson of Oxford is credited with the judgment that no philosophical reasoning can have real depth if it is found capable of translation into French. That seems a hard saying to those who recall the long line of French philosophers, from Descartes to Hippolyte Taine and Henri Bergson. Of these, one knows that the last would have been quoted by Professor Cook Wilson as no exception to his general law, but rather as its most striking recent example. Opinions differ, and perhaps the philosophic originality of Professor Bergson is best proved by the storm he has raised among those who may be profound, but are unquestionably by no means original. At all events, for good or for ill, Anatole France had inherited a spirit of clarity in diction which he believed to correspond with clarity in thought. It was the spirit, for example, of Augustin Thierry, the blind historian to whom it seemed sufficient if he could complete fifteen or twenty faultless lines in one day, and who would wake his attendant at four o'clock in the morning to dictate the alteration of a single phrase in the manuscript of his *Conquête de l'Angleterre*. It was the spirit of Gustave Flaubert, who used to recall with pride how he had expended a week's labour upon "the avoiding of an assonance."

III

The subjects treated in *La Vie Littéraire* are very various. Most of them were prescribed, or at least suggested, by books of the hour—whether by those which had enjoyed a *succès d'estime* or by those that won only a *succès de scan-*

dale. All was fish that came to his net. Perhaps Leconte de Lisle had published a new lyrical drama, or Father Didon a new *Life of Christ;* Boissier had rewritten the history of the fourth century, Jean-François Bladé had collected old Gascon ballads and folk-lore, Madame Dronsart had brought out a book on Bismarck, Zola had been more shocking than usual in a *roman* or Guy de Maupassant in a fresh set of *contes*—whatever it might be, Anatole France had an opportunity to speak his mind, partly on the writer, but still more on the topic. With greater knowledge or with slighter, but always with a piquant suggestiveness, our critic would help the reading public to some novel *aperçu.* And the papers he wrote were always personal. He would describe his own "adventures among the masterpieces."

One is more struck by the abundance and variety than by the exactness of his learning. The experts were often exasperated, for Anatole France's interests were too miscellaneous to allow him to become an authority in any single field of research. With equal readiness he would discourse on legends of Buddhism, on a collection of old Chinese tales, on the latest view of Rabelais, on a monograph about Egyptian monks, on Pierre Loti's diary of a few weeks in Japan, or on a popular account of the stars. And in truth he never aimed at being an authority on anything. His review of a book in *Le Temps* was work of an order very different from a critique in a magazine of archaeological or scientific erudition. When he wrote of poets, of novelists, or masters of the essay, he had indeed a right to speak such as mere learning can never give. But often he was merely popularizing, with knowledge sufficient to guard him against rashness, and suggesting a point of view rather than developing a theory. That there is room for this sort of literary journalism, the work of many gifted masters—from the *Encyclopédie* down

—is evidence enough. And seldom indeed have we seen such an artist of his kind.

He was probably at his best when he wrote, as he so often did, about pagan antiquity. In those papers he was not addressing himself to Mommsen, to Friedländer, to Boissier, to Fustel de Coulanges. Works of pure scholarship, he used to say, were outside his province, and were indeed no fitting subject for a literary article in the press. "The special and the particular are not for us." [10] But just as in his school-days of long ago he had refused to see in Greek and Latin poets no more than the material of the grammarian and the philologue, he always insisted on challenging the scholar's monopoly, and maintained the rights of the general reader in the riches of the ancient world. The *érudit* might catch him tripping, but not often, for he had a wonderful instinct in skirting around the thornier problems so that, whatever one might suspect, one could not easily prove him wrong. As a rule he stopped short at the point where he could not trust himself further; and long before that point had been reached, his vividness of description might well excite envy among the learned. Any pretext was enough to start him on the enterprise he so loved, the enterprise of making the ancient poets and thinkers to live again for the modern imagination. Victorien Sardou had written yet another play on the fortunes of Cleopatra, Lecomte de Lisle had essayed a French version of the *Ion*, or perhaps the stimulus was no more than a new study by Theodore Reinach of the medals and coins found in Pontus and stamped with the image of Mithridates—anything would serve the turn. Sardou, Leconte de Lisle, Reinach would be dismissed with a few sentences of polite but rather constrained compliment, and the critic was off upon the subjects which they had obliged him

[10] *La Vie Littéraire,* IV, p. 350.

so much by making topical. As a neo-pagan himself, he would so depict Euripides in relation to the Athens of the fifth century that many a Frenchman would forget the flippant scorn about dead languages, and turn to the Bibliothèque Nationale for an edition, or at least a translation, of the *Bacchae* or the *Troades*. Taking as his text a page from Jules Tellier's account of a voyage out of the port of Marseilles, he would remind his reader how this was the same sea on which Odysseus had sailed, and that column of *Le Temps* would be made to glow with such pictures from the *Eleventh Odyssey* as the reader would never be able to forget. Or a new book entitled *La Fin de Paganisme* would inspire a fresh account of Julian, in which the Apostate of sacerdotal abuse would give place in the public eye to the real emperor of history. "I do not fail", said Anatole France, "to absorb the specialist's ideas, and to report such of them as I have been able to grasp." [11] But he made them quick and powerful with a quickness and a power that no specialist could rival. One can indeed hardly overestimate the educational value of those most suggestive papers for the audience to which they were directed, or the interest they were calculated to arouse in a past that was so brilliantly portrayed.

At times the subject would be of a very different sort. Anatole France would write about "Children's Playthings", and when he wrote for children he had a touch more delicate and a style more imaginative than almost any other writer of such pieces that one could name. No one could talk more delightfully about school holidays, or more wittily about contemporary spiritualism. Somebody's election to membership of the *Académie française* would call forth a column on the principles by which such a choice should be governed,

[11] *loc. cit.*

ending with the quaint remark that unless a bad choice were known to be made occasionally, the tribunal could not survive the mortification of the rejected. A casual speech delivered in the Senate would stir him to a discourse on "The Eloquence of the Tribune", and the various styles of French public speakers would be analyzed with rare acumen. In these days of newspaper degeneracy, how jealous one feels of those Parisians who could look forward once a week to such a column by such a pen in *Le Temps*. Without undue aspersion on the "Magazine Supplement" of our daily press, one may be permitted to say that, in comparison, its writers are inspired by a laborious but somewhat pedestrian Muse.

IV

Brilliant as it was, it was not book-reviewing in the usual sense, and for book-reviewing in the usual sense there is an important place. The title of some volume was commonly mentioned, and some hint was given of the contents, especially in the case of novels whose plot was summarized more or less in outline. But there was no systematic survey of merits and faults, no list of *errata*, no detailed justifying or controverting of the author supposedly discussed. The reader's interest was thus withdrawn from the book reviewed to the method and opinions of the reviewer. As Anatole France discourses about a volume of poetry by Paul Verlaine, about a new novel by Daudet, about another *Life* of Pascal or Balzac, it is not the poems or the novel or the biography that we come to know. Verlaine, Daudet, Bourget almost disappear when they have furnished a pretext to the critic for explaining, not how they wrote on their subjects, but how the subjects impressed himself. And the wonder of the critic's work is that herein it seldom provokes impatience. He is himself so much more interesting than nearly any of the authors he has set out to criticize.

For this practice Anatole France did not escape reproach among his literary countrymen. More than thirty years ago, Brunetière arraigned such a method in an editorial of the *Revue des Deux-Mondes.* It was subjective, he said, not objective. Perhaps the *causerie* was something better than a review, but at least it was not genuine reviewing. Quick as a flash came the reply that a man's own feelings and sentiments are all he can possibly know, that there is in truth no such thing as "objective" criticism, and that the real deceit would lie in affecting to do what is impossible.[12] Great admiration has been expressed for this humorous preface to the Third Series of *La Vie Littéraire,* and it is often jauntily assumed that Anatole France was altogether victorious over his heavy-handed assailant.[13] But the real point of Brunetière's attack seems rather to have been simply ignored, with characteristic Francian subtlety and grace.

A later volume of *La Vie Littéraire* dwelt at length on this subject. The assignment of literary values, said Anatole France, is purely capricious, and there is no objective standard implied in the fact that certain works are almost unanimously approved. For it was originally the judgment of a very small number of men that set the example, the rest have followed by imitation, and it is well known that the works everyone professes to admire are just those which hardly anyone examines. Victor Cousin had discovered sublimities in Pascal which turned out to be no more than the errors of a copyist. Eminent authorities had seen genius

[12] Preface to Third Series of *La Vie Littéraire.*

[13] *Anatole France, the Man and his Work,* chap. xiii, J. L. May.

in certain passages which they mistakenly supposed to be by Descartes, and had judged them by that token alone. Ossian had been declared equal to Homer when he was believed to be ancient, but fell into contempt when he was known to be Macpherson. And some years previously all France had been laughing at a piece set for dictation in a military school, deriding it as uncouth in style, until the mockers were silenced by the news that it was a piece from Michelet—and from Michelet at his best.[14]

All this sounds like an indictment of the *Académie française.* For of the two purposes for which the great literary Cardinal three hundred years ago granted letters patent to the Academy, one was just the provision of such a tribunal as Anatole France has derided. The Forty were to criticize one another's manuscripts, and to bestow or withhold an official approbation. They were likewise to pass judgment upon the works of authors outside their own circle which might be submitted to their scrutiny. It was Richelieu's idea to set up an authoritative guide for public taste, which should at the same time keep watchful guardianship over the French language in such constant peril of corruption from four specified sources: the colloquialisms of common speech, the jargon of lawyers, the misusage of the Court, and the abuses of the pulpit. Three hundred years ago the darkest peril of all, known in modern times as the daily press, had not begun to impend. How far the enterprise of the Academy was successful, either in the periodic revisions of the Dictionary or in the effective sifting of wheat from chaff in the manuscripts upon which the "Immortals" adjudicated, is still matter for keen debate. But at least two critics, for whom Anatole France had profound respect,

[14] Preface to Fourth Series of *La Vie Littéraire.*

have declared that the project was admirable and that the measure of its success has been great.

There was need, said Sainte-Beuve, for just such a *haut jury,* a "sovereign organ of opinion." The Academy, said Renan, had unique advantage for combatting the insurgence of inferior literature, and for creating an intellectual form which would *impose itself all round.* And the Forty had been, on the whole, good craftsmen at their job. *Ils ont fait un chef-d'œuvre,—la langue française.* Such an institution, in the view of Matthew Arnold, was one which his own countrymen would do well to copy. For it was from lack of just such a tribunal that public taste in England had become so "lamentably uncertain." [15]

Naturally, then, Anatole France was eager to point out those defects which he could find in the actual working of a system whose very basis he considered unsound. It was easy for him to dwell upon the errors of judgment which had marked a tribunal with three centuries of adjudication behind it, though it is less easy to understand how on his own principles he could be sure that what he quoted as errors were really errors at all. Where no standard can be set up, it is surely impossible to go wrong. But he could at all events draw attention to writers and books authoritatively praised or condemned by the Academy, pointing out how later criticism, such as it was, had pronounced in a contrary sense. So our novelist fairly revelled in his list of cases which showed at least confusion of taste, and he revelled still more in the cases where the Forty had been facile victims of deceit. The Academy of our own time is connected by little more than the name with the Academy of

[15] Cf. Matthew Arnold, "The Literary Influence of Academies" (*Essays in Criticism,* p. 48 sq.)

pre-Revolution days. But it was not to be forgotten how those early censors of literature had depreciated Corneille's *Le Cid*, and how they had found merit insufficient for the dignity of a place at their table in Molière and La Bruyère. There had been odd preferences and rejections too in Anatole France's own time. It was truly singular that Balzac, Comte, Michelet, Daudet had applied for admission in vain, and that Lamartine and Hugo should have been honoured so late. Our novelist did not hesitate to suggest that the Academicians habitually neglected even to open the books written by candidates for election. How could they have done so, he asked, in the case of Leconte de Lisle, whom they had chosen—to Anatole France's personal knowledge—on the ground that he was a "Christian" poet? The Duc de Broglie had procured his election by canvassing for him, and had urged upon the voters that since he was a poet, he must necessarily be Christian. Thus the religious imprimatur of the Academy was placed upon *Poèmes Barbares!* The appeal, too, had been further advanced by the fact that most of the Immortals mistook Sully-Prudhomme's *Le Vase brisé* for a piece by Leconte de Lisle.

We get various other stories of the same sort. Louise Colet, for example, used to win a poetry prize every year. Once at least she was successful with a piece of verse which Flaubert had written for her,—copying it word for word from Lamartine. But the Immortals never knew how they had been hoaxed until Flaubert long afterwards acknowledged the trick. And perhaps it did no one any harm, "for no one read the verses." [16] The truth about an Academy election, Anatole France used to confide to his friends, was that men were admitted or rejected through political intrigue. And herein the Academy was reproducing a very old prac-

[16] Cf. P. Gsell: *The Opinions of Anatole France*, V.

tice. It was not for his literary merit, but rather because his play glorified Athens at the expense of Thebes, that Sophocles won such plaudits by his *Œdipus Coloneus.* What delighted the audience at *The Knights* of Aristophanes was to see the comic dramatist "grabbing Comrade Cleon by the seat of the trousers." Vergil had been a subtle propagandist for Augustus. Voltaire, Diderot, Rousseau were admired professedly for their style, but really because their books supplied inexhaustible arsenals of political argument. Nothing else had helped Victor Hugo to his chair like his diatribes against Napoléon le Petit. And coming to the crucial case of his own election, Anatole France openly declared that he could not have won entrance to the Academy except through a bargain, in which the electors of the Left agreed to vote for a certain nobleman for one vacant chair on condition that the nobles among the Forty gave votes to "the anarchist" for the other.

Scandalous gossip of this sort was sure to accumulate. There is indeed something that lends itself to ridicule in a Society for the organization of literature, one of those "well-finished hives"—as Carlyle called them—"to which it is expected that stray agencies of Wisdom will swarm of their own accord, and hive and make honey." [17] There is something grotesque, too, about the canvassing for votes among the Immortals, or about the cocked hat and sword and green coat with black braid that constitute an Academician's uniform. But despite all that can so easily be said in derision of its ways, the Academy seems to have fulfilled a real purpose. It has again and again been mistaken about men of real genius whom it has excluded; and it has opened its portals to others on grounds, remote from merit, which it is all too easy to detect. But in three hundred years of life

[17] *Signs of the Times.*

it can support the reproach of many an error and many a fault.

Naturally such an institution must be conservative and cautious, a restraint upon the adventurous innovator in letters, as the organized Church is a restraint upon the heretic. If it was obstinate in resistance to Romanticism, there were eccentricities about the Romantics which it was desirable that some influence should resist. And the danger to originality is far less than at first sight appears. The literary genius, like the brilliant heretic, will make his own way, —an individual pioneer, neither much helped nor much hindered by mechanical agencies. It is for the great body of valuable though not surpassing talent that a tribunal of taste has its important guidance to supply. In a mocking mood Anatole France declared that the Academy had existed "to prevent all improvements in the French language", but he may well have meant this as no more than a stinging paradox, with that touch of truth which the paradox needs. The *Académie française* has the credit of having made French literature less amateurish, more painstaking than literature elsewhere, as anyone can see who compares the mastery of the graces of speech in the average French writer with the clumsiness of writers in other lands. How much might be gained, for example, by the institution of any sort of genuine tribunal with a prestige to which American journalists might be forced to bow!

Anatole France was an active Academician for only a very short time. He was elected in 1896, and retained his *fauteuil*, but ceased to attend the meetings through disgust over the Dreyfus case. This at least he seems to imply in one of his conversations recorded by M. Brousson. When canvassed by a candidate for his vote, he explained that it would be outrageous for an habitual absentee to appear only at an election, and that the hall porter at the Palais Mazarin would not be able to recognize him. One suspects that the atmosphere of the place had become less and less congenial. In 1914, abbé Dimnet was able to boast that on the roll of the Immortals, so Voltairean in Renan's day, thirty-five out of the forty names were those of men "either practising Catholics or favorable to Catholicism", and that most of the remaining five were careful to give no religious offence.[18] So it was hardly an intellectual resort that our novelist would care to frequent, and he may well have been critical of its transactions.

One knows, indeed, that strange things can be done by the pundits of literature, as by all other pundits. As Oliver Wendell Holmes pointed out, there is much humbug in "conventional reputations", and the expert often bends before a popular storm. There is a tacit understanding, says *The Autocrat of the Breakfast-Table,* that this or that electro-gilded celebrity shall not have his face dimmed. For perhaps he is old, or rich, or goodnatured, or "such a favourite with the pit that it would not be safe to hiss him from the manager's box." But there is likewise a certain acidity of criticism that prevails among men of letters, who seem to believe with St. Paul in the duty of being able to admonish one another. Richelieu indeed dreamed of establishing a sort of European headquarters for the literary elect of all nations, where they should live together, commune together, and co-operate in guiding the taste of the common herd. But one feels that such a Temple would not have been without that friction which the elect of such an order have usually developed. It was assuredly no such gathering that Rabelais had in mind when he sketched the serene and harmonious life of the Abbey of Thelema.

18 Article by abbé Dimnet in *The Nineteenth Century.*

But it is less important to decide whether any such group of critics is very likely to agree than to consider whether in the nature of their task there is any obstacle which makes at least a fair measure of agreement impossible. It was a favourite contention of the late Frederic Harrison that the great assize of letters has now been closed, with the first prizes at least everywhere awarded by a judgment so gradual and so unanimous that it can hardly be supposed in error. The gates leading to the Elysian fields, said Mr. Harrison, might slowly wheel back on their adamantine hinges to admit now and then some new and chosen modern. "But the great company of those who know, and in especial degree of the great poets, is a roll long closed and complete, and they who are of it hold ever peaceful converse together." [19] How shall we adjudicate between such diverse views of criticism?

At all events, we may fairly quote Sainte-Beuve against a disciple who called him in literary matters "the master of us all." "The first consideration", said that sagacious critic, "is not whether we are amused and pleased by a work of art or mind, nor is it whether we are touched by it. What we seek above all to learn is *whether we were right* in being amused with it, and in applauding it, and in being moved by it." And though Anatole France might profess to think one judgment on such an issue quite as good as another, he is often very peremptory indeed in insisting upon his own. If he was diffident about the value of his personal taste, we have to take his word for this, for there is no trace of diffidence in his actual apportionment of praise and blame. Mounting the literary judgment seat, he could pontificate with the very best. He tells Georges Ohnet, for

[19] F. Harrison: *The Choice of Books,* p. 23.

example, that he has achieved nothing great, though his book has reached its seventy-third edition in a single morning, for the "mentally poverty-stricken" must have their ideal too.[20] Zola, he agrees, is a famous man, detestably famous, for he has erected for himself a monument in such a pile of ordure as none ever built before. He warns schoolboys that when their masters put Thiers's *Le Consulat et l'Empire* into their hands, they are being introduced to the worst French prose ever written.[21] These are some examples of his literary condemnation, and he is no less definite in his literary approvals. In an admirable passage of criticism he once laid down the principle that taste in letters is necessarily of slow development, because it is the outcome of long and often sorrowful experience. Did he then really mean to imply that there is no natural superiority in one taste over another, in the more mature over the more crude?

V

But though his critical practice was for the most part better than his rule, one has to regret some consequences of this haunting idea about "subjectivity." No doubt it is important to explain the genesis of a book that is being criticized; but there are many books whose main interest is not exhausted, or even very seriously affected, by knowledge of the personality of their authors. They have an origin, but they have also a content.

Curiously enough, it is in his studies of reminiscent work that Anatole France leaves one specially discontented. For many a reminiscent work is more important as history, or as professedly historical, than as a revelation of the character of him who wrote it. For example, when the *Journal* of the Goncourts appeared, it would have been interesting to

20 *La Vie Littéraire,* II, p. 64.
21 *La Vie en Fleur,* XIV.

know how far Anatole France—who had lived in the same city and at the same time—was able to confirm or refute their picture of Parisian life under the Second Empire. What he has given us is, instead, a few pages of admirable reflection about the autobiographic art in general, comparing the *Confessions* of Rousseau with the *Confessions* of St. Augustine, and both with Chateaubriand's *Mémoires d'Outre-Tombe*. Only at the end, and apparently as a sort of afterthought, does he speak of the Goncourts, in a few paragraphs of subtle psychological analysis, which nowhere tell us whether those brothers observed well or ill in the society of their time. His study of many another autobiographic book is open to similar objection. He could indeed have had no personal knowledge of the time of Benjamin Constant. But he knew at least as little at first hand about Constant's love affairs, which are not very important to posterity, as he knew about those public events of which the writer was so keen a contemporary critic and which the world will always be concerned to understand. One would rather hear about Constant's attitude to Napoleon, whom he called "a Genghis Khan", and to the administration which he called "a government of Mamelukes", than about the variety of his relations with Madame de Krüdener and Madame de Staël. When Anatole France wrote about the letters of the Empress Marie-Louise, he had indeed a subject, if not after his own heart, at least exactly suited to the gifts of his own genius, for the interest there was of a morbidly psychological character alone. But elsewhere that tendency to "divination", which he thought such a fault in Zola, has prevented his studies of autobiography and correspondence from having the value we might well expect. Nor is he free at times from a precisely opposite fault. When he reviewed Madame de Gronsart's *Life of Bismarck*, he simply wrote a brief and very sparkling *Life* of that prince himself; but whether Madame de Gronsart had written it well or ill, we are not given even a hint.

His book reviews were thus often chats with the reader about some problem which a book raised. In these *causeries* one becomes accustomed to certain recurring moods of mind. There is an ever present note of pessimism, not indeed what Margaret of Angoulême called "the boredom shown by every creature who is well bred", nor yet the dark despair of Anatole France's earlier period, but a gently fatalistic expectation, often lit up by the saving grace of humour. From time to time, for example, he would raise the question of human responsibility in its special bearing upon the criminal, abjuring Lombroso's idea about the *criminel né* because the famous stigmata had so often been found in harmless folk, and yet insisting that the offender should be pitied rather than punished. What, for instance, he asks, had been the guilt of the unfortunate woman in the *Affaire Clémenceau* by Alexandre Dumas? She had followed certain perverse instincts, and for our instincts, received through heredity, we were in no way responsible. Education and inheritance were decisive. And no doubt the same was true of inhabitants of other planets. Astronomy showed how in the heavens there is a like action of those pitiless laws by which evil is perpetuated on the earth. But evil was necessary, and so was pain. Mankind had an obscure consciousness that whatever is great in life must have its roots in an experience of suffering.

In a lighter vein, and thrilled with the spirit of his country's past, he would discourse on old ballads and stories of the France of long ago, including particularly those occult and marvellous things that have lived in present remembrance. Or he would dwell upon the contrast of the old *régime* and the new,—the manners of certain graceful ladies of monarchic times, which compared so favourably with those of *la jeune fille* of democratic days—and he would glorify the immortal Balzac for showing so faithfully the features of a vanished past. One night Anatole France had seen *Hamlet* played at the Comédie Française. Next week his column was filled with thoughtful reflections about the deathless interest of that piece for all who can think, and the obvious tedium it inflicted on those ladies who were eating iced fruit in their boxes! For it was mankind's eternal problem that was on the stage, unrelieved by amorous adventure in the world of high finance. And there is always an undercurrent of impish scepticism. Men, he said, can live without thinking—and they generally do.[22]

Yet he quickly reminds us that there is a danger in refraining from thought, at least in so far as a humanitarian spirit must be formed by appreciation of the limits of knowledge, and this can never be reached except by trial. Only those who knew how futile it is to affect a wisdom higher than that of one's neighbour would make the necessary allowance. With great justice had that notable unbeliever, Pyrrho of Elis, been elevated by his fellow-citizens to the priesthood, for his life was indeed holy, and amid all his doubts he conformed to those general customs in which all morality consists.[23] A sceptic, Anatole France has again and again contended, will never be a revolutionary, for he has no expectation that for even the worst laws any better code can be substituted.[24] He will yield a formal, but not a persecuting assent, even as that most worthy man, the abbé Gassendi, could profess theology without believing in God.

[22] *La Vie Littéraire,* I. p. 11.
[23] *ibid.,* II, p. 133.
[24] *ibid.,* I, Preface.

A point at which our author's critical hospitality always breaks down is the point at which he finds some writer who has been censorious either towards the spirit of the French people or towards the spirit of mankind as a whole. It was upon these that he would release streams of indignation such as one had seldom seen flowing in the whole history of criticism. Hermant's book, *Cavalier Miserey*, had been contemptuous towards the French patriot, and the author had to hear in no measured tones what one French patriot thought of himself.[25] Georges Ohnet had argued in *Volonté* that man alone of the animal creation is endowed with such free will as to merit all the punishment which fate can bring upon him for his misdeeds. M. Ohnet, said Anatole France, had not argued, but only asserted, and it was sufficient to meet him with an equal vigour of denial. Every page of the book had been shocking, offensive, and melancholy. There was nothing tolerable in it except the title page, but one should not flatter such a writer by calling him detestable; he was just mediocre and a snob.[26] Nowhere else can I recall an instance where Anatole France's work has degenerated into a piece of reviewing that is so near to mere abuse.[27] But his favourite doctrine of Determinism had been slighted, and with it his apology for the faults of mankind. On the whole, however, his judgments were mild. He had learned to expect comparatively little from contemporary authors, as from contemporary politicians, recognizing—as he says

25 *ibid.*, I, pp. 73 sq.

26 *ibid.*, II, pp. 56 sq.

27 Long afterwards, in a talk with M. Ségur, Anatole France admitted that there might have been a modicum of spite in "the very unkind article which, contrary to my usual custom, I wrote a long while ago on Georges Ohnet." But he did not atone for it very much by explaining that Ohnet was indeed worthy of his fame, because he never shocked the public by introducing a new idea, and all his work was so "attuned to the diapason of universal mediocrity."

in *Le Petit Pierre* [28]—the all-pervading mediocrity of men and things. And to a writer whom he judged of really outstanding merit he could pay such a tribute as would never be forgotten.

* * *

One who has chanced to read Anatole France's other works before taking up *La Vie Littéraire* will become very curious about its date. For he will observe a difference in tone, comparable to that which separates a book like *Sylvestre Bonnard* from a book like *Histoire Comique*. In his literary criticisms at least, our author's Muse was restrained under the rule "virginibus puerisque." One even reads there with astonishment that marriage is an institution which Anatole France would not see deprived of "a single jot of its power and majesty." The symbols of religion, too, are treated with studied decorum, for example, in such a paper as that on *La Tentation de Saint Antoine*, which contrasts so strongly with *Thaïs*. In one extraordinary passage the writer points out how the arguments used against miracle by sceptical disputants are absurdly inconclusive, though he hastens to add that in the miraculous he has no personal belief.[29] And he tells us in a prefatory note: "Those who are good enough to read me know my respect for sacred things." In view of its context, this last remark cannot be taken as ironical. But the date of the writing had nothing to do with its peculiar character, and the explanation is indeed obvious. *Sylvestre Bonnard* was meant to be crowned,[30] and *La Vie Littéraire* was for serial publication in *Le Temps*.

28 chap. xxxiv.

29 *La Vie Littéraire,* IX, p. 105.

30 We have his own statement, recorded by M. Brousson: "*Sylvestre Bonnard.* Toujours *Sylvestre Bonnard.* Mais c'est de tous mes livres le plus fade, le plus ennuyeux. Je le fis pour gagner un prix à l'Académie" (*Anatole France en Pantoufles,* p. 352).

PART II

THE MIDDLE YEARS (1893–1905)

CHAPTER VI

SATIRIST AND SCEPTIC UNDER THE THIRD REPUBLIC

Satire is a sort of glass, wherein beholders do generally discover everybody's face but their own, which is the chief reason for that kind reception it meets in the world, and that so very few are offended with it. But if it should happen to be otherwise, the danger is not great: and I have learned with long experience never to apprehend mischief from those understandings I have been able to provoke. For anger and fury, though they add strength to the sinews of the body, yet are found to relax those of the mind, and to render all its efforts feeble and impotent.

SWIFT

France resembles a region where volcanic forces have been recently active. Here and there the ground is seared by explosions. Deep chasms have opened. Rumblings are heard which may betoken fresh eruptions. The passions roused in three Revolutions are not extinct.

LORD BRYCE

There is a stage at which humour ceases to be a saving grace. For there are situations in which the critic, to be effective, must try the cutting edge of satire. To believe in one's contemporaries while one can is perfectly consistent with disbelieving in them when one must. It was in the years of the long drawn-out *affaire Dreyfus* that Anatole France passed decisively from humorist to satirist. And the cause was adequate.

I

We are indebted to a Parisian psychologist for our best

account of what satire intrinsically means. In that striking monograph, *Le Rire*, M. Bergson has analyzed the work of the great literary caricaturists: of Cervantes, of Swift, of Molière, of Le Sage. He has found the essence of this in its simplest form, that of the political cartoon. The cartoonist draws a face, ridiculous in expression, and yet undeniably resembling some well known person who may never have impressed the casual observer as looking ridiculous at all. There is exaggeration, no doubt. But what is exaggerated is something really present in the original, something one can identify with a thrill of amusement—as soon as it has been so magnified as to be made noticeable.

M. Bergson further points out that the aspect chosen for cartoon is always of the same kind. The human face ought to be mobile, flexible, adaptable, but these qualities are never found in perfection. Always there is a trace of rigidity,—some habitual bias that persists amid differing circumstances. In short, there is a lurking touch of *mechanism* as contrasted with *life*, and it is this which the cartoonist makes obvious by exaggerating it. If there is in the original a hint of the austere, he deepens it into gloom. If there is just a suggestion of fixed meditativeness, he exhibits it as an unquestionable stare.

English readers will recall at once what the comic papers have made of Gladstone's eye, of Dean Inge's sorrowful countenance, of that enduring boyishness which no political affliction could ever remove from the figure of Mr. Winston Churchill, of the "majesty of true corpulence" that gave the late Lord Salisbury so much of his weight with the public, or of that unmistakably Anglo-Catholic physique which so greatly helps Lord Hugh Cecil on a platform of the English Church Union. In caricature there is, of course, tremendous intensifying of such mechanical melancholies, rotundities, or austerities. But the caricaturist shows what is incipient there, what the ordinary observer may well have missed because it was lost or masked in a general view. It must be isolated as well as magnified if it is to be really seen. Thus, as M. Bergson says, the comic artist "makes his figures grimace as they would do themselves, if they went to the end of their tether." Perhaps Dickens has come nearest to disclosing his own method in a passage which expresses exactly the Bergsonian account of caricature. Writing in *Bleak House* about the likeness of Mr. Guppy which hung in his mother's room, the novelist says: "There was a portrait of her son which, I had almost written here, was more like than life. *It insisted upon him with such obstinacy, and was so determined not to let him off.*"

It is thus that Anatole France has burlesqued French society in the years of the Dreyfus case. In the figures as he drew them there is a sort of obstinate insistence on some lurking disposition of the public official, the priest, the soldier, the man of business, the lady of the château,—some quality that might not have been noticed had it not been obtruded by such cunning intensification. Anatole France isolates it and magnifies it, stripping off, as he would himself have said, those conventional disguises which enable men ordinarily to look upon others of their species without horror and disgust.[1] The later historian cannot dispense with the help of such contemporary satirists. We need the *Clouds* of Aristophanes to supplement Xenophon's *Memorabilia.* We need Boccaccio and Rabelais to cast their own light upon the *Lives of the Saints.* We need *Tom Jones* and *Joseph Andrews* to illustrate the presentation of eighteenth century Deism in Collins, Butler and Berkeley. And it is safe to say that the historian of France for the years between 1895 and

[1] *Histoire Comique,* p. 59.

1900 will find priceless material in the ludicrous gossip of château and salon and city bookshop, distorted and intensified just enough to make it suggestive, in the pages of *Histoire Contemporaine.*

There the models are indeed made to grimace as they would grimace if they went "to the end of their tether" and dared to be utterly consistent. There the historian will find a picture of social life as drawn by the keenest spectator and most brilliant artist of the period,—the France of royalist intrigue, of masonic lodges and government contractors, of apparitions of saints and diplomacy under the Concordat and the manœuvring of patriots with an axe to grind. If coming historical literature would be poorer for want of the caricatures in *Punch,* it is not less true that generations yet to come will turn for light upon that epoch of French affairs to *L'Orme du Mail, Le Mannequin d'Osier, L'Anneau d'Améthyste,* and *M. Bergeret à Paris.*

These books are not for the simpleminded, who want their instruction absolutely direct. Anatole France once hailed Mr. Bernard Shaw as the Molière of England, and in French fashion publicly imprinted a kiss upon his cheek. Whether the English Molière was more gratified by the compliment or embarrassed by its accompanying expression, one may well wonder. But at all events two caricaturists of exactly the same type were on that occasion face to face. They are both, of necessity, paradoxical, and the habit of artistic paradox passed beyond their formal writings into their conversational epigrams. I suppose Mr. Shaw does not expect us to look for his considered judgment about soldiers in *Arms and the Man.* When he writes to the daily press that the practitioners of surgery in England have not enough manual skill to manipulate their own shoelaces, he is clothing a truth under a form which only very dull people can misunderstand. And when Anatole France, irritated by the Philistinism of the early Christians amid the antiquities of Rome, says that the great mistake of the emperors was in throwing far too few of this sect to the lions in the Flavian amphitheatre,[2] he is not responsible for the crass ineptitude of those who take this outburst literally. Sharp antithesis and vivid paradox are the satirist's stock-in-trade. Consequently, much of the reproach so often urged against our novelist for "bias" and "onesidedness" is as pointless as a complaint against "Toby, M.P." of *Punch* and F. C. Gould of the *Westminster* for failing as exact photographers.

II

The main outlines of that *cause célèbre* which provoked the writing of Anatole France's next four books may be briefly recalled.

It was on October 29, 1894, that the anti-Semite newspaper *La Libre Parole* contained a very sensational item. It referred to a report that there had been "an important arrest for the crime of high treason", and inquired whether the report was true. The reply was given that one Alfred Dreyfus, a French officer of Jewish descent, had been accused of selling military secrets to the German War Office. At once the anti-Semite press informed its readers that the Minister of War was trying to hush up this scandal because the culprit was a Jew. During the first week of November there was an incessant flow of such articles, arraigning the whole Cabinet and even the President of the Republic for complicity in a scheme to exculpate "the Traitor."

It was an effective press campaign, in an atmosphere prepared throughout the preceding four years by the continu-

[2] J. J. Brousson: *Anatole France en Pantoufles,* p. 32.

ous anti-Jewish propaganda in *La Libre Parole.* The public temper rose high. By the end of the month General Mercier, the Minister of War, had not only promised that Dreyfus should be forthwith brought to trial, but also intimated—three weeks before the court-martial was to meet—that the guilt of the accused was absolutely certain. In a communication to the *Figaro,* on November 28, he said that the Cabinet had seen the "abhorrent proofs", that there was no room for doubt, and that certain persons in civil life were the traitorous officer's accomplices.

So far there was nothing to excite more than a ripple of foreign interest. *Prima facie* it seemed not improbable that there might be a French officer with a German name who was pursuing this nefarious trade. It struck the English reader as odd that there should be such wholesale indictment of the ministry, and in particular of President Casimir Périer himself, for "aiding and abetting." But the journals that brought the charge were known to be of the sensational type, and Frenchmen were known to take their politics rather violently.

On December 19, 1894, the trial began. The witnesses were examined behind closed doors, and the president of the court explained that this was necessary because "there are other interests in question besides those of the prosecution and the defence." In secret a verdict of "Guilty" was reached, and it became generally understood that the evidence had consisted of a single document. The counsel defending Dreyfus said: "They have put a padlock on one's lips." But it was supposed that high national interests had made secrecy imperative. And on 5th January, 1895, in presence of a furious mob howling for his death, Alfred Dreyfus was degraded from the army. He continued to protest his innocence, but he was sentenced to confinement in Devil's Island, off the coast of French Guiana. All seemed to be over, except for an immediate movement by the anti-Semite papers demanding that every officer of Jewish descent should be expelled from the army.

Two years afterwards the matter was recalled to public notice by an article in *L'Éclair,* a journal inspired by Colonel Henry, who was then deputy chief of the Information Department of the French General Staff. It was to the effect that all reason for concealment had now ceased to exist, and that citizens of the Republic might now be safely told upon what proofs the court-martial of 1894 had acted. They were informed that a letter, written in the cipher of the German Embassy, had been intercepted, and that the key to the cipher had been obtained. This purported to be a communication between the German and Italian military attachés, and it contained the words, "Decidedly this animal Dreyfus is too exacting." The mysterious "single document", upon which so much had turned, was the famous *bordereau*—a memorandum apparently sent by Dreyfus to his German paymasters, in which confidential information about the plans of the French War Office had been disclosed. It had no signature, naturally enough, but handwriting experts had determined the authorship, and it was now given to the press for photographic reproduction.

Still the foreign observer was but mildly excited. A handwriting expert does not inspire everywhere the same degree of confidence. That sentence which was alleged to have passed between the two attachés did indeed look rather damning. But it was at least not the British way to withhold from an accused man's counsel the most significant evidence on which a court meant to rely. A few British critics were aware, too, that such a proceeding was expressly forbidden in Article 101 of the French Code of Military Justice. But there was no more than a shrug of the shoulders by suspicious folk across the Straits of Dover, and the incident might soon have become forgotten.

Several months passed before M. Scheurer-Kestner, vice-president of the Senate, raised the matter once more in a letter to the press. He expressed the doubts which had come into his own mind regarding the guilt of Dreyfus, and intimated that in a personal interview with the Minister of War he had given his reasons for suspecting the *bordereau* to have been written by someone else. The minister, he said, had promised to make inquiries, and let him know the result. But he had waited in vain. Since then he had had a visit from the prisoner's brother, who had stated his own conviction that the writer of the *bordereau* was one Commandant Walsin-Esterhazy. This conviction rested on the evidence of a banker he named, who had had many opportunities of becoming familiar with Esterhazy's handwriting through the transactions of his bank, and who had identified it at once when he saw the newspaper facsimile of the *bordereau*. Mathieu Dreyfus, on 15th November, 1897, published a letter which he had sent to the Minister of War, and in which this definite charge was made.

Immediately there was a renewed outburst in the anti-Semite press, alleging that there was a "Dreyfus syndicate" still hard at work, and reviling the vice-president of the Senate for complicity in its designs. Esterhazy was a man of the vilest record, and on such *prima facie* case against him inquiry was inevitable. It was held behind closed doors. The handwriting experts were again called, and Esterhazy was unanimously acquitted, amid the vociferous congratulations of his military friends at court.

Next scene in the *affaire* was the intervention of Émile

Zola. On January 13, 1898, appeared the indictment called *J'Accuse*—an open letter to the President of the Republic, in which the novelist charged the first court-martial with violating French law in its use of a document as evidence which had not been shown to the prisoner's counsel, and the second court-martial with having "knowingly acquitted a guilty person." The premier, M. Méline, at once ordered the prosecution of Émile Zola. But that trial was of necessity before a civil court, with a jury.

It was a strange trial indeed. A ruling was obtained that, since the Dreyfus case was *chose jugée*, the witnesses for the defence might not say a word suggesting the innocence of the man who had been duly and legally condemned. But the officers who appeared as witnesses for the prosecution were given every chance to dwell upon his guilt. Shrieking mobs of anti-Semites crowded the courtroom. The *Écho de Paris*, which could not be thought biassed in favour of Dreyfus, described thus the difficult task of Zola's counsel:

> An outbreak of insults drowned the voice of the advocate. The audience stood up; they whistled; they hooted; sticks struck the floor in regular time. On shutting one's eyes, one had the illusion that the Palace was being swallowed up by a cataclysm. Minute by minute the audience became more excited. Now it breaks out. Menacing cries increase, mixed with whistling. One by one, under the fixed looks of the assemblage, the jurors quitted the court.

In such an atmosphere, while the accused and his friends were being threatened with death, and counsel for the defence barely escaped from attempted assassination, there was a verdict of "Guilty", and a sentence of one year's imprisonment. It was annulled on a technicality by the Court of Cassation, but before the case could be retried Zola had escaped to England. By this time British interest was becoming rather intense. It was a spectacle of "justice" that was very novel to British eyes.[3]

Within a few months, in the summer of 1898, there was a general election in France, and the Dreyfus issue dwarfed every other. A growing sense of uneasiness about what had been done was quite apparent, and it became harder to ignore the suspicious criticism abroad. French scholars and scientists united in solemn "expostulation", demanding that the whole Dreyfus affair be revised. For a time the usual method was adopted to suppress these doctrinaire intellectuals. In an article of *La Revue des Deux-Mondes* the editor assured them of his "complete contempt." Several professors who held government chairs were suspended or placed on the retired list. The mob, taking its cue from the men in authority, began to duck the revisionists in the Seine, and a sort of pogrom was carried out week by week against Jewish shopkeepers. Those were the days when one heard so often on the streets the cry *A bas Zola, mort aux Juifs.* In the election there was a sweeping victory for the anti-revisionists, men like Jaurès and Joseph Reinach losing their seats in the Chamber. The most effective plea for catching votes was that of a national emergency. It was declared impossible to disclose the whole truth, because this would precipitate a war, but the populace was assured that the concealed evidence was ample, and with this cryptic appeal to trust their leaders the electorate had to rest content.

[3] It has sometimes been alleged by French writers that British comment on the Dreyfus affair was prompted by resentment against the Parisian press for its attitude to the South African War, and especially by irritation with the insulting issue of *Le Rire.* A reference to dates will show the absurdity of this. Some of the fiercest attacks in London appeared long before the South African War began, and of those which appeared later some of the strongest were in papers which condemned the Chamberlain policy quite as much as *Le Rire* condemned it.

When the new Chamber met, a fierce anti-Dreyfusite was chosen as Minister of War. This was Cavaignac, son of the general who had so resolutely suppressed the rising of 1848. Among his more interesting proposals was one to cite all the defenders of Dreyfus before the High Court for treason, including even the two advocates, Demange and Labori, whose concern with the case had been professional.[4] In the Chamber, Cavaignac produced yet another mysterious document. It professed to be a letter written in 1896 by the German military attaché to his Italian colleague, and warning him that they must both say the same thing in reply to any inquiries about negotiation with Dreyfus: "For nobody must ever know what happened with him." The Minister of War guaranteed that this letter was authentic, and adduced as further evidence an alleged confession by the accused himself. Naturally the Chamber felt that the *Affaire* had ended at last. By a unanimous vote, on 7th July, 1898, it ordered that Cavaignac's speech should be published all over France. But within two days there was a sensational sequel. Colonel Picquart, who had lately been chief of the Information Department, wrote to the Prime Minister, intimating that he was in a position to prove this last "evidential" document a forgery. This letter was written on July 9. On July 12, Colonel Picquart's house was searched by the police, and on the following day he was arrested. The police professed to have found in his house certain compromising telegrams signed "Speranza" and "Blanche." Colonel Picquart declared that these also were forgeries, and filed a charge against officials of the War Office by name.

So the plot thickened. It was Colonel Henry who had succeeded Colonel Picquart as chief of the Information De-

4 *Vers les Temps Meilleurs,* II, p. 65.

partment. And six weeks after the document read by Cavaignac to the Chamber had been accepted as disposing of the case once for all, Colonel Henry confessed that it had been forged by his own hand! There was then no longer even the semblance of a pretext for resisting revision. Forgers, quarrelling among themselves, began to make revelation after revelation against one another. Esterhazy intimated that he had indeed concocted the *bordereau*, but that he had done this by orders of the General Staff who were now deserting their agents. Henry, he said, was being made a victim, but Commandant du Paty de Clam had counterfeited handwriting too. He was the author of the pretended telegrams to Picquart, signed "Speranza" and "Blanche." Next day after Esterhazy's avowal, Henry committed suicide. The public could not help noticing that there was no official report of this, and no post-mortem examination of the body.

Cavaignac, though he had guaranteed the authenticity of a piece of evidence which a member of the General Staff acknowledged as a forgery of his own, declared that he was more than ever convinced of the guilt of Dreyfus, and on the decision of his government that the case must now be revised he resigned the office of Minister of War. It was plain that the anti-Semite journals were being driven to desperate courses if they would adhere to their campaign. Probably M. Charles Maurras was the man who showed greatest enterprise in devising a new plea. In a letter to the *Gazette de France* he said that Colonel Henry was indeed a forger, but a "forger through patriotism", and proposed that a statue should be raised to his memory! Funds for this pious purpose did not come in very fast. But *La Libre Parole* opened a subscription list for the widow and son of the man who had so nobly sacrificed his morals to his public spirit.

These are the main features of the case upon which Anatole France was to exercise his imaginative gift. To the foreign observer the whole business had seemed foul beyond description. There was, of course, nothing very remarkable about a single miscarriage of justice. Nor was it surprising that the wits of military judges, never very acute for fine points of evidence, should have been misled even on points that were not at all fine in a treason trial of an officer whom they disliked. In many another country such investigators might have been cajoled into accepting documents to be read *in camera* because the "public interest" forbade their publication. How unjust it was to the accused that he should have no chance of knowing the evidence he had to refute, the very dullest minds might have been expected to realize. But patriotic passion has a deadening effect on the judgment. If the case had been no more than a problem in straightening such a tangle as this, it would not have attracted representatives of the whole press of Europe, and focussed the attention of the whole civilized world.

What disgusted and horrified the public outside France was the long and vehement resistance to revision. At least two members of the General Staff were known to have committed forgery in order to secure a verdict. Dreyfus had been adjudged guilty on the evidence of handwriting, though there was a division of opinion among the "experts", and his counsel was not allowed to see the writing in question. Publicists had gravely argued that it was impossible for a court of seven officers to make a mistake—and every intelligent person, who was without bias, of course laughed such an idea to scorn. It seemed indeed impossible that anyone could really believe it. A Minister of War, who had quoted a document as proof, refused to countenance a fresh inquiry when the counterfeit character of his "evidence" was proclaimed by a high official who confessed that he had forged it himself!

And there were far too many coincidences. Dreyfus was a Jew, and it was the anti-Semite feeling that was everywhere inflamed against him. Those who took his side were exposed to every sort of insult and mob violence, turning even an Assize court into a bear-garden of riot. No one was really misled by the fact that certain journals owned or edited by sons of Israel were in the forefront of anti-Dreyfus agitation, or that wealthy Semites had founded anti-Semite papers. Men of that wandering race have never lacked finesse, and to some of them their kinsman was as nought when compared with the advantage of a strident royalism for their business prosperity.

Nor could anyone fail to notice how the leaders of the disgraceful campaign were so often the acknowledged devotees of a movement for kingship or for a dictator. Only a few years had passed since the episode of Boulanger, and there were no opponents of revision more strenuous than those familiar champions of Boulangism—Rochefort, Drumont, Déroulède, Millevoye. One recalls how on the death of President Faure and the accession of Loubet—who was known to have leanings towards Dreyfus—Déroulède led an attempt to capture the "unpatriotic" head of the Republic in the Élysée, how there was no punishment for the rebel, and how for weeks a band of patriots, barricaded in Fort Chabrol, resisted all efforts of the police to dislodge them, amid the plaudits of the mob and the mocking laughter of everyone abroad.

It was indeed a hectic time, with the surge and swell of public feeling manipulated for many a purpose quite outside the single case by which it had been aroused. In French politics there is always a possibility of a *coup d'état*, and in 1897 Parisians hourly expected that such a blow would fall. The Republic, only twenty years old, hated by the nobility of a bygone time, by chauvinists aflame for *revanche*, by men of wealth alarmed for property, was over and over again in imminent peril. That the plot against Dreyfus had been hatched by the army, no reasonable man, aware of the evidence, could long continue to doubt. The evidence did not rest on the confession of such a creature as Esterhazy, nor on the acknowledgment made by Colonel Henry to his own shame. Damning proof, far more than sufficient, lay in that long campaign against reopening a case which had been "closed" on proofs so obviously precarious.

It would probably be too much to say that behind that campaign had stood the serried ranks of the priesthood. There were, of course, exceptions; but the clerical papers, and the ceaseless propaganda by the Jesuits, left no room to doubt how the Church was exerting herself. It is perfectly futile to plead that the matter was one for the courts, and that the clergy had no responsibilities in regard to it. Unless and until it is accepted as a principle that the Church has no prophetic office in a situation where popular passions are being stirred to a fury of racial injustice, to savage attacks on honest men, to disregard of every maxim of ordinary—not to say Christian—fair play, the Roman ecclesiastics in the France of 1897 cannot be exculpated. Instead of calming the public mind, bidding the populace leave an affair of justice to the courts of justice, they were in the foreground of inflammatory fanaticism. Not one bishop raised his voice for the victim.

Even before it ended, and men were able to look back upon it as an incident of singularly discreditable intrigue, Anatole France found in *l'affaire Dreyfus* just the material he wanted for four volumes of mordant fiction.

III

It is a curious social life that these four volumes present. Some of the figures are familiar enough to be met anywhere —thoughtful professors, lost in their own learning, for whom the world is too hard and wives are too light-headed; army contractors who furnish shoes at a price too high for the cardboard soles with which they are equipped; [5] rich tradespeople with aspirations after the world of *ton*, who bind to themselves, by the cords of accumulating debt, such persons as can secure for them the necessary introductions; [6] sprightly ladies who love the uniform, and would cut short the nonsense of popular government by sending a colonel with his regiment straight into the hordes of Socialist deputies; [7] patriotic townsmen who look on, without approval, but also without interference while street hooligans wreck the windows of a Jew bootmaker, shouting *A bas Zola, mort aux Juifs.* Scenes like these, so typical of modern democracy, belong to no land in particular. With a little alteration of names and war-cries, they might be transferred to the England of Mr. H. G. Wells. *L'Anneau d'Améthyste* and *M. Bergeret à Paris* resemble at many points such a book as *Mr. Britling Sees it Through.*

There are some very piquant snapshots of magistrates and officials under the Third Republic. Vagrants seem to be condemned, like Humphrey Clinker, for the offence of sick-

[5] *M. Bergeret à Paris,* p. 48.

[6] *L'Anneau d'Améthyste.*

[7] *ibid.,* p. 51.

ness, hunger, wretchedness and want. An interesting figure is M. Laprat-Teulet,[8] a retired *préfet,* one of those great democratic citizens whom his countrymen load with honours. He has completed a quarter of a century in office, with notable success in ruining his enemies and enriching his friends. M. Laprat-Teulet is in the Senate now, with special aptitude for serving on secret commissions, in much demand as a speaker at a Prize-Day in schools, where he always tells the children that he is a poor man. His admiring friends and jealous enemies know how he contrived a thousand channels for draining public money into his own pocket; but they have no proof, until it chances that a new Keeper of the Seals does not belong to M. Laprat-Teulet's particular syndicate, and on the evidence of certain documents passes him over to "the astonished hands of justice." That happens, by ill luck, on the morning of the day when he is to preside at a banquet of the Social Defence League. But M. Laprat-Teulet will come back. He is a splendid financial orator, trusted for his zeal in supporting "property rights", and a bulwark against Socialism. When he has served his short sentence, he is sure to be re-elected, and it is probable that he will act on next year's budget commission.

Another typical *préfet* is M. Worms-Clavelin.[9] He learned corruption early, for he was a young civil servant under Jules Grévy, at the time when the President of the Republic was distributing largesse at the Palais-Bourbon on a scale that it was impossible to check. Since then he has been in many a dark affair that needed to be hushed up, and he has become a master of concealment. In the maturity of his powers he has come to look upon dishonest politics

8 *Le Mannequin d'Osier,* XII.
9 *L'Orme du Mail,* IX.

as part of the nature of things. But he is unpleasantly alone at the job in his district, for those engineers and financial men once influential in the councils of his party are for the most part either in prison or in hiding. But M. Worms-Clavelin plays his lone hand well. The "vast irony of things" has entered into his soul, so that he has become easy-going, mocking, indifferent. Keeping a semblance of zeal for what he is ordered to do, he manages to defeat his own apparent policy by furtive contrivances against its fulfilment. He believes that herein he would have the real approval of most Frenchmen if they understood just what he is doing, and he knows that they would do the same if they were in his place, with his ability. Madame Worms-Clavelin is a Jewess, and consequently, on public occasions, a vigorous anti-Semite.

One listens with great interest to the talk of the Duc de Brécé. As he walks with his guests round his estate, he points with pride to a tree whereon an ancestor of his line had hanged six hundred and thirty-six Huguenots, and speaks of his own longing to prove worthy of such high descent.[10] Again and again he remarks that people may say what they like, but he feels sure the Jews will never be of any benefit to France, and that no one can really believe it possible for a court of seven officers to make a mistake. A feature very French in these books is the scene where a lady of easy virtue bargains, at the price of her charms, in the office of some freethinking *préfet* for the nomination of her favourite abbé to a bishopric.

But that which recurs most frequently is the conversation about Dreyfus and the Dreyfusards. There is discussion about the best method for embarrassing the finances of some

[10] *L'Anneau d'Améthyste,* p. 21.

revisionist newspaper.[11] First among the problems of the hour is that of the Hebrews who have crept into France, and argument about it is not very much exaggerated or distorted from the tone of the famous book in which it historically took its rise, *La France Juive*, which appeared in 1889. Disputants in *L'Anneau d'Améthyste*, talk not very differently from Edouard Drumont in *La Libre Parole.* We listen to devout Catholics in conference about the baffling ways of a divine order under which the Jewish race is permitted to survive.[12] They are undecided on the question whether a converted Jew is better or worse than one who is unconverted, and they interrogate an experienced ecclesiastic on the practical issue of accepting or rejecting Semitic subscriptions for a Christian purpose. In particular, what should be done with the golden *ciborium* offered to the chapel of the château by a lady who now calls herself Madame de Bonmont? The abbé is doubtful, but he takes the *ciborium* in his hands, finds it very solid and heavy, and becomes latitudinarian. This might, he thinks, be treated as a special instance in which the promptings of an uncanonical grace had visited the mind even of an unbeliever whose original name was Gutenberg. The ladies press him to say whether, if the gift is accepted, pious Catholics must face the harder trial of adding such a name to their visiting list.[13]

* * *

Of interest deeper than belongs to scenes like these is the

[11] *ibid.*, p. 49.

[12] *ibid.*, p. 64. Cf. abbé Guitrel's explanation: "We must not go so far as to say that God purposely made the Jews obstinate and blind, to serve as living proof of Christianity. But he uses their free and voluntary stubbornness to confirm us in our belief. It is for that reason that He allows them a place among the nations." (*ibid.*, p. 23.)

[13] *loc. cit.*

picture of a royalist conspiracy as late as 1900. Many rumours, and some prosecutions, had been provoked by the attempted *coup* at the funeral of President Faure. It may be assumed that such conspirators did not confide in Anatole France, but he was in close contact with the events so far as they were public, and so far as they constituted the gossip of the time. His imaginative account in *M. Bergeret à Paris* is thus good historic material, when examined under the precautions requisite in dealing with caricature.

We watch strong committees at work, drawing up a list of the more meritorious royalists who are to have their reward when the Republic shall have been overthrown.[14] They toil at their register and at their propagandist pamphlets, under the benediction of abbés who remind them how "France must be saved", and amid the radiant smiles of splendid ladies always willing to exchange a large cheque for an autograph letter of thanks from the Duc d'Orléans which they can carry next their hearts. Old generals of 1870 who are sure that under all republics the army will be insulted, nobles anxious to have their titles of rank once more authenticated as only a king can authenticate them, owners of broad acres who will never feel safe until the *ancien régime* is brought back,—in short the whole "gentry of the cornflower and the white carnation" can be seen in these pages as Anatole France thought he saw them in the Paris of 1900, plotting and scheming for the great day when "Philippe" would re-enter the capital in a coach drawn by six white horses.[15]

But the organizers of the campaign are by no means so sanguine as those who merely encourage it. A quaint figure of the party is Joseph Lacrisse, secretary to "The League

[14] *M. Bergeret à Paris,* p. 105, sqq.
[15] *ibid.,* p. 93.

of Royalist Youth." He has to point out to his colleagues that their cause has of late lost two very valuable men. President Faure had been of great service to them, for the magnificent pomp that he kept at the Élysée had an educative effect. It had accustomed Parisians to a certain display by the head of the state, and had thus prepared them for real kingship. But Faure was dead, Loubet was in his place, and the street attack on Loubet had been a failure. Worse still, Méline was no longer premier. A perfectly invaluable man Méline had been! Trusted as a republican, with a facial expression that seemed so perfect a guarantee of honesty, he had worked for royalism as a declared royalist could never have worked for it. "He told the people we were the true republicans, and the people believed him." [16] So everything had been in proper hands in those days. In a riot, for example, under Méline's *régime*, the police could always be depended upon to pass by the royalists and club the republicans. But those days were gone.

It was true, indeed, that Dupuy—his successor—was not without merits, for he had given time to the stalwarts of Philippe to pull themselves together after their abortive *coup* at President Faure's funeral.[17] But he had not the same power to serve them that Méline had had. No one would have believed Dupuy if he had declared the royalists to be the real republicans. And of course his position required that he should take a certain attitude. But the change had been for the worse, and under Waldeck-Rousseau things were worse still.

Rather a wet blanket upon the enthusiasm of those committee-rooms is one Henri Léon.[18] He cynically reminds

[16] *ibid.*, p. 107.
[17] *loc. cit.*
[18] *ibid.*, chap. xi.

his friends that if the king does come back, his chief rewards will not be bestowed upon those who have braved peril for him when his cause was least promising. "Must I, then, teach you the A. B. C. of Restorations?" When Louis XVIII came back, it was no *émigré*, no companion of his wandering exile, that he made Minister of Police. It was one of the regicides. Philippe was by no means as clever as Louis, but "we must not think him devoid of intelligence", and he would favour first and foremost those republicans who might join him at the eleventh hour. From them he would have something to expect and a great deal to fear,—not from those who at the risk of life and limb had long committed themselves so far that they could not possibly recede. Kings, in M. Léon's judgment, and as attested by all history, were thankful for favours to come. Ingratitude was their first duty, and no Bourbon had ever failed to observe it. The royalist committee was just wasting its time on a list of the men to be rewarded in proportion to their services. Even the trimmers would come before them, and before the trimmers would come "the faithful republicans who reserve their treachery for the supreme moment." To them would go the portfolios and gold-laced coats, the titles, the endowments. For such as had borne the burden and heat of conflict when it was at its worst and least hopeful stage would be reserved just such trifles as the republicans might leave.[19]

[19] An interesting parallel may be found in *The Diary of Samuel Pepys*, March 7, 1662. It is in the account of a sermon, preached before Charles II two years after his Restoration, on the text, "Roll yourself in the dust." The preacher, says Pepys, was just such a man as Hugh Peters: "saying that it had been better for the poor Cavaliers never to have come with the King into England again; for he that hath the impudence to deny obedience to the lawful magistrate, and to swear to the oath of allegiance etc., was better treated nowadays in Newgate than a poor royalist, that hath suffered all his life for the king, is at Whitehall among his friends."

All this sounded very depressing, especially to the royalists in that committee-room who were taking very large risks, consorting with the underworld of Paris to arrange street riots, organizing "spontaneous" outbursts of public sentiment against President Loubet, or dodging the detectives who waited just opposite their hall-doors at night. How far Anatole France was a true diviner of the moods of such men, one cannot tell. But his picture was at least *ben trovato*, and he would not have amused Parisian readers as he did if there had not been a basis of truth in it.

* * *

The most fascinating figure of these books is "M. Bergeret, Professor of Latin Literature." He is indeed the masterpiece of Anatole France's pencil: learned and consequently indigent, a henpecked husband, timidly contemptuous of his surroundings, with much goodwill towards everyone, even towards his colleagues whom he knows to be intellectual frauds—a man amused at himself and at the rôle he has to play, Dreyfusard in his sympathies, and with that gift for the mordant phrase that always makes a professor disliked in a prosaic community.

M. Bergeret frequents the local bookstore, to read books rather than to buy them, for his wife and daughters have taught him to be economical. In his home he has a very poor room for a study, kept in confusion by Madame Bergeret's disposal of millinery on his chairs and around the desk. In college the Dean has assigned him the worst available lecture quarters, where in a damp and gloomy cellar he expounds the *Æneid* with German scholarship and French subtlety. To eke out his livelihood he has to write, not the sort of books that are of value and that he could produce if he had time, but the sort that will sell. So for three years he has been at work on a *Vergilius Nauticus,* for which he is to get five hundred francs when it is finished,—"A task foisted upon my poverty by a grasping bookseller in league with a pack of pseudo-scholars." [20] They want to prove that French learning has no need of German tutelage, and for this purpose they bribe M. Bergeret to "take part in the philological pastimes of 1820." He agrees, reluctantly enough, thinking of himself as a sorry spectacle, and of the strange ways of the world for which the repute of French learning has decayed in consequence of the defeat of 1870. Ever since Sedan it has been assumed that no nation can be great in scholars unless it is likewise great in the casting of cannon! The professor has little hope that this pedantic execution of a *Vergilius Nauticus* will help France back to fame in the international academies. But he is to get five hundred francs for it. His wife and daughters need the money, and much more. So he toils on, seeking occasional relief in "silent orgies of meditation." And like Bonnard, he moralizes to his dog. That listener, he reflects, does not laugh at him, as young persons of his own species would do.[21]

M. Bergeret has a few friends in his provincial town, men whom he meets at the local bookshop, or with whom he sits beneath an elm-tree in a public square, and who relish the ironic goodwill with which he talks about things in general. Though a *libre penseur,* he is on good terms with at least one ecclesiastic, drawn to him by a common interest in "general ideas" which the rest of the townsfolk do not share. To abbé Lantaigne the professor speaks in a tone of conventional deference, putting little problems which his friend as head of the local seminary may be expected to resolve. Is it really

20 *Le Mannequin d'Osier,* XVI.

21 *L'Anneau d'Améthyste,* p. 137.

true, for instance, that astronomy as discovered by human reason may be something quite different from astronomy as known to God? M. Bergeret has read somewhere that when Joshua made the sun stand still, this was done only in a sense relative to the human point of view, and that thus understood the miracle implies no absolute interference with planetary law. But he is puzzled. Will the abbé tell him directly whether the sun stood still or did not stand still? [22] And what about the monument so soon to be unveiled to Joan of Arc? M. Bergeret is haunted by some doubts about the miracles of the Maid, especially about her alleged restoration of life to a dead child, and he is not quite certain that she was more than a "mascotte." "But abbé Lantaigne did not hear." [23]

Talk constantly comes round to the Third Republic and its ways.[24] The ecclesiastic is certain that democracy has gone far to ruin France. But M. Bergeret thinks it is not so bad as that. He agrees that the Republic has indeed many faults. It is full of administrative corruption, probably worse and certainly easier to detect than corruption in monarchies. The expenses of government have become excessive, for popular leaders have many poor relations, and they are spendthrifts in the cause of their kindred. Everyone knows that the financial situation is bad, and one may guess that it is worse than has been made public. Under present management, France is incapable of any great national designs, for not only is money scarce, but the State is weakened by lack of cohesion.

However, M. Bergeret observes that there is a good side to this. Great national designs are commonly warlike, and

22 *L'Orme du Mail,* v.
23 *ibid,* x.
24 *ibdi.,* XIII.

it is gratifying to know that certain incapacities—financial and political—make the Third Republic a friend of peace. Expenditure, unreasonable as it is, would be more dreadful if it had to sustain monarchic luxury. It was recollection of the Second Empire that made one welcome the change. Public virtues, or what passed for public virtues, were helped by lack of cash, and a republic which had neither majesty nor even general esteem to preserve was saved from some of the more shocking extravagances. There was personal liberty, too, under so weak a government. It at least left people alone. And so long as it could get enough money for immediate wants out of the taxation of the poor, it would be strong in the support of those important people, the economists and the financiers. It would meet its real peril some day, perhaps, when it should be forced to ask for contributions from the rich. Men working with their hands would pay for a long time with mechanical regularity. But as soon as the State should venture to touch large capital, as it might yet be compelled to do, it would be lost.

A very reflective man was M. Bergeret, amid all his troubles in the "Main Street" of that drab provincial town, and in the surroundings still more drab of his home and family. Sometimes, as he looked out upon the scene on his daily walk, he would mutter to himself, "this hateful place." But as a rule his meditations were just quaintly humorous, and any trifle was enough to set up a train of thought. He would stand before a shop-window in which was displayed a model of the Farnese Hercules, a hero he liked to picture to himself not in terms of comparative mythology about those Twelve Labours that meant the signs of the zodiac, but as a barber of Thebes or an herb-vendor of Eleusis might be supposed to have pictured him in the time of the Persian wars. M. Bergeret would think of Hercules resting wearily on his club, after heavy toil undertaken through kindness of heart for people in a difficulty, not seldom doing "foolish things for women of little worth", and gaining in the end the reward of death which then—as always—was the only guerdon of life.[25]

M. Bergeret refuses to be a politician. On the noisiest issue of his time he is, of course, less opposed to the anti-clericals than to the clericals; but he will not join any group, for he will not clip the wings of his mind "in order to force it into a political compartment."[26] What really interests him is the prior question which neither clericals nor anti-clericals will ever raise. They differ in the origin they assign to their rules of conduct, but not in regard to the rules themselves, and the antiquarian point of "origin" is not worth a quarrel. In truth, as this tranquil spectator contemplates the history of social usages, he sees that they depend hardly at all upon what men believe, but almost wholly upon habits, upon "the period and clime", so that there never have been and there never can be two rival codes in any community. He points out how Julian the sun-worshipper was as ascetic in his ways as the Christians from whom he theoretically differed. And he asks wherein do the *libres penseurs* of contemporary France profess any moral ideals distinct from those of the men who go to Mass. The priests have their own striking way of presenting those ideals, but they are the common aspirations of Frenchmen of every type. A man who believes, or professes to believe, that his abiding city is in Heaven will yet urge military service here and now just like the most profane patriot. Duelling originated in a superstitious belief that God will intervene in a dispute to make the "right" disputant able to kill

25 *L'Anneau d'Améthyste,* p. 99.
26 *Le Mannequin d'Osier,* xvii.

the "wrong"; but the priests, who have dropped this view in deference to other parts of their creed, are as unwilling to condemn so fashionable a practice as the atheists who never believed in its divine foundation at all. In like manner all agree, though for different alleged reasons, about private property, about capital, about the organization of labour, and about practically everything else that matters. If the nation were to become Socialistic, the Church's creed would show a similar power of adaptation to a national *fait accompli.*

With these sentiments about his public, it is not surprising that the professor should be a Dreyfusard. Stones hurtle through his window, "arguments" as he calls them, "rhomboid in shape", while screams of "To hell with Bergeret" are heard from the crowd below. Only the Socialists and anti-clericals, the people suspected of "anarchism", seem to have any lingering sense of justice and fair play. It appears indeed to the professor that the case for Dreyfus is part and parcel of the larger case for "Social Revolution", and he rails with fury against those established authorities that still maintain their inhuman systems of punishment for crime.

* * *

It is in M. Bergeret's opinions that we have the most detailed picture of Anatole France's attitude to the *affaire.* The professor reads to a little circle of friends an article entitled "The Government", obviously written by himself, which has appeared that morning in the *Figaro.*[27] It dwells upon the source of popular delusion as rooted in a *naïf* idea of the Army. The crowd, says M. Bergeret, loves soldiers, thinking of them for the most part in terms of spectac-

[27] *M. Bergeret à Paris,* chap. xiii.

ular display,—parade, march past, review, manœuvres, uniforms, high boots, spurs, epaulets, guns and flags. Such are features that catch the eye. The national trade in pictures has confirmed the error—those brilliant little sketches by military painters, with their spotless uniforms and "nice tidy battle scenes." All this is reinforced by the ever potent conception of *gloire*. And it was hard for the crowd to think of officers differently. They clutch at any pretext for discrediting painful evidence:

> The officers who rode past on horseback with their swords in their hands, amid the glitter of gold and steel, to the sound of music and the roll of drums,—how was it posible to believe that they would shortly be bending over a table, behind locked doors, *tête-à-tête* with anxious agents from the prefecture of police, handling the eraser and the india-rubber, handling the gum-brush or sprinkling pounce, scratching out or putting in a name in a document, forging handwriting to ruin an innocent man, or thinking out ridiculous disguises for mysterious appointments with the traitor they had to save? [28]

M. Bergeret even commends the popular dislike to deface this lovely image of the early morning march and the chivalrous battlefield with such drab colouring of the secret office, the sponge and the eraser. Yet these were the hard facts. Such was the whole ghastly drama of fraud, covered and buttressed until it could be neither buttressed nor covered any longer, by lazy plotting scribblers of a suborned press. The impostors, forgers, and tricksters of all preceding time had not accumulated in the course of the centuries as many lies as the Parisian public had to read in their newspapers in a single day. "And after that, how can we be surprised that they have so many bogeys in their heads?" [29]

[28] *loc. cit.*

[29] *ibid.*, chap. xx.

In many a critical appreciation of Anatole France he is freely quoted as "M. Bergeret"; and in truth if ever an author drew his own likeness in a work of fiction, it is here. There are exceptional passages, of course,—outbursts by the professor at a time of conjugal hardship, which must not be taken as Anatole France's view of his age, or even as M. Bergeret's own. When he said that the savagery of civilized peoples was beyond anything ever known in barbarism, that the idea of ever making life on this earth bearable should long since have been given up by all intelligent people, and that almost all of the human species are either hateful or ridiculous, he had just had his sky darkened by his wife's infidelity. Dr. Fornerol made a shrewd guess when he whispered to his neighbour, "Bergeret wouldn't gird at the universe in this way if he had not some special trouble." One thinks of the dyspeptic Carlyle, declaiming about the world as a fuliginous chaos and Europe as a huge suppuration, denouncing his maidservants as "sluttish harlots", and avowing that he can reverence no existing man.

In short, Anatole France was not only expressing through M. Bergeret his judgments about the Third Republic. He was creating a character, worried with domestic infelicities, and reacting to his environment in a mingled condition of academic detachment and academic incompetence. What Bergeret says has to be carefully examined in the light of the circumstances, and those critics who have accepted all his opinions wholesale as those of his creator have done less than justice to Anatole France the imaginative novelist. Yet these four volumes of social satire are very eloquent of the author's views about much that he had to watch during the Dreyfus period. He too was in a mood of disgust, and may well have used a heavier brush, with more lurid colours, than the situation could justify. If there were reckless chauvinists in the Paris of that time, there were likewise reckless anti-clericals. If there were some who joined in a pogrom against Jews, there were others who joined in a like pogrom against the Army and the Church. It was a time when heads were split open in the Champs Élysées by rival mobs. Here is the picture as drawn on behalf of one side, which was fortunate enough to command the services of an inimitable artist. It is persuasive, convincing, no doubt in its essentials true. If the other side have an equally plausible case to present, they have unfortunately never presented it with like vividness and power.

* * *

Not long ago, in an English country town, occurred the death of a quiet gentleman, who spoke English with a foreign accent, and was known to his neighbours chiefly as an enthusiastic gardener. Within a few days after his funeral it was learned, with a thrill of interest, that the name under which he had passed was not his own. His real name was Esterhazy. At once there came back to all readers of the British press, who are concerned in foreign events and have passed middle age, how dark was the record of the forger of a generation before. But except for an occasional reminder, all thought of Dreyfus and his fortunes has long passed away. The expiation has been made, and there will be few to dispute that in its great essentials the picture as drawn in *Histoire Contemporaine* is fair.

But there is another aspect of that satiric series about which no such consensus can be maintained. Is the whole story of a royalist plot in *M. Bergeret à Paris* to be dismissed as a novelist's ideal fancy, incapable of disproof, and yet destitute of evidence that it describes anything actual?

In the very year when Anatole France's book appeared there was founded a singular organization under the title *Action Française*. The conspiracy upon which our novelist dwells is supposed to have been in process of formation about eighteen months before. And what was the purpose of the *Action Française?* To avoid all reproach of bias, I shall quote the words of a writer of great competence who is among the most enthusiastic friends of that movement, Mr. Georges Chatterton-Hill. Writing twelve years ago in *The Nineteenth Century*, he thus defined it:

> The Association in question has as its object to galvanize into life the latent antipathy of many people for the Republic, to unite as it were in a single sheaf all the individual movements of revolt, and to place the forces thus collected and organized in the service of the King of France.

The subsequent history of that organization is now known to all. In fierce revolt against the advice of Pope Leo XIII, given eight years earlier, that French Catholics should "rally" to the Constitution of their country, these professed sons of the Church have been unremitting in their efforts to bring back the kingship, and with that end in view to make the republican administration unworkable. On every issue of their daily paper stands a motto from the "Pretender" described as *héritier des quarante rois qui en mille ans firent la France*. They have their campaign of lectures, their publishing house, their students' associations, their women's auxiliaries, their *camelots du roi* who specialize chiefly in the disturbance of gatherings at which a republican monument is unveiled and in creating disorder at all commemorations of the great Revolution. As I write these lines, a principal evidence of their spirit is being shown in the obvious rejoicing of their journals at the collapse of their country's currency in the chief money-markets of the world.

It is indeed a curious spectacle, not easily paralleled either in the present or in the past, this open campaign by citizens of France against the very basis on which their government rests. One feels that under the Republic there must at least be immense toleration of free thought and free speech. Excepting only the *Confédération Générale du Travail*, which so threatened Paris in 1906 that it was necessary to import some sixty thousand troops for protective purposes, there is no other menace comparable to that of the *Action Française* which the republican government has to face. There is needed no further explanation of the wavering and unstable policy which Anatole France had to deplore, when one thinks of a government thus assailed on different sides by groups which violently disagree with each other, but are ever ready to coöperate for the overthrow of the Constitution under which they live.

If such a movement was nascent about the year 1899, if Mr. Chatterton-Hill is right in saying that it aimed to "galvanize into life the latent antipathy of many people for the Republic", shall we regard Anatole France's picture of the royalist committees as probably overdrawn? Rather one must conclude that what he represented as a chimerical enterprise of a few fanatics of the old *régime* was in truth a serious, even a grave, tide of insurrection. And if it has swollen to such dimensions within a few years, we are driven to suppose that, like *Le Temps* and the other papers which think it policy to leave unreported each huge royalist meeting, he erred in minimizing rather than in exaggerating what was at work underground.

CHAPTER VII

THE SCEPTIC AS SOCIAL REFORMER

While the Positivist faith professes to base itself upon science, its emotions centre in humanity, and we are therefore treated to the singular spectacle of a religion in which every advance in the doctrines which support it dwarfs still further the dignity of the object for which it exists.

LORD BALFOUR

It was not surprising that the Dreyfus case should have turned Anatole France from humorist to satirist. But it was remarkable that it should have made him, temporarily at least, a sort of prophet. In the years from 1898 to 1906 he appears in a new rôle,—social pamphleteer, platform speaker, not unlike Mr. Bernard Shaw in his "cart and trumpet" days. The pamphlets and the speeches have been collected in a volume, with a title very significant of the author's change. It is called *Vers les Temps Meilleurs*.

I

Those bad times which he proposed to improve may be sketched from material thick strewn in the novels. And he must have intended these, or at least some of them, as no mere pieces of caricaturist exaggeration. For Anatole France allowed the soliloquies of M. Bergeret and the conversation of abbé Coignard to be republished as his own by the *Bibliothèque Socialiste*. The Socialists too, apparently with his approval and certainly with his consent, reprinted *Crainquebille* as a half-franc pamphlet in aid of their cause.

For instance, he attacked the bourgeois administration of justice. *Crainquebille* is a picture of the hardships of an old man struggling for a livelihood as a street-hawker. He sells leeks and cabbages from his barrow, the butt of urchins, and often swindled by his customers. A gendarme tells him to "move on", and in the crowd, amid a babble of voices, he is thought to have hurled an offensive epithet at the officer. It is in vain for witnesses to plead that Crainquebille said nothing of the kind. The policeman gives his evidence, the court ignores all that is urged in rebuttal, the prisoner becomes confused, and the sentence is passed. When this harmless old street-hawker comes out of jail he is still in public disgrace, takes heavily to drink, falls lower and lower into destitution, and is with difficulty prevented from throwing himself into the Seine. The piece is not very convincing, and it is hard to suppose that any court in France would be so grotesquely unfair. It is not, perhaps, less credible than the scene in *Oliver Twist*, where the London magistrate deals "summarily" with Oliver for stealing a book from a counter, and one knows how Dickens shared with Daudet the special admiration of Anatole France. Perhaps the police magistrates of Paris are not yet better than those of London about ninety years ago. At all events, the author of *Crainquebille* should have been in a position to judge. The story recalls a passage in *Le Mannequin d'Osier* about the tramp Pied d'Alouette, whom a magistrate had tried for murder, and in the complete absence of proofs against him had sent to jail for six months "in the vague hope that unforeseen charges would be laid at his door."

Crainquebille has been dramatized and acted, to the great delight of the social revolutionists. It is a French counterpart of Mr. Galsworthy's *Justice* or Mr. Bayard Veiller's

Within the Law. But reliance could not always be placed upon the author as champion of a "proletariat" system which would "democratize the courts." There is a passage in *Les Dieux ont Soif* which we may be sure that the *Bibliothèque Socialiste* would not care to reprint. It is in the congratulatory address by Brotteaux to Evariste Gamelin, who had just been appointed a juror on the court of the Revolution. You are to act, he says, on a tribunal more trustworthy than any other, because it has to "search out good and evil, not in themselves and in their essence, but solely in relation to tangible interests and plain and obvious sentiments." Judgment was to be given, not between truth and falsehood, which was impossible, but between love and hate, which was easy. And there could be no risk of mistake, for every verdict would be good so long as it satisfied popular passion, and in a difficulty one could always invoke the arbitrament of the dice!

A social reformer is plainly under some disadvantage when he is likewise a cynic.

The Third Republic, as this writer has portrayed it, has features one may easily specify. It is a State in constant peril from revolutionaries, tolerated for a time with sullen acquiescence by powerful interests—monarchic, military, financial and religious—which lie ever in wait to overturn it. In ceaseless danger, and hence driven to ceaseless artifices of compromise, its government is weak and vacillating. On the whole, the greatest single influence is that of *la haute finance*. Officials are corrupt to the core, looking upon bribery as normal and integrity as peculiar, ever contriving disguise or concealment for an administrative scandal. Militaristic passion is readily stirred, and the public mind is very inflammable. Men best fitted by intelligence or enlightenment to be the guides of policy are either persecuted by those in power or terrified into silence by a fanatical mob. The press is manipulated by forces plutocratic or sacerdotal. Courts of justice are unworthy of the name, for they are but courts of law. And underlying all these faults is the obstinate adherence to certain traditional ideas about property, about guilt and punishment, about religion, about nationalism—ideas long since outgrown by the keener minds, but used by dexterous rogues for their own purposes.

This indictment may not appear to be specially applicable to France. One notices in it various counts that are no less conspicuous in the complaint of reformers against other lands and other forms of polity. Here and there our novelist takes the view that the case is irremediable, as for instance when he says about Penguinia that it was ruled with "the weakness, indecision, flabbiness and heedlessness common to all governments", and adds that no government has ever departed from this without falling into arbitrary and violent courses. Yet for some reason, in the decade after 1896, he encouraged the hope that there might be a change for the better. For the method by which this was to be accomplished, we have to turn to his public appeals in *Vers les Temps Meilleurs*.

II

There are some fifty speeches in the collection: on politics domestic and foreign, on social reform, on contemporary literature, on the outlook for science. Some of them were delivered during the Dreyfus days, when tempers were hot and words were high. To an English reader many an epithet sounds rather lurid. The President of the Republic has his policy characterized as *l'égoisme tortueux et bas de Felix Faure.*[1] The Prime Minister is *le blême Méline,*[2] while a Minister of War is described as preparing *de nouveaux mensonges et de nouvelles forfaitures.*[3] Half a dozen of these speeches were made at meetings of protest held by friends of Russian freedom in those dark weeks of 1905 when Tsarist troops were knouting or slaughtering the distressed workers of St. Petersburg. Three or four, belonging to the same time, were in support of European action against "Abdul the Damned." There are others on world-peace, on the abolition of slums, on the project of a co-operative store, on the movement for separating Church and State. A group of special interest consists of complimentary addresses at a banquet to some popular leader, at the funeral of some chieftain in the army of Freethought, at the unveiling of a monument or the commemoration of an anniversary. Most illuminating of all, for those concerned to trace the growth of the speaker's mind on social subjects, are those in which he encouraged the enterprise known as *universités populaires.*

This was a sort of University Extension scheme. Not only in Paris, but over the country, groups of workers were being organized for night study, under such suggestive names as *The Society of the Awakening,* or *The Emancipation League.* Anatole France was among their favourite visiting orators, and in each short address he had very much the same thing to say. Always and everywhere he was appealing for revolt against the traditional in institutions, in usages, in beliefs. And always it was the foundation in *beliefs* that he aimed to shake. Like Pierre Proudhon, he would have said that at the basis of every political dispute

[1] *Vers les Temps Meilleurs,* I, p. 10.
[2] *ibid.,* p. 11,
[3] *ibid.,* p. 12.

in France was to be found some difference that was theological. Hence one of his speeches was quite unlike the familiar speech of an English man of letters to a Labour audience at Toynbee Hall or in Bethnal Green. Mr. Lloyd George at Limehouse is a closer parallel, except for the attacks upon religion which Anatole France never omitted. We know that strain, mingling sympathy with admonition, which is thought appropriate when a man of learning speaks to English manual workers. But in every Francian harangue there was the definite ring of a class-war. The listeners were always and everywhere warned of a conspiracy among "privileged people" to cheat them of their rights, especially through maintenance of those superstitions which are the tyrant's most effective ally.

A typical speech from this collection is one which begins with a few congratulatory words to those who were willing to give their nights to study as well as their days to toil.[4] They are complimented upon their superiority to the sons of the rich, who desired to forget what they had learned as soon as an examination had been passed, while the men of the *université populaire* wanted knowledge which they might keep and use. The speaker would next assure them that the value of such knowledge was boundless, for it was the key to mastery over circumstance—as the great inventors, studying Nature that they might control her, had again and again illustrated. The subjects best fitted to open their minds were such as astronomy, biology, anatomy. And why? Because their most urgent need was to escape from "superstition." Even yet there were wretched people enslaved to dogmas about a Devil and about Hell—hideous folly which a little acquaintance with cosmic facts would soon put to flight. Out of this misunderstanding of the phen-

[4] Cf. esp. *ibid.*, pp. 17–22.

omena of Nature had arisen a barbarous morality, a hateful myth disseminated by the priesthood to the effect that there is merit in suffering and in self-denial. Herein was a mere trick to perpetuate the social tyrannies, and to make men neglect their own amelioration in "the only world of which we are sure."

Liberated by such knowledge of natural history, man would proceed, said the orator, to fashion his own destinies. Other-worldliness had kept him passive and hopeless under wrong. The advance guard of the army of progress had already made its way into the light, but the masses were still lost in the darkness of that entangled forest.[5] Too long had the discoveries of science been monopolized by a few.[6] It was time for the workers to become conscious of their strength, to assert their right to a share in the intellectual riches of the world. The natural history of human development from the days of the caveman to the days of steam and electricity would suggest many a line of progress yet to be achieved. Most important of all, perhaps, would be the unbiassed inquiry into changes relatively recent; above all, the examination of the beginnings of capitalism. For mastery of the capitalistic forces, upon which the proletariat should set its heart and direct its effort, it was necessary to know just how these forces had arisen and how they had grown. Let them scrutinize and discuss with one another the places of *les privilégiés*. Let them wage unceasing war against those successors of the old Catholic League,—the Jesuits, the Dominicans, the Assumptionists, no matter how cunningly these foes of all freedom might disguise their purpose under some deceptive phrase. At

[5] *ibid.*, p. 31.

[6] Cf. *ibid.*, p. 29: *"les richesses intellectuelles longtemps renfermées dans la classe bourgeoise."*

length the battle had been joined, and only through knowledge could it be won. Confronting each other in deadly feud were *l'esprit théologique* and *l'esprit scientifique.* There could be no compromise. The latter for the proletariat was the spirit of life, the former was the spirit of death. And the fight would be hard, for the organization of the enemy was centuries old: *une innombrable armée d'esprits rétrogrades que commandent des moines fanatiques.*[7]

A passionate address during those years was that entitled *La Barbarie Coloniale.* In the early weeks of 1906 all Europe was ringing with tales of atrocity from the French and Belgian Congo. Twenty-five years earlier, the energetic and humane administration of de Brazza had established a protectorate which had won the loyalty of those West African tribes to *le drapeau français.* It was the proud boast of the imperialists that the old colony of Senegal had been extended as far as the Niger, that Timbuctoo had become a French city, that the Sahara itself might now be called "a French desert." But with the coming of other and very different administrators the savage story of exploitation had begun. At a meeting of protest in Paris, on 30th January, 1906, Anatole France pled that the hideous example of the *régime* on the Belgian Congo should no longer be imitated, and that the Republic founded on the Revolution should show how it regarded the black races in a spirit very different from that of the infamous Leopold.

At present, he exclaimed, there is no commerce with these native races except the commerce which shows itself in enslavement and massacre. The peoples called "barbarous" know the European nations only by their crimes. Well had a young Chinaman declared at the congress of Lucerne that his own race, originally so peaceful, had by contact

[7] *ibid.,* p. 26.

with Europeans been made as savage as the invaders who came to "civilize" them. What was chiefly to be feared in the Far East was the copying of western patterns.[8] Bursting into lurid rhetoric, Anatole France suggests that the French exploiters of the Congo might fitly address the natives thus:

> Toujours les explorateurs vous tireront des coups de fusil et vous enfumeront dans vos huttes: toujours le fier soldat chrétien amusera son courage à couper vos femmes par morceaux: toujours le marin jovial, venu des mers brumeuses, crèvera d'un coup de pied le ventre à vos petits enfants pour se dégourdir les jambes.[9]

And of course it all came back to the one great principle: colonial policy was founded upon *la politique capitaliste.*[10]

This point was driven home with special energy in the days of crisis over the Morocco question, and the diplomatic bargaining at the Conference of Algeciras. Speaking at a peace meeting in Paris on 20th January, 1906, Anatole France freely admitted that there was no desire for an outbreak of hostilities in the mind even of the fiercest chauvinist. But, he said, there was a very real desire that the *threat* of war should be constantly available to impede every movement for social reform. It was not so much the War Office as the financiers and the politicians that had been pursuing a sinister policy. For they knew that a people kept under ever-present dread of European conflict would be all the easier to govern in domestic relations. *Inter arma silent leges.* The surest way to block proposals about the extension of rights of trade combination, or about a statutory eight hours' day for labour, was to point out that the national peril forbade such schemes for the time. The

[8] Cf. *ibid.*, II, 82. *Le péril blanc a créé le péril jaune.*
[9] *ibid.*, III, p. 77.
[10] *ibid.*, p. 76.

reply must always be kept in reserve: "*Proletaires, ce n'est pas le moment d'améliorer votre sort. Nous ne devons penser qu'à faire fondre des canons.*" Patriotism was the great plea of financiers and manufacturers greedy for gain. Six weeks of threatened war would injure the Socialists more than twenty years of bourgeois speech-making and votes.

But let not such children's bogeys frighten the proletariat any further. Let them no longer give up their legitimate demands at the warning, "Be good, or the great Algeciras devil will eat you." Above all, let them remember that international relations, by the eighth Article of the Constitution, are a matter not for the President of the Republic alone, but for the two parliamentary Chambers. And how had this been observed, for example, in the recent treaty with Russia? On the pretence that national security demanded it, these two Chambers had been allowed no voice in settling a bargain with the "criminal autocracy" of St. Petersburg, under which milliards had been lost in the guise of loans, milliards more would yet be lost, and an inexpiable shame had been inflicted on the Republic by partnership with despotism. Even yet, twelve years after that treaty had been concluded, the French people were very imperfectly informed of its provisions, and it was currently reported that it might even commit the country to armed intervention in a war with England or Japan. In truth, there was as little opportunity given in practice for popular choice on the issues of peace and war under the Republic as had been given under Napoleon or Louis XIV.

One of these days, the speaker went on, the morning newspaper might announce that the Foreign Minister had precipitated a world conflagration. What had the President of the Council recently said? He had said that if Delcassé had remained twenty-four hours longer in office, war would have been inevitable! And he had added the assurance that the danger was past, because he had himself "put his foot on the match." This in a nation which professed to be in control of its own destinies! It seemed that the very indiscretion of an attaché might be enough to provoke a European horror. Had the days of Louis XIV come back again? There was indeed this difference, that it would not be hired mercenaries, but the soldiers of France whose lives would thus be at the hazard of an official's indiscretion. The changed times called for a changed diplomacy, a diplomacy open and public. If it required a Revolution to effect this, then a Revolution let it be:

> Aveugle qui ne voit pas le danger. Une grande partie du prolétariat craint, et non sans une apparence de raison, que le pays ne se trouve engagé un jour ou l'autre dans des expéditions lointaines, dans des guerres d'intérêt capitaliste. Et comment ne le craindrait-il pas? Sur les ruines du passé, sur les débris des aristocraties et des sacerdoces, le capital assied aujourd'hui sa masse colossale. Il règne sur les empires, il règne sur les républiques. . . . Nous voulons que tous les citoyens sans exception, que le prolétariat tout entier donne son concours à cette œuvre et serve de tout son dévouement et de toutes ses forces les intérêts veritables du pays. Et il faut pour cela que ces intérêts ne restent pas le secret du Quai d'Orsay.

Capitalist, militarist, clergy—all united in an unholy alliance—were fighting for their very lives to preserve the atmosphere of delusion by which they had so long profited. Conjuring with the watchwords of "nationality" and "patriotism", the army contractor was keeping up a lucrative myth about the need for more and yet more armaments, drowning the voice of that nascent internationalism which would work rather for a good understanding among the poor of all nations alike. Only by fostering the imperialistic mania could such men maintain that "organized barbarism and regularized injustice" which one saw in French society. Thus isolated from the common life of mankind, and urged to think of France alone, the nation was led to look on Armenian massacres and the savagery of Tsarist police in the streets of St. Petersburg in the spirit of him who asked "Am I my brother's keeper?" Only a short time before there had been a visit of the Tsar to Paris, and under capitalist instigation the French people had shouted "*Vive la Russie*", never reflecting that the alliance had been contrived behind the scenes by secret diplomacy in order to float a loan in France which might pay for the Russo-Japanese War.

Such burlesque of republican institutions must come to an end. Let it be understood that the war bogey was a mere pretext. Not by competitive arming would the peace of Europe ever be assured. Peace had its enduring basis, not in "preparedness", not even in improvement of human character—which was largely chimerical—but in an intelligent grasp of economic principles by a public that would thus take its own interests into its own hands. And the reforming public would be opposed, of course, by those who profited so much from the *status quo*. One recalls the remark in *Coignard* about the cook who, as was natural, had little affection for Lent.[11]

There is a curiously familiar ring about all this. It sounds like the summary of a pamphlet issued in London by the *League of Democratic Control over Foreign Policy*. And one thinks of Mr. Norman Angell. But the gospel according to such evangelists has had need of a finer subtlety of apologetic since August, 1914.

[11] *Les Opinions de M. Jérôme Coignard*, V.

III

These are somewhat vague and misty generalities. But the heart of Anatole France's campaign during his years of active political work lay in his support of certain proposals that were very definite indeed. Those were the years in which a succession of French ministers was pressing forward a new scheme of popular education. It was plain that only by a people educated very differently from the people of the past could the reins of government be snatched from hands that had so long held them. The old type of school had produced the old type of *citoyen*. For a new type there must be a preparation in new schools. Such men as Waldeck-Rousseau, Combes, Clémenceau, were fighting a hard battle for such reform. And Anatole France was with them, heart and soul.

For nearly twenty years before he took up this cause, there had been more or less intermittent strife that had forced the question forward from stage to stage. In the belief that "it was the German schoolmaster who conquered at Sedan", the French had developed a new zeal for popular education. By the Jules Ferry laws of 1881 and 1882 this had been made both compulsory and gratuitous. It had also been made secular, for teachers were to be appointed by the local *préfet*. Anti-clerical enthusiasts had even proposed that no unauthorized religious community should be allowed under any circumstances to teach, but the Senate had vetoed so drastic a change. By degrees, however, between 1881 and 1900, the friars and nuns were disappearing from common schools, and lay teachers were being appointed in their places. The resistance of the priesthood was naturally fierce. France, it was declared, had adopted a policy of official "godlessness." It was in vain to reply that the new schools were just secular, and that by the elimination of religious dogma from the curriculum they had been made "religiously neutral." No one who understands the Roman position on such matters will require to be told how such a term as "religious neutrality" must sound in sacerdotal ears.

Thus in the period preceding Anatole France's platform campaign there had been a warfare, sometimes open but more frequently covert, between schoolmaster and priest in every French village. Those who owed their appointment to republican politicians made no secret, in their more exalted moods, of the thought that the priests of knowledge had displaced the priests of dogma. Not the Ten Commandments, but the "Immortal Principles of 1789" formed the basis of their ethical instruction. It needed no seer to guess how, all over rural France, such discord would develop between the *maître d'école* who guided the minds of children during the week and the *curé* who addressed their parents on Sunday from the altar. Many a tale of petty village persecution, incited or at least sanctioned by the priest, raised the anti-clericalism of the teachers to a white heat. They in turn became propagandists for the secular gospel, and talked of the need for forming the thought of young France not on the obsolete superstitions, but on "the principles of modern civilization." When the Dreyfus case gave an opportunity for still closer battle, teachers were in the vanguard against *le parti noir*. As soon as that crisis had passed, a further step was taken by the ministry of Combes towards ridding the schools completely of the last vestige of clerical control. In 1904 it was enacted that within ten years all those managed by the religious Orders should be either secularized or closed.

* * *

Externally at least, the agitation was successful. Émile Combes delivered his final blow. Completing the great pressure, half open and half concealed, of twenty years, the anti-clericals had removed the majority of French children for six days in each week from sacerdotal influence, and had placed them under lay teachers who could be trusted not to inculcate a single word of "dogma." To the eyes of the older generation it was indeed a portent. Far behind were those days of Napoleon III when no fewer than seven Articles of the school code of France had been concerned with the religious side of teaching, when the Catechism was officially prescribed, when each day some part of "Sunday's Gospel" had to be read and all the parts were repeated in sequence on the Saturday, and when such exercises of enforced piety were left to be arranged in detail in every case "according to the instructions of the parish priest." As late as 1880 that code had been in force. In 1902, not only in theory but in actual working practice, all elementary instruction was *laïque.*

And with what result? The difficulties which might so easily have been foreseen were left to reveal themselves in practice. They arose at once in connection with that moral side of school teaching which even the most determined secularist minister could hardly ignore. Provision, of a kind, had indeed been made for this under the Jules Ferry law of 1882. The extraordinary circular issued to the schools on July 27 of that year deserves a place in such archives as preserve the record of a doctrinaire legislation which ignores the facts of human nature.

It was pointed out in that famous memorandum that the school-teacher must assume his pupils to have "some previous knowledge of good and evil", because the vast majority of them would come under his guidance with some measure of religious preparation. They would know at least a divine Author of the universe, who was also the Father of men, and they would be familiar with the traditions, beliefs and practices of either Christian or Jewish worship. It would be for the teacher to develop such moral notions—the ideas of conduct that are common to every doctrine and necessary to all civilized peoples. But since the dogmatic associations of such ideas were not essential to them, the teacher could do his ethical work without personally adhering to any such dogma or opposing it. His instruction would be distinct from dogma, though not necessarily anti-dogmatic. Priest, father and teacher would thus combine to "make a good man of each child", and it would be the function of the school to "give all these children an emotional apprenticeship to the moral life."

The devout Catholic objects to this,—and it does not seem to require any remarkable gift for appreciating a point of view other than one's own if even a Protestant, devout or undevout, is to grasp the ground of the objection. Those moral principles which the child is supposed to have learned from parent or from priest are, apparently, to be re-inculcated and developed, but with all that gave them their original appeal sedulously pruned away. If one turns to a typical textbook, prepared by a leader in such undenominationalism for use in the common school, one has no difficulty in seeing how it outrages what a Catholic holds dear.

Take, for example, such a book as the *Cours de Morale*, by M. Jules Payot. The writer has done his best to present for children a groundwork of morals which will be independent of religious dogma without being contradictory to it. So he calls upon the child—with some lack of humour—to discover within himself his idea of "national life in which the highest freedom is included." When the child has risen to this idea, it seems that he can next be led to realize how such national life is possible "only in and by human co-operation." It is not a first course in ethics for the university student that is here outlined, but a course for the elementary school! And the textbook which Catholics are supposed to have denounced on such unreasonable grounds proceeds to explain that "religions have had a common origin in the fear of hostile forces and in a naïve interpretation of death"!

Truly it is hard to draw up a work in strict fidelity to the limits which M. Payot has prescribed for himself. Thackeray once said that Dean Swift's sermons might have been preached with equal propriety from the steps of a synagogue, the floor of a mosque, or even the box of a coffee-house.[12] But Swift had a flexibility of homiletic which the French undenominationalist does not seem to share.

The British Moral Education League has long been occupying itself, somewhat fruitlessly, with a like enterprise. It is well meant, but the Church of England schools have resisted with a vigour comparable to that of the religious Orders in France. The High Church parents have taken their stand, like French Catholic parents, upon the right of the taxpayer, and have told the advocates of undenominational teaching that the Anglican conscience is as much opposed to "godless" schools as the secularist conscience can be to schools of denominationalism. Moreover, without being suspected of priestly prejudice, one may perhaps deplore the unfortunate lot of the French village child under this new *régime*. To those who think in terms only of Protestant countries it may not be obvious that such

[12] *English Humorists,* p. 156.

"Cowper-Templeism"—hard enough in England—would be wholly impossible in France. The French parent, if he is concerned for the moral education of his child, does not desire that he should have two instructors, working at cross-purposes on the discipline of the juvenile mind. And if anyone thinks a child will not be quick to notice such adult discords, he must know very little about children. One may be too young to understand "religious neutrality", but not too young to observe that the *curé* thinks the *maître d'école* a scoundrel, while the *maître d'école* thinks the *curé* a fool. Apart from the delight afforded by so engaging a spectacle, there is a great chance provided by it,—a chance for juvenile free will amid such conflict of authorities, each of which may be disregarded in turn, under the high sanction of the other.

What has happened in practice, according to one very keen and by no means prejudiced spectator, is that every textbook not agreeable to Catholic parents is denounced by the priest. So is "every unguarded word of a freethinking teacher." Lawsuits on this subject have been multiplied. "Thus every village school is a battlefield, and the new generation is brought up in an atmosphere of hatred." [13] Moreover, in secondary education the victory lies for the most part with the Church. Those who can afford to pay fees at private schools ignore the government pressure, defy every artifice of government boycott, and send their children—"at least half of the children of the middle and upper classes"—to Church schools as of old. There, they say, is a home for childhood, not a prison. And so far as girls are concerned, the religious instructors have almost everything in their own hands. One notices, too, with interest how it

13 A. L. Guérard: *French Civilization in the Nineteenth Century*, pp. 241, 2.

was in such Jesuit institutions that both Combes and Anatole France had been trained. How far this experience influenced their later attitudes, we may conjecture at will.

IV

It is the fine optimistic ring of *Vers les Temps Meilleurs* that surprises the reader most. Anatole France seems to have had an interval of intense faith in the power of democracy to look after its own destinies. Democracy had tried this, on a great scale, more than once before in his own land. But the great Revolution which had so stirred the hearts of men like Michelet had roused little more than a mocking spirit in the author of *L'Étui de Nacre.* And in the various efforts made since then he had seen no more than "an incoherent succession of insurrectionary governments." The outburst of fresh faith in a democratic order succeeded, strangely enough, to the pessimism of the Dreyfus days, and it was to be followed by the cynical bitterness of *L'Ile des Pingouins.* Yet those Dreyfus days had not, in our novelist's view, been wholly dark. As M. Bergeret observes in his glowing tribute to Colonel Picquart, they had revealed a villainous state of public morality, but they had likewise raised up some noble characters.[14] And one remembers how Sir Francis Jeune said that his long experience in the Divorce Court had led him to "believe more in human nature"!

Anatole France's new prophetic faith could be justified only on the assumption that the masses might be educated as they had never been educated before. The reform of schools was but one item in his plan for this. Another was the scheme for *universités populaires,* of which our once

[14] *M. Bergeret à Paris,* chap. xiii.

gloomy pessimist became an eager advocate. The title was, of course, a misnomer, for it was impossible to provide for the working masses that "university" training which demands all a student's time. On the whole, the plan was closest to what is known in England as the "Workers' Educational Association", with some features consciously borrowed from Toynbee Hall. It was not just an outcome of the post-Dreyfus enthusiasm, for at an earlier date there had been two tentative projects of the same kind, the one known as "Co-operation of Ideas" in which a joiner had taken the lead, and the other a sort of University Settlement at Belleville initiated by Jacques Bardoux. But it was the shock of the Dreyfus period which awakened men otherwise phlegmatic to the need for educating democracy. In the association of workers with brain and workers with hand Anatole France thought for a time that he could see some real promise of better days. So he raised his voice for that curious venture in which, under the varied names of "People's Palace", "Freethinkers' Club" and the like, it was hoped that the liberating and broadening influence of knowledge might prevent a repetition of the follies of 1897. But the scheme was shortlived, and our apostle sank back into a mood of disillusionment. Not thus was the Republic to be made "safe for democracy."

The disillusioned mood was not hard to recapture. Anatole France had but to recall what he had so often said already about the impossibility of rousing the masses to anything better than a stupid violence, about their temper of revenge, about the plebeian hatred for all the fine things of life." [15] His actual contact with Demos made him revert quickly to that reflection in *Le Puits de Sainte-Claire* [16]

[15] Cf. esp. *L'Etui de nacre,* XI, XII, XV.

[16] p. 245.

about changes of government in the town of Siena, comparable to the turning backwards and forwards of a sick man in bed, who vainly seeks by change of place to circumvent his disease. After all, was it not best to resume his study chair in the Villa Saïd, contented—with his own Coignard—that things should remain as they are, for the mournful reason that plainly they cannot be improved?

* * *

In such a temper he wrote that savage burlesque called *L'Ile des Pingouins.* Nowhere else, perhaps, except in *Gulliver's Travels,* can we find such bitter distrust of progress. It is a fantastic and impious tale of an island inhabited by creatures originally penguins, but raised to human status through the inadvertence of a missionary. The birds, almost anthropoid in appearance, had been evangelized and baptized before the error was known. So at a celestial council of the Saints, where Irenaeus, Augustine, Tertullian, Gregory of Nazianzen and others proffer advice for circumstances so difficult, it is decided that the penguins must be advanced to a rank commensurate with the privilege in which they have shared.

This prelude prepares the way for a history of the stages of civilization. The penguins begin to wear clothes, and thus become for the first time conscious of those inhibitions and disguises that make it possible to be immoral. They fight with one another, not occasionally as in their bird state, but with the continuous pugnacity of human beings, for private rights to parcels of ground. On the basis of successful slaughter the stronger among them found noble houses, with a title to permanent social superiority for their descendants, and the more thoughtful among them who construct a theoretic account of this are the founders of civil law in Penguinia. Out of the cunning deceit of a few, seeking pretexts for monopoly over the rest, emerge a mythology and a priesthood. They develop a cult of kings and warriors, a system of "morality" which is but the legal sanction of dominance for groups that are ingenious enough to overreach and strong enough to suppress the others. Through the "Ancient Times" the "Middle Ages" and the "Modern Times" of the Penguins is gradually unrolled the long series of usages, ignoble and selfish in origin, but consecrated by time and put beyond the reach of criticism by a steadily fostered superstition.

Clearly the Dreyfus case was still in the author's mind. It is not hard, for example, to identify the original of Pyrot, accused of stealing eighty thousand trusses of hay from the stores of the Penguin cavalry, and of selling this to their national enemy, the Porpoises. There is no proof against Pyrot until after he has been convicted, but then proofs accumulate to order, and forged evidence is held to be the most persuasive because it has been made to suit exactly the case. And the Penguin leaders explain that it is really best to have no proofs in such a case, for evidence lends itself to criticism. One "Colomban", thrown into a sewer by an infuriated mob for posting up notices "Pyrot is innocent", recalls at once the hairsbreadth escapes of the author of *J'Accuse.*

But most cynical of all in the reaction from the cheery optimism of *Vers les Temps Meilleurs* is the figure of Dr. Obnubile, the Penguin sociologist who is certain that wars will disappear with the disappearances of dynasties and the establishment of an enlightened democracy. He journeys to "New Atlantis", where republican legislators are sitting in cane-bottomed chairs, discussing—he does not doubt—some project of pacifist progress. Alas, when he enters that republican legislature, he finds them debating various economic wars,—"wars for the opening of markets." They have had a cotton war, a pig war, and a war against the inhabitants of Third Zealand, where they have killed two-thirds of the population in order to compel the remaining one-third to buy the Atlantan umbrellas and braces. Dr. Obnubile decides that it would be the part of a wise man to get enough dynamite to blow up this whole planet as "some satisfaction to the universal conscience." But then, he remembers with a sigh, "this universal conscience does not exist."

* * *

What had led to Anatole France's temporary illusion about the possibilities of improvement? Whence this new-born faith in democracy? Not long before, he had felt with Benjamin Constant that the human race is born foolish and is guided by knaves. He was later to say about the democrats of 1848 that they would have enthroned the Comte de Paris if only his mother had been eighteen inches taller.[17] And so far had he been from pinning his faith to popular education that he had again and again deprecated all disturbance of the salutary proletarian superstitions. His earlier, like his subsequent, pessimism had been based on what he knew of human nature. Had anything happened to human nature which might elevate its prospects in the years between 1894 and 1898? The pictures in *Histoire Contemporaine* would not lead us to think so. But something had happened to the temperament of the novelist.

He could lapse into enthusiasm for one cause if he had been sufficiently irritated by another. Anatole France could attack democracy, or he could attack monarchy, but not both at once. An existing state of things cannot be assailed

[17] *Le Petit Pierre,* XVI.

with very much effect unless one will, for a time at least, extol the possibilities and promise of a change. The philosopher may amuse himself in his study demonstrating how the opposite kinds of evil are exquisitely balanced. But he will never rouse the crowd by this, and Anatole France was indignant enough with certain interests to desire that the crowd should be stirred up against them. So in *Vers les Temps Meilleurs* he took his part, with such show of zeal as he could muster, for "the undenominational school."

As he did so, he may well have had misgivings, for he was neglecting the advice of his master. Renan had said, *il faut une religion pour le peuple.* "Do not interfere with what we teach, with what we write, and we will leave the people to you. Do not control our places in the university, in the Académie, and we will abandon the village schools wholly to you."[18] That, exclaimed the indignant Mazzini, was the strangest and most immoral compromise which ever occurred to a thinker.[19] But sometimes Anatole France felt that Renan was right, and Mazzini a mere doctrinaire. He even declared in a very candid moment that his former confidence in scientific education was more than half lost, and that he was much disappointed with the slow progress towards universal rationalism. But for the time his warfare was with *le parti noir*, and he was doing one piece of propagandism at once. Professor Saintsbury has conjectured that his liking for Joan of Arc was due to the fact that she "made royalty and the Church and the nobility look disgusting."[20] He may have acquired a temporary enthusiasm for "Social Reform" on grounds not very dissimilar. But he was speaking his real mind when he said

18 E. Renan: *Réforme Intellectuelle et Morale,* p. 99.

19 Cf. Article by Mazzini, April 11th, in *Revue Politique et Littéraire.*

20 *Quarterly Review,* Jan., 1923.

that the fruits of the Tree of Knowledge had turned to ashes in one's mouth.[21]

A character in one of Mr. H. G. Wells's novels has remarked that all our public enthusiasms are based on hatred, that patriotism—for example—is just hatred of foreigners, and that morality is just "hatred of rotten goings-on." Such a negative sentiment will indeed carry some people far, but it is not very lasting in its effects. The apostle of progress, though stirred by disgust with the defenders of inertia, needs some more positive equipment if he is to persevere. He must be badly handicapped if at bottom he really believes change of every sort to be merely apparent, and regards even those forms of error which look new as nothing else than the old errors in disguise. As Lord Morley used to say, he is entering upon the race of life "intellectually ham-strung." And though he may start with great vigour, he will soon be tired.

[21] *La Vie Littéraire,* III, p. 7.

CHAPTER VIII

THE SATIRIST AS HISTORIAN

History is but a parcel of tricks that we play upon the dead.

VOLTAIRE

To M. Lamartine belongs the credit of having raised history to the level of fiction.

DUMAS

We get very wearied of the persistent identification of the Church throughout the Dark Ages with fraud and imposture and sinister self-seeking, when we have once learned—what is undoubtedly the most important principle in the study of those times—that it was the churchmen who kept the flickering light of civilization alive amid the raging storms of uncontrolled passion and violence.

LORD MORLEY

A man, in whatsoever craft he sails, cannot stretch away out of sight when he is linked to the windings of the shore by the towing ropes of history.

DE QUINCEY

Among the more interesting *sequelae* of the Dreyfus period was Anatole France's resolve to complete and publish his long projected *Life* of Joan of Arc.

The closing years of the nineteenth century had witnessed a French revival of the cult of "the Maid." Her name had haunted the restless imagination of royalists ever since the founding of the hateful Third Republic. In 1873 the plot for a Bourbon restoration had broken down, through an obstinate refusal of the Comte de Chambord to accept the tricolour in place of "the flag of Jeanne d'Arc."

Since then, the memory of the Maid of Orleans had become more and more a rallying cry for the monarchist revolutionaries. That memory they now sought to establish for ever by a shrewd spectacular stroke. Why should not Joan be canonized?

If we may trust those who profess to know, there are methods of cautious agitation by which the supreme pontiff is induced to confer Sainthood, just as there is a subtle propagandism by which the friends of an aspirant to the British peerage manage to influence the course of "His Majesty's pleasure." As early as 1904, Pius X had granted that preliminary decoration which entitled Joan to be called "Venerable." By Decree, four years afterwards, she was beatified. Watching the movement close at hand, Anatole France suspected the purpose for which this patent of spiritual nobility was being sought, and it was a purpose which he had the strongest motive to counteract. In it were the unmistakable echoes of *l'Affaire*. Such canonization would emphasize tremendously the link between French patriotism and the Catholic Faith. Before that tribute of the Holy Father to the warrior Maid, Church and Army might cement again their alliance. It was at such a thought that Anatole France became enraged. Resorting as ever to his pen for a weapon, he determined that the picture of Joan should be drawn another way.

Whether a piece of genuine historical work can be done under an impulse like this, may well be doubted. One may doubt, too, whether history has ever been successful in the best sense when written by one endowed to a superlative degree with the gift of satire. Even the example of Tacitus cannot be said to answer these questions decisively. The case of Anatole France certainly does not decide them in the affirmative.

I

His biographers say that he was engaged for some twenty years on the *Vie de Jeanne d'Arc.* But during the same twenty years he was busy with at least twenty-five other books, as well as countless pamphlets, on quite different subjects. So it would probably be more accurate to say that he began his *Jeanne d'Arc* in 1889, but did not finish it until the end of 1908.

Anti-clerical propagandism was not indeed his sole motive. Anatole France plainly desired that this book should establish for him a new sort of fame. He would be known not only as a versatile and imaginative writer of *contes,* not only as a piercing satirist of contemporary follies, not only as a Socialist reformer and a fearless critic of reaction, but as an historian of vast learning and creative insight into the remote past. This kind of glory he knew had so far been denied him, and it had scarcely even been sought. He had still no repute among those lovers of research who insist that a book on the past shall be "thoroughly documented." So he resolved to bring together his innumerable jottings about Joan of Arc, and to engage a secretary for the purpose of documenting them.

M. Brousson's account of his employment on this enterprise is among the droller parts of his very droll memoir.[1] The Master, we are told, presented him with a sackful of memoranda, which he guessed might weigh about one hundred and twelve pounds. "All that rubbish", he exclaimed, "is yours—yours to be burned, torn to pieces, or blue-pencilled." It contained the rough notes for the *Vie de Jeanne d'Arc,* scrawled on the backs of envelopes, visiting cards, and tradesmen's bills. Much of this had been jotted

[1] *Anatole France en Pantoufles,* p. 22, sqq.

down at railway stations, where the author was waiting for a train connection. Much consisted of "essential passages copied from goodness knows what books." But it was a secretary's business to work up such a mess for his employer, upon whom the incessant demands of magazines for yet another short story were such a burden that he had no time to work it up by himself.

Obviously the first thing to be done was to divide the material into chapters, arranged so that each would lead up to the next; for, said the cunning artist, "it is essential to string the reader on." There would be two volumes, and the second must "carry such a full cargo" that the reader would not stop short with the first. Both must be sold in order to ensure success. Above all, scholars must be placated by an abundance of "the best and most learned references." The secretary must spare no pains to make these precise. Some years before, there had been an unfortunate historical slip in the author's short piece called *Le Procurateur de Judée*. It had depicted Pontius Pilate in his invalid chair overlooking the Bay of Naples, while "Vesuvius smoked below". But this vivid touch had been wrong, for a score of crazy specialists had pointed out that Vesuvius was never in eruption until Pilate was in all probability dead, referring the writer in disgust to the narrative by Pliny, so that in later editions he "had to put out Vesuvius." There must be no oversight of such a kind in the *Jeanne d'Arc*,—no picturesque mistake, for example, about the trees that grew in the garden of the d'Arcs, such as a wheezy old archivist familiar with the orchards of Champagne might detect, and quote a mass of fifteenth century deeds or wills to expose. M. Brousson must understand his task, and have no fear of hard work in the Bibliothèque Nationale. He must hurry, too, for the canonization of the Maid was at hand.

Such, according to his very candid secretary, was the genesis of Anatole France's great historical monograph. If it suggests the efficiency of American business advertising, rather than the patient erudition of a Gibbon or a Mommsen, we must remember the versatile adaptability of the Parisian mind.

II

Although produced by such a method, the *Jeanne d'Arc* is a notable book. It is indeed no addition to hagiography. The exploits of Joan are explained on purely naturalistic grounds, first through reduction of their legendary vastness to a more manageable size, and next by allowance for the immense psychological effect—five centuries ago—of a portent reputed to be supernatural. The Maid, we learn, was able to relieve Orleans because her followers were hypnotized, and because the enemy was terrified at the thought of an angel—or a demon—fighting on the side of the Dauphin. That thought worked wonders in the Europe of 1429. It was helped by the quite mundane circumstance that the troops besieging the city were in truth far fewer than the troops defending or relieving—not far more numerous, as the pious myth had insisted. Joan, in Anatole France's view, deserved no special credit for military skill. She was a peasant girl, seventeen years old, of stainless character and glowing patriotism, intensely devout after the manner of her time and upbringing. But the whole story of a precocious Napoleonic gift was concocted to build up a situation that only supernaturalism could explain. All the real facts were explicable otherwise.

She was a *béguine*, and in her childhood piety she thought she heard the voices of angels. There was nothing strange about that in the village of Domrémy, A. D. 1429. In a few rapid strokes, Anatole France introduces his readers to a scene like that which Lady Gregory has described in the West of Ireland, among peasants for whom the veil of the unseen has scarcely thickened since the days when some messenger from Heaven talked with Abraham in Hebron or with Columcille in the oakwoods of Derry.[2] He makes us think of a scene like that which Moore had in mind when he wrote *The Loves of the Angels:*

> When earth was nearer to the skies
>   Than in these days of crime and woe,
> And mortals saw, without surprise,
>   In the mid-air angelic eyes
> Gazing upon this world below.

To Joan the "miraculous" was quite in the order of things. It came out in evidence at her trial that her godfather, Jean Morel, believed fairies to have been driven from the village by priestly rites, and that periodically at each spring in the parish the Gospel of St. John was recited to purify the spot. Local opinion differed as to whether Domrémy was still subject to ghostly visitants, or whether it had enjoyed spiritual immunity for almost a generation back. Some held that Thursday was the favourite time for an infernal tryst. Joan's own opinion was that witchcraft was at work; and though she had never met fairies under the tree herself, she would not say that she had not seen them elsewhere.[3]

As a child, she began to have visions, which a medical correspondent of Anatole France has found intelligible on certain physiological grounds that he has been able to conjecture from evidence given about her at her trial. Like

[2] Cf. *Visions and Beliefs in the West of Ireland,* II, p. 89.

[3] *Vie de Jeanne d'Arc,* Vol. I, chap. i.

Samuel of old, she had heard a supernatural voice calling her by name, and at the third call she had recognized it as the voice of St. Michael, the patron saint whose figure she knew so well on the church pillar, and to whom a chapel had been dedicated on a familiar hill in Lorraine. He was the archangel of sacred legend. The message he brought to Joan was that two other saints were coming to see her, the saints Catherine and Margaret, with advice about what the Lord would have her to do. Joan, who was thirteen years old at the time, was overwhelmed with amazement and delight.

The expectation so created was, of course, fulfilled. Those holy women began to visit her daily in vision, queenly in their apparel, wearing golden crowns, with countenances of dazzling light upon which her eyes could not look, but permitting her to kiss the hem of their garments. She curtsied low, heard herself addressed as the daughter of God, was bidden live well and go to church. Such were the preliminary visits, in which no very exciting message was delivered, but which accustomed the Maid to supernatural intercourse, especially in the woods hard by the church when the bells rang for matins or compline. But of all this experience she said nothing to her priest. Clearly the heavenly Powers were choosing to act without the usual intermediary, and it was not for Joan to obstruct their plans.

Some ecclesiastic heard of it, however, for the Maid could not keep the secret altogether to herself. And the ecclesiastical mind began to form its own plans. Things had become desperate on the countryside. The national misfortunes were pressing hard on the priesthood. A devastated district could no longer contribute to the expenses of public worship. The abbeys were being overrun by a plundering soldiery, and churchmen were driven to beg their bread from door to door. Some extraordinary expedient must be devised, and nothing else would serve the turn like a miracle.

So sacerdotal ingenuity recalled an old legend, traditionally received from Merlin and the Venerable Bede,—a prophecy that France should be saved by a maid. Let Joan be presented in this Messianic rôle, and the broken *morale* of the soldiers of the Dauphin might be restored as by magic. She must first be duly coached for her part. Joan would be no party to fraud, so the miracle must be made very real to herself. But let her once be convinced, and it would be only natural for her to sing her *Magnificat* and act in unison with it. When she had been told, on authority, what the angel visitors were going to say, she might be trusted to hear them say it. Thus the good advice about conduct of life was expanded into a call to leave her village and seek an audience of the Dauphin. It was to be her high mission to anoint the true king of France with the holy chrism. Merlin had said so. And the saints, Catherine and Margaret, would say so next time they called.

The scheme worked. If any further proof were needed, who could resist the suggestiveness of the single circumstance that for some reason or other she had vowed her virginity to God? Later tradition said she had done this at the age of thirteen—a story which needs no refuting—but she may have done it four years later, under advice. Our historian thinks he has evidence that the neighbouring peasants of Domrémy knew nothing of Merlin and his prophecies. But someone must have effected the passage from the first angelic appearance to the divine commission for liberating France. *Cui bono?* And in what sort of mind did that idea of consecrated virginity originate?

Merlin's prophecy was retailed to her with a further gloss. She was told that the Maiden Redemptress had been announced as coming from the borders of Lorraine. "This local addition", remarks Anatole France, with an air of triumphant certainty, "is not the work of a cowherd. It suggests rather a mind apt to direct souls and to inspire deeds." [4]

Such, in outline, is the Francian theory about Joan's inspiration, and about the priestly imposture which wrought such marvels alike of enthusiasm and of dismay. In his own judgment, he had rendered the sequence of events quite natural. All that was needed was to escape from the myth, to see the alleged marvels as no greater than they really were, and to conceive adequately the strength of a religious enthusiast "indoctrinated" by sacerdotal cunning in a mediæval neighbourhood. A genuine historical method, combined with modern psychological analysis, had thus "restored the Maid to life and humanity." [5]

III

But the historians and the psychologists have shown no great haste to acclaim this triumph of science. They have pointed out how freely Anatole France filled up the *lacunae* of evidence by the most daring guesswork, and how the witnesses who are against his conclusion are dismissed as liars, while those who can be construed as favouring it are believed implicitly. They have found that in several places he has reversed what we have good ground for supposing to have been the real order of events. M. Brousson's task of devising safeguards against disproof of detail seems to have been too heavy for him. His employer was not convicted of mistake regarding the sort of trees that grew at Domrémy,

[4] *ibid.*, chap. iii.

[5] Author's preface to the English edition of the *Vie de Jeanne d'Arc*.

but he was interrogated as to his knowledge of mediæval artillery, on the basis of which he had made some confident but quite undemonstrable statements. About the folklore current in Lorraine he was rudely called in question by a "wheezy old archivist" who wrote from St. Andrews, Scotland, producing a mass of evidence that the Lorraine peasants of the fifteenth century had long been familiar with just those legends which Anatole France declared to have been unknown. And the expedient of hiring a man to decorate one's book with "the most learned references"—such as will "look fine" because they quote precise pages from folio volumes—is not without its risk. The learned, though often very simple in other respects, are quick enough in detecting the artifices of pseudo-scholarship, and some of them have as keen an eye for the imposture of footnotes as our author had for the imposture of a priesthood. It is not safe to assume that they will not look up references for themselves. Thus Andrew Lang coldly informed readers of his *Maid of Orleans* that Anatole France had many a footnote reference to what was found on investigation to have no relevance to the statement in the text for which it was invoked as evidential. He instanced precise cases of this remarkable habit, and added: "I know not how to understand the method of making very strange statements and supporting them by references to books and pages in which I can find no such matter." [6] Bishop Lightfoot's reply to the author of *Supernatural Religion* will occur to many as a parallel. When Anatole France, in the preface to a later edition of his book, declared that he had suffered no severe criticism except from "the hagiographers", Andrew Lang must have had difficulty in recognizing himself under such novel description.

[6] A. Lang: *The Maid of Orleans,* Vol. I, Appendix C.

A book, however, may be great, though the writer in a hurry has confused his authorities, and even though—flinging scruple to the winds—he has deliberately cited authorities that do not exist. The peculiar distinction of the *Jeanne d'Arc* lies in its blend of the spirit and method of two very different historical epochs. Voltaire knew how to describe the past with a pictorial fluency that was as fascinating as it was inaccurate. Lord Acton knew how to record it with cumbrous and tiresome precision. Herein lay the contrast of two centuries; for if we describe the historical movement of our time as "the revolt of the nineteenth century against the eighteenth", we shall have stated more truth than is usually compressed into an epigram. It was to the eighteenth century that Anatole France by temperament belonged. But his *Jeanne d'Arc* is not more like Voltaire's *La Pucelle* than Renan's *Vie de Jésus* was like Paine's *Age of Reason.*

For, pagan in spirit as they both were, Anatole France was separated from the sage of Ferney by that whole significant interval which we call the period of Romanticism. Beginning with Rousseau and ending with Lamartine, it had left its deepest mark on those who disliked it most. It was John Stuart Mill, for example, who rejoiced that the Oxford Tractarians had at least served the cause of history by disinterring the Christian antiquities from that forgotten grave in which Protestant resentment had entombed them,[7] and in this the Tractarians were but one section of Romantic zealots. No man appreciated more keenly than Anatole France what this new historical spirit meant, and no man stated its requirements better than he stated them in a column of careful analysis contributed to *Le Temps.*[8]

[7] J. S. Mill: *Dissertations,* p. 263.

[8] *La Vie Littéraire,* I, p. 96, sq.

However much we despise the past, we must, he said, begin our criticism by depicting it as it really was. The better we understand it, too, the less we shall despise it. Leconte de Lisle might see in the Middle Ages nothing except famines, ignorance, leprosy, and burnings at the stake. That was enough for the purpose of writing admirable verses, "if you are a poet like him." [9] But other equipment was needed by the historian. We must take warning from the error of Livy, who had made the shepherds of Latium speak like contemporaries of Augustus; the error of Racine, in whose tragedies the invariability of custom seems to be childishly assumed; the error of eighteenth century *philosophes* who viewed Solon as but an ancient anticipation of Turgot, and clothed Semiramis with the royal mantle of Catherine II. Our critic here instanced specially the art of the Middle Ages, which decorated old Jewish kings with the Hand of Justice, the Crown, and the *fleur de lys*.[10] Account must be taken of archæology, of ethnography, of philology, —weapons of historical investigation which were the peculiar recourse of nineteenth century scholars. In this matter, he said, Ernest Renan had notably shown the way.

But Anatole France was more successful in formulating these requirements than in fulfilling them. The spirit of the eighteenth century was his spirit, much as his judgment might condemn it, and hard as he might struggle—like Baron d'Haussonville whom he compliments—to be "just towards ideas that he does not share." [11] And he occasionally wonders whether he has not proceeded too far in his constrained reaction against a tendency he so much liked:

[9] *loc cit.*
[10] *ibid.*, p. 325.
[11] *ibid.*, II, p. 47.

> Je ne sais . . . s'il ne faut pas admettre de temps en temps l'hypothèse de la fraude consciente, s'il n'y aurait pas lieu enfin, sur ce point, comme sur plusieurs autres, de concilier Voltaire avec Renan.[12]

He once said that the author of the *Origines du Christianisme* had undertaken a work for which he rightly judged himself fitted by the nature and extent of his talents. But if Renan had lived to see the publication of the *Jeanne d'Arc*, it may be doubted whether he would have felt able to reciprocate the compliment.[13] He would not, I think, have upbraided the author simply for indulging in guesses, for he could often guess very wilfully himself. Nor would he have been over-sensitive to certain inaccuracies, mortal sin though they be in the eyes of exact scholarship, for Renan had his own slips of the same kind, and one notes with amusement how Anatole France admired him for "not bothering about references." But he would have noticed that the guesswork and the inaccuracies are uniformly at the service of a certain conception of the priesthood borrowed from a period far later than the fifteenth century. That priests of the time of Joan of Arc were often as simple-minded as the Maid herself, that they too were equally the victims of enthusiasm and of terror about ghostly visitants, that the legend they propagated may have been their own genuine belief,—this is at least as possible as the hypothesis of wilful deceit. Whether it is the actual explanation or not, depends on its power to bring together all the facts, and it may well be impossible to decide. But Anatole France had no difficulty in deciding. The wholesale attribution of fraud

[12] *Vers les Temps Meilleurs*, II, p. 38.

[13] It is perhaps significant that Renan rather disapproved of Anatole France's project in writing the *Jeanne d'Arc*. Cf. Brousson, pp. 125, 6.

to some conjectured but unnamed ecclesiastic, the constant recourse to an assumed falsifying of oracles and legends, the dismissing of contrary evidence as probably perjured and the acceptance of favourable evidence no matter how inconsistent with itself or how expressly contradicted by witnesses of average credibility,—whence comes that attitude of mind in an historian? No critic will be at any loss to name the century within which such was a characteristic way of thinking. It is not the nineteenth century. One can imagine how the massive head of Renan would have been shaken in protest. Our author once said that he had resolved, for literary purposes, to dream again the dream of the Ages of Faith. But dreams cannot be made simply to order, even under the stress of an historian's necessity.

IV

The *Vie de Jeanne d'Arc* was a comparative failure. This disappointed Anatole France, for he had supposed it might have a success comparable to that of the *Vie de Jésus* forty-five years before. He thought, too, that, like Florian, he had shown "the genius of the opportune" [14] in choosing his time for publication. Here was one of his curiously Parisian mistakes. The most prosaic of his English or German friends could have told him that a naturalizing of the experiences of Joan would create no such sensation as a naturalizing of the Gospels. Mr. Shaw, indeed, declares that if Joan was mad so was all Christendom at the time, so was Luther a hundred years afterwards when he threw his inkhorn at the Devil, and for that matter so are all the orthodox to-day, "for people who believe devoutly in the existence of celestial personages are every whit as mad in that sense as the people

[14] *La Vie Littéraire,* I, p. 192.

who think they see them." [15] But this, whether true or false, has no bearing on the prospects of literary success for a book on the Maid. Exhaustive proof, with copious citation of references, regarding the quite natural origin of Luther's optical error about the Devil would have fallen quite flat too. Our world still takes much interest, wisely or unwisely, in "the existence of celestial personages", but not much interest in the vagaries of Luther's digestion.

It is indeed with a certain feeling of amazement that the English reader at least lays down these two bulky volumes on Joan. He can understand the curiosity aroused by the subject in a psychical researcher like Andrew Lang or Frederick Myers. He can enter into the poetic enthusiasm stirred by such a heroine of romance in a Schiller, a Coleridge, even a Southey. He can appreciate Mr. Bernard Shaw's quickness of eye for material that will make such a diverting piece on the stage, especially when the saintly protagonist becomes in Shavian treatment a "boss" [16]—like Florence Nightingale under the pen of Mr. Lytton Strachey. There is at least a field here for the poet, a chance for humour, for a touch of the satirical. But why Anatole France should have undertaken such immense toil to disprove a monstrous dogma about the Maid, is rather a mystery to the insular intelligence. If he had not been at work upon it for some twenty years, the explanation would be plainer, at least when one realizes the vogue that still belongs to the miraculous in rural France, and the political possibilities of this legend upon such a soil. Our author had a very obvious purpose in hurrying this work at the end. There was a movement, he said, to hoist Joan on the

15 G. Bernard Shaw: Preface to *Saint Joan.*

16 G. B. Shaw: Preface to *Saint Joan.* Cf. Lytton Strachey, *Eminent Victorians,* p. 135, sq.

sacerdotal altars; a republican monument should be erected before that of the priestly and royalist coalition; with the assistance of M. Brousson, he would "race them to the church door." [17] The priests beat him by about twelve months. Perhaps the terrific pace he made at the close must be his apology for inadequate verification.

But the marks of disastrous haste, so obvious in its frequent lack of the literary charm that belongs to the writer, are not the worst faults of the book. Anatole France was a sceptic about history in general, and no man can do very well a task which at heart he rather despises. The physician in *Histoire Comique* [18] asks: *Peut-on consoler et soulager sans mentir?* And for those anxious to have the past set before them in an ordered sequence, our author declares that only the rhetorician can serve. "History can never be interesting without lies." What the *Jeanne d'Arc* shows us, however, is that history may be made dull by causes other than strict truthfulness. A tale of the expiring Middle Ages is full of interest, if it is well told, but not if it is used as just so much material to stoke the furnace of twentieth century *anti-cléricalisme.* The kindling of that furnace is an enterprise by itself.

An English reader, indeed, must bear in mind that if it is ever justifiable to write "history with a purpose", the *Jeanne d'Arc* may well be justified for the sake of one sort of effect —not in the least political—which it may have served at the moment in the country where it appeared. The Parisian *philosophe* has a sort of traditional apostolate to the less sophisticated of his countrymen. And just two years before the publication of this monograph there had been an oc-

[17] J. J. Brousson: *Anatole France en Pantoufles,* p. 23.
[18] p. 171.

currence which makes the book seem opportune. The Paris correspondent of *The Times* had occasion to send the following despatch to London:

> French Catholics are awaiting with concern the report of a special commission on a mysterious affair known as the Miraculous Hailstones of Remiremont. On Sunday, May 26, 1907, during a violent storm which swept over that region of the Vosges, among the great quantity of hailstones that fell at the time a certain number were found split in two. On the inner face of each of the halves, according to the local papers that appeared the next day, was the image of the Madonna venerated at Rémiremont and known as Notre Dame du Trésor. The local Catholics regarded it as a reply to the municipal council's veto of the procession in honour of the Virgin. So many people testified to having seen the miraculous hailstones that the Bishop of Sainte-Die instituted an inquiry; 107 men, women and children were heard by the parish priest, and certain well-known men of science were consulted. The report has just been published in the *Semaine Religieuse,* and concludes in favour of the absolute authenticity of the fact under inquiry. . . . The last word rests with the bishop, who will decide according to the conclusions of the report of the special commission.

So, for a Parisian, there was more than an antiquarian interest in the mystery of the Maid.

But the immediate interest for Anatole France was of a quite limited and practical kind. It is revealed, among other places, in the first chapter of the Second Volume of *Jeanne d'Arc,* where he sets forth the peril of belief in supernatural directors. There happened to Joan, he says, that which necessarily happens to all who suppose themselves entrusted with a divine mission. For such persons inevitably constitute themselves a spiritual and temporal power superior to the established powers, and by nature hostile to them. It is a most dangerous illusion, productive of shocks in which enlightened people are the first to suffer.

Herein we have the moral, drawn from the fifteenth century, which underlay the campaign for the Briand Law, and inspired the argument of *L'Église et la République*.

PART III

THE PROPAGANDIST OF ANTI-CLERICALISM

CHAPTER IX

THE CAMPAIGN FOR CHURCH DISESTABLISHMENT

The Concordat is a method of inoculating against religion. In fifty years there will be no religion left in France.

NAPOLEON I

The question of the truth or falsehood of this or that positive religion is a purely theological one, which does not concern us. Even if they are false, religions have this advantage, that they are a hindrance to the spread of arbitrary, independent teaching. They form a faith-focus for individuals. Governments are at ease with regard to ascertained dogmas which do not change. Superstition is, so to speak, regulated, circumscribed, confined within certain bounds which it either cannot or dare not overstep.

PORTALIS

Le cléricalisme,—voilà l'ennemi.

GAMBETTA

Traiter avec le chef étranger d'une Église à laquelle appartiennent des citoyens français, sur le régime du culte, s'engager vis-à-vis de cet étranger à des obligations pécuniaires ou autres, c'est aliéner une part de la souveraineté de l'État, et admettre une ingérence étrangère dans nos affaires intérieures.

FRANCIS DE PRESSENSÉ

It was indeed a fight *à outrance* that was so curiously heralded by the movement for Beatification of the Maid. Should the French State be republican and secular, or royalist and Christian? In those closing years of the nineteenth century, such was the issue which in French politics began to dwarf every other. And if to the English reader these alternatives do not seem exhaustive, it is because he is forgetting the difference between the Anglican Church in England and the Roman Church under the Concordat in France.

I

That the clergy had for twenty-five years been enemies of the Republic, was beyond doubt. "France awaits a Head, she awaits a Master", exclaimed the Bishop of Poitiers to a vast audience on May 27, 1873; and the audience, knowing well what he meant, shouted in unison the name of the Comte de Chambord. Ever since 1875 the republican Constitution had been in constant peril, and the force more dangerous to it than all other forces combined had been the hostility of the priesthood and the religious Orders. More precarious than even the Constitution of Weimar among German monarchists of to-day, it had survived less through the support of its friends than through the discord of its foes. Until the death of the Prince Imperial in 1879, a watchful eye had to be kept upon Bonapartism. But when there was no longer anyone who could conjure with the name of Napoleon, it was clear that the remaining Bonapartists would make common cause with any species of autocrat rather than with the men described by Bismarck as *chevaliers du pavé*. To those "knights of the pavement" had fallen the thankless task of post-war reconstruction in a desolated country, and one does not need to be told that the success of such men had to await the tribute of a later time, while the resentment against their necessary exactions was immediate and fierce. For long years, in the memory of relatives and friends, the blood of the thirty thousand Communards seemed to call to Heaven for vengeance against Adolphe Thiers and the *régime* which Thiers had established. In such a troubled sea every monarchist had his chance. The choice of Marshal MacMahon, like that of von Hindenburg so recently and in a situation so similar among the Germans, was achieved by an alliance whose purpose was well known. And again and again those curious allies were on the point of success. Even a Boulanger was able for a time to cast his spell.

The consequence of all this for republican administration is not hard to conjecture. Beset behind and before, such statesmen as Gambetta had been forced to rely upon counter coalitions,—some cunning bargain among groups mutually hostile, but held together by a common dread. One sees to-day the political inheritance of such "Opportunism", so scathingly indicted in its first years by radicals like M. Clémenceau, but quite inevitable in the circumstances that suggested it. Government by *bloc* means instability, feebleness, indecision. But what else was possible? Members elected to a legislative Chamber were often there with the avowed purpose of overturning the Constitution under which they served. Thus every programme of national advance had to yield priority to one desperate expedient after another for keeping the Republic in existence.

And the chief intriguers were well known. "Unhasting, but unresting", and comparatively careless as to who the leader of the anti-Republicans might be, *le parti noir* stood ready in every election to use its strength against the government in office. Its hope lay in effecting that administrative chaos from which a tired country would demand relief sooner or later in some vast constitutional reorganization. And the Church which was thus plotting for the Republic's overthrow was itself a Department of State! One can well understand the fierce outcry against officials placed in positions of high influence and trust, drawing salaries from the public purse, and yet using every opportunity to make government more difficult. Was it even safe, in view of the external foes by whom France was menaced, that men clothed with such power—and with the awful prestige of the guardianship of souls—should exact allegiance to a ruler in Rome who could scarcely even pretend friendship for the policies of the State?

Nor was it only on the side of the State that divorce might fairly have been asked from so unnatural and so ill-assorted a union. There was much in the working of the Concordat that must have seemed increasingly intolerable to churchmen who were in earnest with their faith. It was satisfactory enough to the gay latitudinarian,—the French Catholic who resembled the Anglican in Newman's *Loss and Gain*, with his motto "There is no harm in holding beliefs; the harm arises in insisting upon them." But insistence upon a belief is of the very spirit of a real Catholic. The devout might well ask, for example, whether it was any longer to be endured that militant unbelievers should determine spiritual preferment, that every civil servant and every schoolteacher should find in aggressive impiety the route to professional advancement, that bishops and archbishops should accept or resign their Sees not at the behest of the Holy Father, but by the votes of Jews and atheists in the Palais Bourbon.

It was *l'affaire Dreyfus* that brought things finally to a head, for in that strange business it was the worst side of French Catholicism that seemed at least temporarily to prevail. How far the Jesuits were acting with the approval of that Authority to which they pay a nominal deference, and how far they were insurgents against not only the State but also the bishops of their own Church, no one can be sure. It was they, at least, who were supposed to be representatives of *l'ordre religieux*. And it was truly in a fearful light that they caused the "religious" spirit to be seen.

For it became plain to every unbiassed witness that in 1899 the republican government was staking its existence upon a principle of justice. Not only the existence of the Cabinet in office, but that of the Republic itself was being risked, and for a time it appeared on the very point of being lost. With almost a unanimous voice the Protestants of France took the same righteous side. But, as so often before, the chief peril came from officials of the State Church. It was in the organs of Catholic opinion that one found in those days a ceaseless ridicule of pacifists and internationalists. It was there that one met most sedulous propagation of the myth about "an international conspiracy", supposed to be financed against France by foreigners, and carried on in Paris itself by the paid agency of Protestants, Freemasons or Jews. In the clerical papers, in countless publications of *La Bonne Presse*, every revisionist was denounced as a traitor. By every artifice the clerical journalist inflamed anti-Semitism. Belief in the guilt of Dreyfus was erected almost into a dogma. At that *moment de la conscience humaine*, the French clergy for the most part were on the side where one had a right to expect that clergymen at least would not be found. And all men knew how the previous generation of army officers had been trained in the schools of Jesuits or Dominicans. Can we wonder that the cry of the Radicals was against the alliance between *épée* and *aspersorium?*

The storm was weathered, and the Republic did not fall. Dreyfus was restored to his command, promoted to the rank of Major, decorated with the cross of the Legion of Honour. Colonel Picquart, who had literally fought for him at the risk of his own life, was made Brigadier-General and afterwards Minister of War. The remains of Zola were transferred to the Pantheon. But while M. Clémenceau and his associates were pressing forward these measures of expiation, a deeper consequence was revealing itself in the drafting of a "Separation Law."

It began on a mild scale, but as it encountered opposition it was strengthened rather than diluted. Waldeck-Rousseau first proposed to subject the religious Orders to a measure of State supervision. Each was to be required to register a copy of its statutes, with a statement of its membership and of the property it held. A comparatively slight requirement, not very objectionable except to such Orders as disliked compliance with factory laws, such as had managed in the past to dodge taxation, or such as were unwilling that the extent of their wealth should be known. So far, there had been no suggestion of abolishing the Concordat. But there was bitter strife over the carrying out of Waldeck-Rousseau's enactment. French villages became the scene of riotous conflict with the police, where country folk set up barricades to protect some unregistered brotherhood from disturbance. Very soon the premier retired from office, recommending to the President that Émile Combes should be chosen as his successor.

What that nomination meant, was quite obvious. Combes was a man with all the traditional rancour of an apostate candidate for the priesthood. Not regulation but suppression of the religious Orders was the policy of the new *régime*. There followed, naturally enough, a series of unpleasant incidents between the French government and the Vatican. They may well have been contrived for the purpose which they undoubtedly served. Pope Pius X summoned two bishops to Rome to answer certain charges that had been brought against them, and the government forbade them to attend. They were deposed for disobedience, and the supreme pontiff refused to confirm the selection of the men whom Combes appointed to succeed them. Next in order came the visit of President Loubet to Rome, the insult to the Vatican involved in his meeting the "usurper" king within the precincts of the Eternal City, and the note of protest to the Powers of Europe. Immediately France recalled her ambassador from the papal court, and the papal nuncio was expelled from Paris.

It was clear that a Separation Law was now inevitable. But before the battle was joined at the polls, there was a vigorous war of pamphlets. In the forefront of that war was Anatole France. Probably no other single publication contributed quite so much to strengthen the hands of Combes as the now celebrated monograph *L'Église et la République.*

II

Its argument is very unlike that of the more familiar attacks upon the political activity of the Church of Rome. One often hears it said that the French priests had been to blame for abandoning their proper function, that they had invaded politics to the neglect of their spiritual duty, and that Disestablishment was thus the fitting nemesis of a Church which had "de-spiritualized" itself. Anatole France had no such charge to bring. His attack was not upon men who had been unfaithful to their office. It was upon the office itself, which—just so far as men are loyal in fulfilling it—he judged hostile to the ideals of modern civilization.

The pamphlet begins with a survey of what is necessarily meant by "a spiritual power." [1] We are reminded that such a power can never remain only spiritual, and that the at-

[1] *L'Église et la République,* p. 7, sqq.

tempt thus to delimit boundaries is absurd. For the priest believes himself to hold a super-human commission, which he cannot regard as contingent upon the will of man or as subject to any pledges which the secular State may impose. Raised above all worldly things, the Church must thus include and penetrate them all, for submission of the soul must involve also submission of the body which is the soul's subordinate. Hence, our critic proceeds, a Minister of Public Worship who says a bishop should "confine himself to things sacred" is forgetting altogether what a Catholic bishop is.[2]

For if the Church means anything at all, it is an institution which undertakes to disclose the real purposes of humanity, and to prescribe methods for their accomplishment. It has to "save" the world, and with this in view it enjoins certain formulas or rites which affect social life at many points. It interferes, for example, in sexual matters, in usages about education, holidays, days of rest, food, and much more. Herein its authority may well collide with that of the secular government and the State police. The French citizen was thus under two rival jurisdictions, and the Church had spoken with a voice that had never varied regarding the paramount place of the spiritual power wherever there is a conflict. In 1904 the Bishop of Séez had made this plain in a pastoral, wherein he argued that the Church has *des droits imprescriptibles* over both individuals and society—rights which no human power can abrogate.[3] Moreover, as sole custodian of truth, she must fight against "error", and for this purpose she had historically requisitioned again and again the aid of the secular arm. Anatole France insists that in doing so the Church has simply been

[2] *ibid.*, p. 9. Cf. *Vers les Temps Meilleurs*, II, p. 69.
[3] *ibid.*, p. 10.

loyal to the divine commission she believes herself to possess. The real point at issue was whether such commission should continue to be recognized in the French Republic of 1905.

A spiritual power, entrusted with such rights and obligations, may indeed enter into "treaties" with a secular State. In certain circumstances, this may be a counsel of prudence, which the Church is not justified in neglecting. But Anatole France bids us observe carefully the limits within which such negotiation is authorized. As proclaimed by successive theologians and ecclesiastics, the civil rulers of States which have disobeyed the papal direction are holding illegitimate sway. But, in the words of the Bishop of Séez, "particular situations oblige the Church to concede some points for the sake of the greatest possible good." [4] What, then, our inquirer asks, is to happen when these situations have ceased to exist? Do treaties thus concluded under duress remain binding? The Church, he declares, has an indubitable policy at such times:

> Elle cède a la violence. Elle aura toujours le droit de révoquer les concessions arrachées à sa faiblesse. Elle peut toujours dire qu'elle signa contrainte et forcée. Tout pouvoir qui traite avec elle la violente et la force, par cela même qu'il traite au lieu d'obéir et dispute avec sa reine dépouillée quand il devrait baiser la poussière de ses pieds. Elle aura toujours le droit de protester qu'elle n'était pas libre. Elle n'est pas libre tant qu'elle ne commande pas.

The reader is next invited to review the historic application of such principles during the preceding quarter of a century under the Third Republic. Anatole France points out how the *régime* inaugurated in 1872 had been marked at first by a subservience to Rome such as had not been

[4] *ibid.,* p. 17.

seen even in the days of Charles X. Not a shred had been left of the old Gallican Liberties. A National Church, enormously endowed, knew no master but the pope! In the spheres of education, of public charity, of national defence, she dominated everywhere. Unpopular with the country folk, and hated by the workmen of the cities, she had drawn back to her standard *la jeune bourgeoisie*. And how? By that force which had always been her chief ally,—the force of fear. *Le spectre rouge* had frightened the bourgeois Frenchman back to the protection of a spiritual police. Manufacturers, merchants, property-owners, *rentiers* small and great, had turned to religion as a safeguard against Socialism. Thiers himself had led the way in this ignominous flight. *Épouvanté de voir les rouges dans la rue, il etait allé se cacher sous le camail de Monseigneur Dupanloup.*[5]

The surrender had indeed been complete. Those timid republican ministers had accepted the pope's decisions upon all candidates for Sees, and the episcopal bench had in consequence been manned by *ultramontains enflammés*. In later years the Department of Public Worship had indeed sometimes plucked up courage to insist on its rights under the Concordat, and to nominate bishops for papal acceptance. But the men thus appointed had proved anxious to obliterate the stigma of such civil promotion, and once they were settled in their Sees had made all the greater display of their ultramontanism. Our keen critic rather admired these princes of the Church for having thus at least surpassed the ministers of State in their courageous independence.

He agrees, too, that the bishops had never declared hostility to the Republic as such. They had followed the teaching of their Church that subjects should submit to the State even when the State is evil.[6] We are reminded that

[5] *ibid.*, p. 20.
[6] *ibid.*, p. 21.

what the supreme pontiff claims is the right of deposing evil rulers, when he can, by ecclesiastical censure; but when the times are not propitious for such Hildebrandic action, the Church restricts herself to the task of opposing an "evil" State in such matters as a law granting liberty of conscience, liberty of teaching, or liberty of the press. Anatole France indicates how, under the Third Republic, there had been secret ecclesiastical scheming to overturn a system which made such impieties possible. For a time, all hope had been in Frohsdorf, and on the fall of Thiers the Church's expectation had risen high. *Dans le monde religieux on annoncait la prochaine entrée de Henri V. à Paris.*[7]

It is a vivid picture which our novelist draws of the planning for that event,—the clergy rehearsing their ceremonial, while pious ladies in the châteaux were embroidering white scarfs with the golden *fleur de lys.* Foiled by the obstinacy of the Comte de Chambord, the clerical group had turned to the House of Orleans, and had relied on the help of President MacMahon. But that stupid old soldier, even when he summoned a royalist ministry to office, found that it was impracticable to suppress parliamentary government by force. Another election had crushed the reactionaries for a time by the triumphant return of Gambetta.

Anatole France subjects the policy of Gambetta to a careful examination. Why did so keen an anti-clerical shrink from a measure of Disestablishment? Because he knew that he dared not risk it. Confronted with reactionaries of various and very discordant types, he realized well that such a proposal would unite them in solid opposition to his government. Only a few years had elapsed since the defeat at the hands of the Germans, and there were still

[7] *ibid.*, p. 23.

high hopes of *revanche*. Under such conditions, what minister could offend the Army? And it was known that the Army was solid for the Church. So Gambetta had played a game of opportunism. He would *ménager l'église*, like Napoleon I or Napoleon III. But he ventured one unforgettable dictum: *Le cléricalisme, voilà l'ennemi.* From that hour, Church policy under the Third Republic had been fixed.

The sequence of the narrative next presents Jules Ferry. That adroit minister, we are told, conciliated the anticlericals by breaking up the congregations, dispersing the religious Orders, sending a *préfet* with a force of police to hunt Dominicans, Capuchins and Jesuits from their homes. But he likewise conciliated the clergy by making sure that it was the symbols of force rather than force itself which was brought to bear, and by taking no step against those monks who when expelled one day quietly returned to their posts on the day following. The whole affair, says Anatole France, was nothing but *une apparence et un amusement.*[8] Before long, Jules Ferry was even making friends of *les pères blancs*. For in his vast colonial schemes he was winning fields for the missions of the Church, just as surely as he was winning lands for the nation, and especially for the financiers. Soon he found himself in less danger from the clergy than from the radicals. But it was undeniable that he had lowered episcopal salaries, suppressed seminary courses, reduced the public budget for religion. He had irritated the enemy, without enfeebling him, and in the elections of 1885 the power of the Church was openly used for the monarchists.

A most interesting passage of *L'Église et la République* is that in which it is explained that the real destruction of

[8] *ibid.*, p. 26.

royalist hopes was the episode of Boulanger.[9] With the fortunes of that adventurer the royalist party had associated itself, and they collapsed together. The aged pontiff was quick to see the situation. As he said himself, he was resolved that the Church should not attach itself to a "corpse", and the encyclical of 1893 bade all good Catholics rally to the Republic. A government bad in Constitution, said Leo XIII, might rule well, and a government whose Constitution was above reproach might rule badly. It was thus the part of all Catholics to respect a *fait accompli*, enter into the work of the government under which they found themselves, and seek to influence its laws in the cause of the Church. That encyclical detached a considerable number from the monarchist ranks,—but it did not detach all. The more unbending even stopped their contributions to Peter's Pence, while devout royalist ladies of Brittany and Anjou offered prayers for the conversion of the pope![10]

Next comes the long familiar tale of priestly machinations in the Dreyfus case. The turmoil that case raised was comparable, says Anatole France, only to the passion which one hundred and sixty-four years previously had followed the publication of the Bull *Unigenitus*.[11] And that too, one might remember, was a quarrel among Frenchmen about an issue of justice or injustice. The Dreyfus affair had been shrouded in such mystery as lends itself to lying. How the anti-Semites who engineered it had been so successful in stirring race hatred among a people so temperamentally tolerant, would be hard to understand, if one did not recognize the work of missionaries of the Roman Church:

9 *ibid.*, pp. 28, 29.
10 *ibid.*, p. 30.
11 *ibid.*, p. 32.

> Aux antisémites se joignit bientôt un parti nombreux, le parti noir, qui dans les salons, dans les faubourgs, dans les campagnes, semait des bruits sinistres, soufflait des nouvelles alarmantes, parlait de complot et de trahison, inquiétait le peuple dans son patriotisme, le troublait dans sa sécurité, l'imbibait longuement de colère et de peur.[12]

They did not yet work in the open day, but in the shadow one could discern an immense horde—reminiscent of *les frocs cuirassés des moines de la Ligue.* When that hidden host had rallied to the call every kind of counter-revolutionary force, attracted to its cause all the malcontents of the republican *régime,* it declared itself in its true colours under the avowed motto of "Nationalism."

Trading on the limitless credulity of the mob, it gathered more and more strength, and threw to the winds its earlier caution. It trusted to *l'Affaire* to atone for the outrage done it by the Constituent Assembly, hoping to effect amid the popular passion a cancelling of the civil rights of Jews and Protestants alike. Conspicuous beyond others, and true to their historic mission of combatting heresy, the priests of the Order of St. Dominic thundered against their ecclesiastical enemies. Side by side with them, the Assumptionists laboured for the "holy Revolution." To exploit the opportunity better, they founded their journal called *La Croix,* with sacred symbols and edifying texts which might cast a halo round *leurs sales injures et leurs abominables calomnies.*[13] From their printing-presses issued a continuous stream of reviews, almanachs, brochures of religious and political propagandism. Ninety-six Catholic *cercles,* disposing of a budget of a million and a half francs, combined their efforts with those of the Orders.[14]

[12] *loc. cit.*
[13] *ibid.,* p. 36.
[14] *ibid.,* p. 37.

In a speech delivered to the Chamber of Deputies on 16th November, 1897, M. Léon Bourgeois had dwelt upon the growing audacity of the "congregations", the all-powerful Catholic influence of the Army, the attendance of officers on Mass lest they might compromise their chances of promotion, the sending of the children of officers to the schools managed by religious Orders where they were brought up in a creed of hatred and contempt for the civil power. The Chamber ordered that this speech should be published far and wide. But the monks trusted to their weight with the thoughtless mob, entered into royalist plots, and seeing that it was hopeless to attempt a restoration of the Pretender, set themselves to bring about a dictatorship.[15]

When the elections came round, they were held in an atmosphere of terrorism:

> Les moines étaient pleins de courage. Ils avaient l'Affaire, la bienheureuse Affaire, suscitée, pensaient-ils, par Dieu lui-même pour ramener la France à la foi catholique.[16]

Our novelist here quotes the famous harangue of Père Didon, of the Order of St. Dominic. Was freedom, asked that militant monk, to be granted to the evil? By no means. If milder means would not serve, a time came for justice to be imposed by force. Government had no more urgent duty than that of discerning the exact situation in which tolerance passed into complicity. Woe to those who would disguise their criminal feebleness behind the plea that it would be "illegal" for them to act with the needful vigour! *Il faut s'armer de la force coercitive, brandir le glaive, terroriser, sévir, frapper.* Thus was the Commander-in-Chief of the armies of France made to listen in silence while

15 *ibid.*, p. 38.
16 *ibid.*, p. 39.

a monk incited his soldiers to revolt and massacre.[17] This was the climax of discord between the civil and the religious rulers of the country. If such a thing was not to be repeated, there was but one way to avoid it.

For the futility of the papal summons of 1893 had become plain. Despite that appeal to rally to the Republic, the most ferocious onslaught the Republic had suffered since its formation had been made five years after Leo XIII had thus intervened. And it was indeed obvious that it was a conflict of principle, not to be patched up by compromise or palliation. In a concluding chapter Anatole France sums up his argument thus: [18]

There must be Separation because of the strife becoming ever clearer and clearer between *l'ordre civil* and *l'ordre religieux*. A twofold jurisdiction was intolerable. This was a reason for Disestablishment not in France alone, but in all States where—despite the progress of modern knowledge—a Church was still endowed and sanctioned by the civil government. Herein was just an indefensible survival of an ancient time when priests were kings and the world was still in its swaddling clothes. It was preserved through prejudice, through irrational attachment to old custom, through the natural conservatism of mankind. It must disappear sooner or later, and the sooner the better.

But this, our critic admits, is an argument which can appeal only to *esprits spéculatifs*. More generally intelligible were some other reasons that bore upon the specific case of

[17] *ibid.*, p. 41. Cf. the passage in *Vers les Temps Meilleurs* (II, p. 65) in which it is stated that the same Dominican had urged the military chiefs to overthrow a pusillanimous government, and had excited Catholic youths to attack on the streets those *orgeuilleux intellectuels* who could not look on in silence at injustice.

[18] *ibid.*, p. 115, sqq.

the Roman Church in France. There was growing antagonism between clergy and laity. As the faithful had more and more fallen away from the Church, the clerical domination had become closer and more despotic. The time had long gone by when the priesthood were leaders in knowledge or in social life, and the time had come when they were antagonistic to both, as shown above all by the Dogma of Infallibility and the *Syllabus Errorum.* In truth, as Émile Ollivier had said, the Concordat had ceased to exist in any real sense when the Syllabus appeared, for that publication indicated a complete breach of "understanding" between the Church and modern society. It was a poor pretence that the State retained, under the arrangement negotiated by Napoleon, any serious control which a Separation Law would abolish. Look at the so-called "Organic Articles." They had never been even recognized or admitted in practice by any pope, never been fulfilled, probably never even been read in detail by the ecclesiastics who were supposed to observe them. The Gallican Liberties they affected to guarantee had been a mere name for at least a century. Meantime multitudes of Frenchmen were being assessed for contributions to a Church which they abhorred, and whose officials abhorred all that these taxpayers held dear. In fact, the French flag had come to fly over a greater number of Moslems than of Christians; yet when the census returns were made, one had to enter one's name as Catholic, Protestant, or Jew!

The case was complete. *Vos évêques sont vos ennemis, vos ennemis irrités.*[19]

III

To the outside critic, free from local passions, it appears

[19] *ibid.,* p. 118.

that this indictment of the Roman Church in France includes charges very different both in force and in relevance.

(1) A State establishment of religion must be justified, if it is to be justified at all, on the ground that it enlists a fairly general sympathy, and common sense must determine how such "general" sympathy is to be recognized. It seems absurd, for example, to suggest—as Anatole France does—that since there is a preponderance of Moslems *sous le drapeau français*, a Mussulman ought to be eligible for the Ministry of Worship so long as such a ministry exists in Paris.[20] And though it is amusing to hear that every French citizen must regard himself as Catholic, Protestant or Jew because there are only three columns for "religion" on the census paper, no practically-minded man will feel that herein is a burning grievance for the resident Buddhists.

But was it true that in 1905 there was no such general sympathy with the established Church as to make it reasonable to levy taxes for the ecclesiastical budget? It was indeed clear enough that during the thirty years after the Franco-Prussian War priesthood and laity had been drifting apart. The term "Concordat" had begun to sound satirical. But was the cause of this such as our novelist has described it? And if it was not, was the real cause such as might be regarded as lasting, or was it not more than transient?

In 1870 there was at first a tremendous return to the churches on the part of a people whose emotional life had been poignantly stirred in the ordeal of battle. The fall of Thiers in 1873 and the election of Marshal MacMahon had been widely hailed as making an end of the Voltaireans in public office. Men were profoundly moved by the thought that the defeat of France had coincided with the calamities

[20] *Vers les Temps Meilleurs*, II, p. 71.

of the papacy. They felt that they had been chastened for their sins, and the national pilgrimage to Notre Dame de Chartres was headed by no fewer than one hundred and forty members of the Chamber of Deputies. Amid tense feeling, and apparently with the approval of the vast assemblage, the Bishop of Poitiers confessed that the nation had been led to disaster because it had set "the idolatrous declaration of the Rights of Man" higher than "the Ark of the Rights of God." [21] On 20th June, 1873, in presence of twenty thousand pilgrims, the Bishop of Autun had solemnly re-dedicated France to the Sacred Heart.[22] The Memorial Church, erected on the hill at Montmartre, was officially adopted by a vote of the Chamber as a symbol of national contrition. Not less suggestive was the public resentment against those few *libres penseurs* who were responsible at such cities as Lyons for the "civil funerals." It was plain that piety had received a real impetus through misfortune.

The wave of religious excitement, like the corresponding wave in the France of 1919, quickly receded. But the chief cause of its ebb was not the growth of a deep religious unbelief. A survey of the sermons, the pamphlets, the addresses at conferences, will help to disclose its more important cause. For what these make plain is that the French clergy killed the "revival" in their eager haste to profit by it. It was the counsel of the priesthood that the hour called for a national repentance, and obviously such an appeal might have been made very effective indeed. But laymen soon saw that the repentance enjoined was a mere intensification of ritual, a cult of miraculous medals and the like, with purely formal pilgrimages to some shrine of the Sacred

[21] G. Hanotaux: *France Contemporaine,* chap. 1.
[22] *loc. cit.*

Heart, and acknowledgment that the national sin had been a facile complaisance towards Freethought. The reformation indicated took the form of increased support for ecclesiastical projects, and especially a united effort at reestablishing the temporal power of the pope. Disillusioned and disappointed, the French people quickly went back to their former conviction that the Church was on the watch for but one object, and that her sole concern with the public calamity was to exploit it for her own selfish ends.

Nor could the incipient return to "religion" find a satisfying outlet in French Protestantism. The Huguenot pastors pursued a policy as ill judged as that of the priests. With a singular lack of discernment in the fitness of things, they dwelt upon the fact that the victorious Prussian soldiers had carried Bibles in their knapsacks! Their heartless aphorists taunted the relatives of the Catholic fallen with the conjecture that if France had had a Luther she would have had no Sedan. It was such ecclesiastical *gaucherie*, far more than any speculative insight into the conflict between science and faith, which so widened the breach between clergy and laity in the first years of the Third Republic.

(2) The antagonism arising, or at least vastly intensified, in this way soon developed into a violent opposition to all that the clergy did, whether good or bad. That the priesthood favoured some project or some law, became in itself a reason why laymen should resist it. In consequence, men like Gambetta began to insist upon such limitations to the Church's activity as must reduce the Concordat to a farce. The *prêtre*, though he had brought much of this upon himself by his ecclesiastical greed, was soon able to complain that in his very best work he was hampered and persecuted.

So long as public policy is determined by one's conception of the values of life, it is clear that the clergy can never treat politics as quite outside their province. On such questions as the law of divorce, moral training in the schools, the licence permitted to certain forms of popular entertainment, any Church which had not degenerated into a mere purveyor of ritual was bound to speak with emphasis and vigour. Again and again the clerical party has protested that its opposition is not to the Republic, but to some specified kinds of law which the Republic has enacted. And if a priest, with such purpose in mind, took active part in advising his parishioners before a conflict at the polls, he was but exercising his undoubted rights of French citizenship. It was, of course, always possible to represent this as an intrusion of "sacerdotalism", and the peculiar position of a priest who is also a paid official of government presents a problem of its own. But the clergy of the English Church, for example, have not found it necessary to observe that abstinence from all political action which has been so loudly demanded from the clergy in France. Nor have they commonly avoided altogether those appeals to "supra-mundane" values which a writer like our novelist must brand as superstitious.

Again, it is to be observed that in *L'Église et la République* objection is taken far less to any political propagandism by the clergy than to the inculcating of a general view of life from which certain consequences for practical politics would logically follow. The priest taught his listeners and his penitents to regard human concerns *sub specie aeternitatis:* and thus whether he spoke of the public questions of the hour or not, he was instilling principles whose application must be expected to make a difference in conduct. It is hard indeed to imagine how any Church which had not the character of mere soothsaying could have acted otherwise. Quite clearly, Anatole France made no demand that the French Church, so long as it existed at all, should be under civil fetters. For him there could be no mending except ending. He recognized that, from their own point of view, the clergy were justified in such interference in public affairs, and would have been blameworthy if they had avoided it. What he denounced was an arrangement under which such sacerdotal action was not only defensible but inevitable in a Department of the State.

(3) His assumption, in short, is that the Third Republic had definitely committed itself to a social order in which "lay" considerations of public advantage are to prevail over "religious" considerations of duty imposed by divine decree. In such a case, he argued, it was manifestly absurd that the State should endow officials to work against its own purpose from the vantage-ground of a public position. For instance, it was perfectly legitimate that *La Bonne Presse* should continue to issue its immense volume of periodical literature, upbraiding the republican government at its will, but only on condition that it did so as an enterprise of free political or religious journalism. *La Croix*, *Causeries du dimanche*, *Le Mois*, *Cosmos*, and all the rest, must bear no State imprimatur. But Anatole France would have been the last to question the propriety of permitting this or any other form of propaganda which writers were willing to promote, and for which readers were willing to pay out of their private pockets. If the ordinary newspapers of the country chose to attack the clericals, the men attacked must be perfectly free to reply. If the ordinary monthlies or quarterlies made it their practice to present scientific and historical progress as always a contradiction of *l'esprit théologique*, it was to be expected that the Church would

not leave "the faithful" without access to science and history presented otherwise. Whether France had thus definitely decided upon professing publicly a "lay" view of life alone, whether her population had come to include so large a number of persons anti-religious in feeling as to make their continued taxation for religious purposes a real grievance, was a matter for France herself to settle. And that she settled this in the anti-clerical, if not anti-religious, direction, was made evident by the success of Disestablishment at the polls. There were isolated and sporadic outbursts of resentment, but on the whole the Separation Law was accepted with very little token of public disturbance.

Yet it may well be questioned whether the French people in general intended by acceptance of the Separation Law any such proclaiming of the dominance of a "lay" view of life as was so obviously desired by men like Anatole France. He might insist that the old *régime* was unjust to freethinkers, because it forced them to pay for the dissemination of a creed in which they disbelieved. But what he proposed to substitute for it was not a system in which social welfare should be promoted, with careful avoidance of "taking any side" in regard to religious issues. In countless speeches and articles he urged the establishment of an order of things under which the beliefs most dear to millions of Frenchmen should be continuously and artfully undermined by paid officials of the Republic, and under which laws such as those relating to divorce should be imposed in exultant scorn of the religious scruples of a great multitude of his fellow-countrymen.

(4) There is obvious rhetorical and dialectic value in the charge that the Church was disloyal to the Constitution. For thirty years the French bishops had indeed treated the Republic as a sort of odious and wearisome jest,

to be endured with quiet contempt until there should be a return to national sanity. And they had put many an obstacle in the way of the State machine. But there is another side to that story, which the foreign observer at least should not overlook.

It is surely permissible, even for men living under a Republic, to believe that a monarchic Constitution would be better, and in the method by which the Third Republic had been established there was much to suggest that it was but temporary. It had been voted into existence by a National Assembly with no popular mandate to do anything of the kind. Those deputies had been chosen for the single purpose of terminating the Franco-Prussian War. The test applied to a candidate at the polls was not "Is he republican or monarchist?" but "Is he for making immediate peace, or is he for prolonging a useless struggle?" Anatole France remembered well, and admitted quite freely, that the Constitution was thus determined by a kind of accident:

> Craignant les républicains toujours coiffés, comme Victor Hugo, du képi de la défense nationale, ils choisirent de préférence de vieux monarchistes, innocents des fautes de l'Empire et des défaites de la République.[23]

He points out that the Assembly of 1871 was thus under the sway of the clericals, that it voted the devotion of France to the Sacred Heart, and that the rural population allowed this to pass without complaint, because they preferred the "Blues" to the "Reds", *craignant moins le rétablissement de la dîme que le partage des biens.* [24]

Hence the group whose very motley elements constituted in the aggregate a majority was, as it turned out, not republican but monarchist in opinion. Frenchmen as a whole

[23] *L'Église et la République,* p. 22.
[24] *loc. cit.*

neither knew nor cared about this, thinking predominantly of the need to get rid of the Prussian troops who were still encamped in the environs of Versailles. The outburst by the Commune of Paris was indeed anti-monarchist, and was provoked by suspicion that the deputies chosen to make peace would go on to restore either a monarchy or an empire. But the Commune was far from typical of the nation's mood.

Out of the 750 members of the National Assembly of 1871, perhaps 250 believed in republicanism. But of these a dozen were violent spirits, like Rochefort and Louis Blanc, more dangerous in their friendship than in their enmity. Of the remaining 500, there were 300 Orleanists, devotees of the Comte de Paris. One hundred were Legitimists, struggling in vain to persuade the Comte de Chambord that if Henry IV judged Paris to be "worth a Mass", he might judge the ancient capital to be worth at least a temporary acceptance of the tricolour instead of the *fleur de lys*. Most of the rest were men of the sort known in the England of the Commonwealth as "waiters on Providence", but in the less pious atmosphere of Versailles they were rather like Mr. Micawber, and they hoped the thing to "turn up" would at least be different from republicanism. There were thirty Bonapartists, who lay low and said nothing, but whose aspirations were no secret. And there was a couple of dozen described in the uncomplimentary language of the hour as *sauvages*, who would not make up their minds until it was obvious which side was going to win. If this miscellaneous crowd voted the Third Republic into existence, it was because, after a delay of some four years' bargaining and intrigue, there was a sudden token that the Bonapartists were planning another *coup d'état*.

Thus the clericals all over the country, so often blamed

for being "traitors to the Constitution", had some ground of complaint about the way the Constitution had been framed. If ever there was a case of what the Americans would call "log-rolling", it was there. In so far as the electors could be imagined to have given any mandate for Constitution-making at all, it was for some sort of monarchy, and a monarchy would beyond doubt have been set up if those deputies could have agreed on the particular person to be named as monarch. Not more than 33 per cent of them were republicans. But, *faute de mieux*, it was on a Republic that they found it easiest to settle. An arrangement thus hastily patched up, by men with no authority to conclude it, and concluding it in a manner against their own convictions, might be argued to be far from final. However dubious were the means used to undo it, the clericals might plead that they were at least as respectable as the means by which it had been inaugurated. These are some considerations which it seems relevant to point out in regard to the case for the Separation Law as Anatole France argued it. But the intrinsic merits of the case itself may be argued otherwise.

IV

The Concordat fell just a century after it had been first established. There were many lamentations, on the part of simple-minded folk who thought of it as indeed what it had been originally named: a Covenant of Reconciliation between apostate France and Almighty God. This Covenant they felt that Combes and his associates had abjured, even as Julian had undone the work of Constantine and Chaumette had profaned Notre Dame. But the event of 1905 had another aspect for those who knew the real history of the Concordat, and had watched its later working from within.

The thoughts of such men went back to that night in October, 1801, when a papal envoy to General Bonaparte had been admitted in a closed carriage under cover of darkness within the walls of Paris, because—as Thiers explains —it was not safe to tempt the risibility of Parisians by admitting him in daylight.[25] He came to negotiate a bargain. In return for State endowment of the priesthood, the supreme pontiff would lend the weight of his sanction to the First Consul's *régime*. That *régime* was indeed remote enough from anything that one might have expected to be blessed from the Chair of Peter, and even the First Consul found it hard to carry his supporters with him along so tortuous a path. His men of science, like Lagrange and Laplace, protested that this fresh compromise with superstition for power would make his consulate a laughing-stock before the world. As negotiations proceeded, and the ceremonial for Notre Dame was being arranged, the generals petitioned Napoleon that they might be excused from kneeling before the Altar. But a petition of that sort was summarily treated, and when the great day came, there stood behind the First Consul, says Thiers, his generals "obedient rather than convinced." [26] There was even a conspiracy to assassinate him, with a volunteer for so perilous a duty, and Moreau appears to have lent the scheme some measure of cautious countenance.

But the same iron will that had triumphed in so many emergencies was not failing here. "Henry VIII", said Napoleon, "who had not the twentieth part of my power, could change the religion of his country. How much easier it is for me to do so." For his officers it was sufficient to put the religious change on their Orders of the Day, but with his

25 A. Thiers: *Histoire du Consulat et de l'Empire*, p. 246.

26 *ibid.*, p. 282.

men of science he condescended to argue a little. To Cabanis he explained, curiously anticipating a very sound pathological principle, that the disease of religion in general could best be warded off by a judicious inoculation with that form of it known as a State Church. To the more reflective Catholics he pointed out that he was following the example of Charlemagne. A few years after the bargain had been struck, he admitted to Wieland that some form of Christianity other than Catholicism would have been more to his own deistic mind, but added that for the all-important purpose of keeping people in order one could not give them too many miracles to believe. And for the men with a single eye to the glories of Imperial France he had the argument which really weighed most with himself, that he needed but to add priests to his other subservient officials in order to have the world at his feet. In Egypt he had proclaimed himself a Mohammedan. What he should proclaim himself in order to consolidate his power in France was plainly neither an atheist nor a Huguenot. But to Cardinal Consalvi, when he arrived for negotiation, Napoleon intimated, in the tones of the parade ground, that just five days would be allowed to close the treaty.

The Cardinal knew his First Consul, and the five days sufficed for signature to all necessary documents. Endowment was assured to the clergy. The Holy See agreed that bishops should be chosen by the French government, afterwards to be consecrated by the Church. All was thus made ready for the public ceremonies. The gold crucifix, which had to be borne before a Cardinal-Legate, was brought, like the papal envoy of a year before, under precautions in a closed carriage within the city. In the gorgeous apparel of a prince of the Church, Cardinal Consalvi publicly presented to Napoleon a copy of the Concordat, which had previously been posted in all the streets. It is the testimony of onlookers that, while this was taking place, the countenance usually so Sphinx-like became suddenly uncontrollable, so that the ritual was interrupted by a burst of laughter from the throne. Two years afterwards, when the supreme pontiff was anointing him, the Emperor shocked all faithful observers by yawning incessantly. A prelate who was on the spot at a later visit of the pope to Paris declared that in the huge crowd there was one moment of intense strain; for if a single person had given the signal by losing his gravity, there would have been "a perfectly inextinguishable Homeric outburst." But, says the good Archbishop of Malines, "the Chief of Police had taken proper precautions, and—thanks to him—Paris kept a serious face."

Thus the Concordat was inaugurated. Anatole France once called it *une bouffonnerie italienne jouée par un cadet d'Ajaccio avec un prêtre romain.*[27] Its latest history was not undeserving of such an origin. Foreign readers of a Paris newspaper of twenty-five years ago, particularly those papers generically termed *La Bonne Presse*, knew what to expect under the heading, *une affaire religieuse*. They looked for details of some squabble about money between ecclesiastics and the republican government. For at least twenty years, Church and State bound together in a fictitious alliance had been thwarting each other's policies in a temper compounded half of hate and half of fear. Locked less in a union than in a grapple, they were most aptly compared to wrestlers, neither of whom will dare for a moment to let go his hold. Hideous beyond description was the manœuvring for appointment to Sees, which a Jew or a Freethinker in political office might assign at will. One recalls the burlesque lines about a situation in England:

[27] *Vers les Temps Meilleurs*, II, p. 91.

> Bishop-making for Palmerston is a queer trade,
> He didn't learn it in the school where the first bishops were made.

But bishop-making for Waldeck-Rousseau! For Combes! For Clémenceau! The thing was indescribable.

* * *

Anatole France, in one of his most successful pieces, has done the situation such justice as he could.[28]

The scene of *L'Orme du Mail* is laid in the later years of the Concordat. A bishopric is vacant—the ancient See of Turcoing—and it is practically in the gift of a secularist *préfet*, M. Worms-Clavelin. His wife has her share in the decision among claimants. Madame Worms-Clavelin is a Jewess, who delights to adorn her salon with historic copes, vestments, chalices and pyxes, torn from rural sacristies, and conveyed to her at a price by complaisant ecclesiastics. In a Church vacancy she is an adept at directing the intrigue of masonic lodges and setting the bureaux in motion. Noëmi, says her husband, is powerful enough to make a bishop by herself.

But the old orthodoxy has its cunning too. That other influences and other wives have to be reckoned with, is made obvious when abbé Guitrel and abbé Lantaigne are rivals for the diocese of Turcoing. They are men of different types. Guitrel is no *intransigeant* priest. He believes in the divine appointment of the powers that be; in the judicious accommodation which adapts theories to facts; above all, in the paramount necessity of preserving the Concordat. So he gently insinuates in a high quarter that Lantaigne is lamentably obstinate in his "devotion to an exiled family", that he has been heard to sneer at the Cardinal's lack of intellect, that his preferment would deepen rather than heal

28 Cf. *L'Orme du Mail,* esp. chaps. I to III, V, XI.

the discord between Church and State, and that he nourishes a fanatical bitterness against the Jewish Freemasons.

Lantaigne plays a counterstroke against Guitrel, accuses him to the archbishop of simoniacal traffic in chasubles with the freethinking world of Parisian fashion, points out his shocking concessions to German rationalism, and even repeats with heartfelt reluctance some village scandal about his private life. Madame Worms-Clavelin has an antagonist of her own sex in Madame Cartier de Chalmot, wife of an old general of 1870, who has his own ideas about worshipping the God of Sabaoth, and knows that the *morale* of an army must be maintained by chaplains who are sound in the faith. He will have no trifling with ancient dogma, for "By what right do you exact of a man the sacrifice of his life if you take away from him the hope of another existence?" [29] And Madame Cartier de Chalmot promises to drop a word in season to Monseigneur.

It was a nice point that Monseigneur had to settle. He was a cautious Cardinal, a little afraid that in his old age he might have a coadjutor foisted upon him, and that the man he declared worthy of a bishopric might be inferred worthy to share his own archiepiscopal See. The scheming Guitrel he believed to be capable of anything. On the other hand, he loathed Lantaigne, would have been glad to see him pope in order to get rid of him, but could not support his candidature for the bishopric because he foresaw its

[29] This is plainly a transcript from an actual incident. In 1873, on the occasion of a civil funeral at Lyons, under the auspices of a free-thinking association, the deceased chanced to be a member of the Chamber of Deputies, and as such was entitled to the honour of having a detachment of Cuirassiers in the cortège. But General du Barail refused to permit the soldiers to take part in such "scenes of impiety", and ordered them back to barracks. When interrogated about this in the Chamber, he replied in almost the exact language of General de Chalmot quoted above. Cf. G. Hanotaux, *France Contemporaine,* pp. 76–78.

failure, and "Monseigneur Charlot never willingly placed himself on the losing side." So when Lantaigne craves an audience, the Cardinal diverts him to the discussion of a serious problem about cleansing a village church within which someone has lately hanged himself. It is a matter on which his Eminence would much value the advice of so learned a priest.

So the manœuvres go merrily on, with much engaging humour on both sides. What, for instance, it is good ecclesiastical statesmanship to do about Mademoiselle Claudine Deniseau, who has set up as a prophetess inspired by nightly visions of St. Radegonde, constitutes a problem like that of psychic mediumship to some English theologians of our own day. It was a hard question, for the girl had been foretellings things that came to pass. All the world was running after her, and the State Church as guardian of public order and patriotism must be eminently judicious. She was even influencing the elections. M. Worms-Clavelin had to see abbé Guitrel about this.

He elicited a wary answer that communications had beyond doubt from time to time occurred between the Church Militant and the Church Triumphant, but that the sayings of Mademoiselle Deniseau did not "bear the hallmarks of a celestial revelation." The *préfet* was less interested in this than in a definite practical suggestion, and was overjoyed to hear that the maid might be "exorcised." That sounded like real business, in view of the coming trial of strength by the ministry. M. Worms-Clavelin was keen to know how this exorcising could be effected, and abbé Guitrel undertook to set the Cardinal at work if the salary of seven poor *curés*, suspended under a former minister, were at once restored. Lantaigne, on the other hand, kept an open mind on such matters. The Church had not yet pronounced, and he must reserve his opinion, lest he should fall either into latitudinarianism or into credulity. And the whole tale is lit up by many an acrid comment from one constitutional ecclesiastic upon another, like the jest of abbé Lantaigne that in learning at least the Cardinal has kept his vow of evangelical poverty, and the terrific charge that his Eminence never speaks the truth except when on the steps of the altar he pronounces the words: *Domine, non sum dignus.*

The picture is exaggerated, no doubt. But the scenes are very droll, and the Christian Church as a branch of the civil service under Napoleon III must have been a droll spectacle. That *L'Orme du Mail* should have been resented as a satire on Christianity is odd, for no figure recognizable as Christian passes before one's eye on the stage. A French Catholic under the Concordat of sixty years ago had been drilled by his environment into singular use of old terms. Language as well as worship was controlled. Even so robust a Huguenot as the late Pierre Loti, when he spoke of "the Church", commonly meant the Church of Rome alone, and one must not forget how in English cathedral towns to-day the same term is curiously limited to the Establishment. Did not the Rev. Mr. Thwackum explain in *Tom Jones* how by religion he meant, of course, the Christian religion, and by the Christian religion the Protestant religion, and by the Protestant religion the religion of the Church of England?

Thus, though there is exaggeration in *L'Orme du Mail*, it is the exaggeration of what was real. Can we wonder that so many religious men in France, when challenged as to their belief in national piety as exemplified in the Concordat, used to answer in words like those of Mr. H. G. Wells: "By faith we have disbelieved and denied"?

* * *

The anti-clerical party was by no means unanimous in

supporting the Separation Law. Whether the public influence of the Church would be reduced or augmented by such a change, was a point that might well be argued. A religious organization which is known—or generally believed—to be a mere branch of the civil service has to share in that popular dislike which the civil service in a divided country is sure to inspire. But under the halo of apparent martyrdom it may acquire new life. Such thinkers as J. M. Guyau, recalling the historic progress of a persecuted Church, urged that Separation would be a mistake, and that the anti-clericals should rather combine in defence of the Concordat, using the chance this gave to mould the priesthood itself, through control of clerical incomes, that they might "act upon this great torpid body and endeavour to raise it up." [30] Guyau was looking far ahead, beyond momentary victory to lasting results.

With the loss of State endowment, the clergy acquired complete freedom from State control. Bishops became chosen simply as the nominees of Rome, with no further negotiation between Vatican and Cabinet. The ultramontanism so long resisted was no longer ever challenged. A Church whose independence and vitality had been in great measure lost in complaisant union with the secular power was revivified into spiritual life by that opposition on which alone real Churches can thrive. In every contested election the party of *le bon Dieu* was contrasted in the public imagination with *la secte satanique*. It was, indeed, a little disconcerting to piety to observe that *le bon Dieu* was so often ineffective in electioneering. But there was many a precedent which Apologetic might quote for such temporary success of the Prince of Darkness, and reference could always be made to those divine mills which grind slowly but

[30] J. M. Guyau: *L'Irréligion de l'Avenir*, pp. 229 sqq.

grind exceeding small. As things worked out, too, the clergy had much to encourage them. What had begun under the motto of "religious neutrality" soon developed into an Anti-Church whose fortunes have been very suggestive of those which attended the substitution one hundred years ago of the *Culte Décadaire* for the observance of Sunday and *Théophilanthropie* for the Christian charities. It is a thrice-told tale. The French *Cultures Mutuelles* has been an institution as dry and impotent as the one so facetiously named "Living Church" in Soviet Russia.

Forecasting the consequences of a great change like the Separation Law is indeed precarious work, and the prophets on both sides have been proved far astray. It was confidently expected, for example, by the priests that the Briand Act would be enforced with such ruthless severity as to rouse a fierce Catholic reaction. But the government was judicious enough to avoid, so far as possible, the risk of making martyrs. It was alive to the need, so aptly expressed by Anatole France, for depriving the Church of that strength which always comes to those apparently persecuted, and for opposing to the sacerdotal Order what he has described as *une invincible tolérance.* The law was applied with scrupulous prudence and an overlooking of such anomalies as it seemed wiser, for a time at least, not to see. So there was almost nothing of the anticipated "reaction."

On the other hand, the law had to be modified again and again. That traditional *finesse* which seems never failing to the Roman Curia was more than a match for the contrivances of the lay politician. Obstinacy and concession were used by turns, as fitted the moment or the place. First came the stern refusal to permit the forming of *Associations*

Cultuelles, and in consequence the whole Church property was sequestered. But the State did not dare to pursue this to its natural outcome, and forbid altogether the practice of Catholic worship in the edifices sacred to this purpose by immemorial tradition. So a new law was enacted on January 2, 1907, by which the churches were to be at the disposal of the clergy under the name of "Historic Buildings" for the practice of religion, and under which the State undertook responsibility for keeping them in repair. A condition was attached, to the effect that there should be a yearly statement of the "religious meetings" thus held in each place of worship. But again the passive resistance of the Church triumphed. No yearly statement was forthcoming, in regard to the places and times at which the priesthood celebrated Mass or heard confession, and within a few weeks there was a further amendment to the law, dispensing with the requirement altogether.

There remained, indeed, much of which the Church continued to complain, much that it continued to include under the name of *lois scélérates.* Apart from the deprivation of endowment, there was the "legal incapacity." No one could bequeath money, for example, to be applied to payment for Masses, because the Church was not a legal person. And when seven years later, in the vast cataclysm of the war, members of the expelled brotherhoods came trooping back to enlist under the tricolour for active service, the most ferocious of *libres penseurs* could foresee that it would be extremely awkward to propose the re-expulsion of such of them as should survive the perils of battle. Hence *union sacrée* was declared. Again, when M. Herriot, in 1925, attempted to carry the spirit and even the letter of the Briand Law into the administration of the schools of Alsace-Lorraine, there followed for him and his government those results which the world knows. It is at least arguable to-day, twenty-two years after the Separation Law, that the Church has been immensely strengthened in popular influence by the very measure which was intended to weaken it. Beyond all doubt, the tone which French ministers think it expedient to adopt towards the Vatican in 1927 is very different from the tone of Émile Combes. No one supposes that M. Clémenceau had changed in disposition as he changed in language. But he had felt the strength of the new *Fédération catholique.*

Those anti-clericals may have been men of great scientific insight, but they were poor psychologists. What they have been forced to witness is the change from a popular odium against State-favoured piety to a like odium against State-favoured Freethought. The exposure of a system of delation, under which "clericals" in the Army were reported to headquarters that "free-thinkers" might be promoted over their heads, produced the resentment which one might have expected. Such a plan had too obvious a flavour of the old *régime,* like the present-day employment of well-known methods of the Tsarist police under the new name of Soviet "Cheka." Once it becomes understood that the road to official advancement through the good graces of a *préfet* is by docile and enthusiastic anticlericalism, many a man of real independence of mind will return after long abstinences to the Mass. All over France to-day there are public employees who are bowing to the Altar because they disdain to bow to the dictation of some local *libre penseur.*

Probably the aggressiveness of the Anti-Church appears in its least attractive light at a "civil funeral." By the side of an open grave, some itinerant apostle of progress pronounces his eulogium on the departed, invariably mingling with it some species of argument for which neither the place nor the mood of the mourners is at all opportune. Something has always to be said, in a tone which the speaker cannot free from derisiveness, about the vanished illusions of a life to come. Whether the school of Freethought will ever evolve a more seemly ritual for the dead, must be left to the future to disclose. So far, these secular obsequies remind one of Mr. Hardy's jest about "interment according to the rites of the Board of Guardians as by law ordained." [31] Nor can it be said that the ingenious parody of the Prayer Book by Auguste Comte has been of much service to the Positivist Church. Perhaps the Positivists are intellectually right and the Christians intellectually wrong. That is not my present problem. The point at issue is whether the Anti-Church in France has been effective for that liberation of the popular mind which it took as its purpose. One thing at least is clear: that the intensifying of the contrast has very often, for the popular mind, been to the Church's advantage.

* * *

Our novelist speculated a good deal about such probabilities when the Separation Law was being discussed. But he guessed that, on the whole, the Church would be gravely weakened. And in a somewhat vindictive passage he has set forth his reasons.

In the first place, he pointed out, there would be a dead loss of the annual appropriation of fifty million francs, and he thought it impossible that this loss could be made good by voluntary contributions, because the French people were by nature so thrifty, and they were already overburdened with dues for Peter's Pence and theological education.[32] The clergy too, he predicted with glee, would feel

[31] *Tess of the d'Urbervilles,* chap. xli.

[32] *L'Église et la République,* p. 104.

the difference when they had to raise their own salaries by canvassing. What an unpleasant change from the regular receipt of the statutory cheque! It was hard to say what the number of "the faithful" actually was, but Taine had estimated the roll of practising Catholics at not more than four millions out of a total population of thirty-eight millions, and a great number of these were women and children. The Bishop of Orleans, our novelist was glad to observe, had admitted that in his own diocese only about thirty-eight thousand out of three hundred and fifty thousand went to Easter Communion.

Pursuing these exultant reflections about ecclesiastical weakness, Anatole France reminded his readers how in many a rural parish the *curé* was the only person who ever entered the church, how in many other cases the women with the children alone went to Mass while their husbands waited for them outside "chatting about their business", and how even among those who attended regularly the motive was often no pious sentiment. For marriage, for baptism of infants, for a funeral, for the sake of company, for the display of a new dress, or just in the practice of *gestes purement ataviques* [33], people of no devotional feeling went to church occasionally. But such "worshippers" would not contribute on any great scale to the depleted ecclesiastical chest. And there would be no such foolishness committed in the French as in the Disestablishment elsewhere, for no vested interests would be recognized, and there would be no compensation to individual priests except in the case of the aged or the infirm.[34]

So in a financial sense the State would be a large gainer, and the Church a heavy loser. What moral consequences

[33] *ibid.*, p. 105.

[34] *ibid.*, p. 107.

would follow, it was hard to predict. It was one of Anatole France's more extraordinary conjectures that an immediate consequence would be a break-up of ecclesiastical unity into divergent groups. It was the Concordat, he said, that had held the different factions together, and when that bond should be withdrawn they would fall apart. Such, one may object, has seldom been the experience of a Church that feels itself persecuted. It was not the case, for example, in Ireland. And that it has not been the case in France, one can see from the recent enormous progress of the *Fédération catholique*. Like the Germans who argued that the British Empire, being held together only by compulsion, would fall to pieces in the crisis of war, our novelist seems to have shown little insight into the conditions of unity. He was delighted, too, with the forecast of the abbé Dubillard that Disestablishment would mean a collapse of faith among the lukewarm, though it would intensify faith among the ardent believers. Those "ardent believers", he reflected, were few in number.[35]

There is something distinctly unpleasant about the tone of this summary of gain and loss; but it had elements of truth, as the event has shown. Anatole France relied above all upon the effect that the Separation would produce for that large body of Frenchmen to whom, as Professor Guignebert has said, the Faith was no more than a label.[36] Once the old religion of the country was placed under the frown of the State, once anti-clericalism was encouraged by the smile of Power, there would result, he believed, a great rallying to Freethought on the part of those for whom the smile

[35] *ibid.*, p. 103: "M. Dubillard croit que ce sera la perte de la foi pour les âmes tièdes. Il est vrai qu'il espère que les âmes ardentes en deviendront plus ardentes. Mais il y en a peu."

[36] Cf. Prof. Guignebert's article on Church and State in France: *Current History*, May, 1925.

and the frown of secular authority are the sole determinants of action. It would be like one of those wholesale conversions of the lawyers which are known to follow upon a débâcle at the polls. Freethinker as he was, and democrat as he tried to be, Anatole France knew well the strength in politics that belongs to a Church with official prestige. When disestablished, it might gain in spiritual appeal to the village, to the country town, but it would lose in social influence with the majority of officials, with most of the men in quest of military or civil promotion, with the society of salon and château, with the *jeunesse dorée* of the capital. The Dreyfus case had shown how great was the power which these classes wielded. A voluntary Church might have a truer and more effective apostolate, but it would have lost its hold on "the Machine." Once it had sunk to the level of a sect, it would count perhaps for more with those who in public affairs counted for least, but for less with those who counted for most. What the change would mean for religion, as apart from the religious element in the State, this reformer was not for the moment concerned to ask. He was doing one thing at a time. *L'Église et la République* was a political pamphlet.

But the author had other things to say about the French Church, and about all Churches. They sprang from a feeling far deeper than any anxiety for *la République*,—towards which Anatole France could at times be as disrespectful as anyone else. And they have an interest for readers everywhere, to whom the vicissitudes of French ecclesiastical politics may mean nothing at all.

CHAPTER X

CHRISTIANITY OR HUMANISM?

The mind and the conscience which have been formed by Catholicism are powerless to rise to any other form of religion. From Catholicism, as from Epicureanism, there is no return.

AMIEL

Je désirerais beaucoup que le fatal dilemme proposé par ce docteur (W. G. Ward) pût se réaliser suffisamment, et que la grande lutte philosophique s'engageât désormais exclusivement, comme je l'ai demandé de mon côté depuis longtemps, entre le catholicisme et le positivisme, en éliminant d'un commun accord la métaphysique protestante ou déiste, dans ses innombrables nuances, Guizot, Cousin, Dupin, Thiers.

AUGUSTE COMTE

Nous ne convertirons pas ni Mazzini ni Garibaldi. . . . Vous qui êtes plus puissants que nous, vous l'avez tenté; avez vous réussi? Vos beaux discours, vos savants écrits, vos protestations, vos superbes articles, ont-ils retardé même une heure le progrès de la révolution?

ABBÉ GAUME

What is it we combat in Christianity? That it aims at destroying the strong, at breaking their spirit, at exploiting their moments of weariness and debility, at converting their proud assurance into anxiety and conscience-trouble; that it knows how to poison their noblest instincts and to infect them with disease . . . that gruesome way of perishing, of which Pascal is the most famous example.

NIETZSCHE

L'Église et la République was the work of an "anti-clerical." But that word, as used in loose popular speech, is ambiguous. Here is a term of the sort beloved by politicians, because it is capable of as many varieties of interpretation as there are varieties of audience upon whose sensibilities it can be exercised. It is often applied, for example, to those Frenchmen who, whatever their creed, resent interference by the Roman Church in the domestic or international policies of the country. The seven hundred and fifty thousand French Protestants are, in this sense, for the most part strongly anti-clerical, but not anti-Christian. They point out that if men are to be branded as irreligious because they oppose a dominating political priesthood, it is the cause of religion which is sure to suffer. For the Church must take the consequence of having associated two different things, in the hope that they will stand together. And the more probable result is that they will fall together.

But by "anti-clerical" is more commonly meant that sort of Parisian who derides ancient piety, speaks and writes for the overthrow of "superstition", and exults in those habits of emancipated life which shock the *mœurs provinciales* of a country still rooted in the Middle Ages. Religion, our novelist once remarked to M. Brousson, is a tendency, congenital for the most part, which the more robust natures lack, and whose ultimate origin anatomists may one day reveal.[1] Upon a man in sound health belief in God had no hold, but the mind was enfeebled with a lowering of the physique, and the poor invalid would turn to Deity as to drugs. The sufferings of life were, however, an irresistible justification for atheism.[2] Among all theological arguments, the best was the famous *credo quia absurdum;* for in proportion as reasoning was admitted to any form of faith,

[1] *Anatole France en Pantoufles,* p. 6.
[2] *ibid.,* p. 65.

it ceased to be divine.[3] One saw this in the ravages which criticism had already made among the beliefs even of the devout. "Everyone chips away at the Church's dogma till he has what suits him." [4] The invention of printing had sounded the knell of the Book of Books. La Bruyère was right in his view that a vigorous man feels no need for piety, but that when he comes dropsical he "leaves his mistress and sends for the priest." [5] What nonsense, however, was that remark by the same writer that it is a very serious thing to die! "It is no harder than to be born. It is the end of the curve. Everyone is successful at that. It may be longer or shorter, more or less harmonious. We come from the womb, to go and rot in the earth." [6]

Thus when he engaged M. Brousson as secretary, he inquired whether this young man from the country had been "liberated", explaining that he hoped for the services of one who was under no bondage to Christian modes of thought. The evidence of the memoir makes only a little clearer and a little more definite what anyone might have guessed from Anatole France's novels. With pathetic simplicity some of his biographers have reminded us of his tender regard for that *Imitatio* which he once commended as a bedside book for a "serene atheist",[7] and they think they have discovered proof that Tertullian would have called him *anima naturaliter Christiana.* Observant readers of the *Patrologia* will probably decide that Tertullian would not have been deceived to that extent. He would not have been impressed, for example, by that deeply religious temper which noted how the rural Italians of to-day are de-

[3] *ibid.*, p. 202.
[4] *ibid.*, p. 236.
[5] *ibid.*, p. 22.
[6] *loc. cit.*
[7] *La Vie Littéraire,* I, p. 349.

manding from the Madonna and the saints just what the men of an earlier Age on the same soil demanded from gods and genii, how guardian angels have been substituted for the old Latin deities of grass and cattle, how the protecting spirits of Christian like those of heathen mythology are still importuned for favours and still reproached for disappointment.[8] Anatole France had indeed a restless curiosity about religious origins. He could have said, in the language and in the very mood of Byron in Athens:

> And yet unwearied still my footsteps trod
> O'er the vain shrine of many a vanished god.[9]

He was known to express his love for the majestic old cathedrals, admired some turns of phrase in the Roman Missal, and would have mourned over the disappearance of those rural churches whose steeples went so well into the landscape. Do not all visitors to his house remember the stoles, chasubles, incense boxes "glittering in their glass cases"? [10] No doubt. He was an antiquarian. And Lord Morley, one remembers, was often seen in Westminster Abbey, where he liked the music.

At all events, these tokens that Anatole France had within him some seeds of devotion were insufficient to protect his books from the wrath of the Curia. The intellectual world, says Mr. J. L. May, was startled in 1922 by news that the whole series had been summarily consigned to the Index. Mr. May thinks the Church authorities made a tactical error, and that it would have been wiser to distinguish those books which on principle they had to condemn from those others which might be regarded as at least harmless.

8 *Sur la Pierre Blanche.*

9 *The Curse of Minerva.*

10 P. Gsell, *Opinions of Anatole France,* p. 32.

Whether there should be any black list of forbidden books at all, is a question which may perhaps be argued. The Roman authorities are careful to point out that in placing a book on the Index they by no means intend to forbid its perusal by anyone, and there is much in what Anatole France has said about the popular intelligence to make such a limited veto by no means obviously wrong. But if there is to be a censorship, we must wonder at an intellectual world that was not more amazed by the tardiness than by the vigour of this particular condemnation. Perhaps nowhere else in contemporary literature can we find such a blend of all that the College of Propaganda has most reason to hate, and the books of Anatole France which do not accuse the Church directly are among the most effective anti-clerical tractates which have issued from that subtle mind. Always and everywhere the view of life which Catholicism holds dear is either openly denied or insidiously burlesqued. A character in *Yeast* remarked about the object of his special detestation: "If the Devil don't get such as he, than I see no use in keeping no Devil." And if Anatole France's books were to be passed, it would be hard to guess for what purpose an Index is retained at all.

I

His antagonism to Christianity was the antagonism of a humanist towards that creed by which humanistic ideals were fundamentally denied.[11] It seemed to Anatole France that so far as a man was really in earnest with the Christian interpretation of the world, he was bound to become what

[11] Cf. M. Salomon Reinach's definition of religion: "A body of scruples that thwart the free exercise of our faculties" (Orpheus, *Histoire Générale des Religions,* p. 4).

Nietzsche called a "world-denier." For he was pledged to set the spirit against the flesh, like that Christian mother in *Les Noces Corinthiennes* who imposed the celibate life on her unwilling child. How inferior was such religiosity to that generous pagan naturalism which meets martyrdom not for a Faith, but for "Eros"! All other superstitions Anatole France could tolerate with a smile, but not the superstition that outrages the human, forbids sensuous delight, hampers the quest for knowledge, decries pagan art and the pagan *joie de vivre.* Did not the Bible open with a warning against the Tree of Knowledge? [12] "As a Christian", exclaims Coignard, "I should have realized the full malignity of that pagan motto, *Felix qui potuit rerum cognoscere causas.*" [13]

Illustrations are multiplied. There is the monk Paphnutius in *Thaïs,* on a missionary expedition amid the luxuriance of the tropics, but selecting that route which takes him along the most cheerless byways, and wrapping his face tightly in its cowl lest the beauties of the world should seduce his eye from its austere devoutness.[14] There is the protest of Vergil in *L'Ile des Pingouins* that to fear pleasure and flee from joy is the worst of all insults to Nature, and that Dante had done him grievous wrong in supposing he would substitute Iahveh for Jupiter. There is the Benedictine in the same piece who had defaced four thousand Greek and Latin manuscripts in order to make four thousand copies of the Fourth Gospel, thus casting a strange light upon the legend that monasteries were a refuge of learning in the Middle Age.[15] Nor was Anatole France any better pleased with Luther. He was "that German monk

12 Cf. *La Révolte des Anges,* chap. xviii.

13 *Les Opinions de M. Jérôme Coignard,* IX.

14 *Thaïs,* pp. 27, 28.

15 *L'Ile des Pingouins,* III, iii.

all swollen with beer and theology", who stopped the Renaissance of paganism, thus saving by his "Reformation" what would otherwise have blessedly perished.[16]

And we learn that it was not only humanism, but at least equally humanitarianism, which Christianity had obstructed. If Joan of Arc's judges had been sceptical philosophers instead of pious fanatics, she would not have been burned.[17] The eighteenth century protest against military and judicial barbarities had come from the unbelieving group of the *Encyclopédie*. Not only had the greatest masters of French thought been sceptics, but their scepticism was what had made them humane, just as the faith of the churchmen had made them savage. Think of Rabelais, Montaigne, Molière, Voltaire, Renan:—one and all had struggled against the intolerance that tyrannizes, the cruelty that tortures, the hatred that kills. Well had Diderot summed it up: "I have only a small flickering light to guide me in the darkness of a thick forest. Up comes a theologian and blows it out." [18] It was the dogmatists who were ever nerved to inhumanity by their belief in a divine mission, while mercy belonged to those who had learned with Montaigne to lay their heads upon the pillow of doubt. The sceptic, so often abused for his overweening confidence in reason, was in truth well aware how weak and precarious are the intellectual faculties. But it was just this *docta ignorantia* which inclined him to commiserate his brethren, forbade him to make others suffer, urged a sympathetic kinship among all who realize the desperate position in which they are placed amid the useless and eternal flux of things.

[16] *La Révolte des Anges,* XXI.

[17] *Opinions of Anatole France,* p. 81.

[18] *ibid.,* pp. 78, 79.

* * *

For Anatole France the typical Christian was Pascal. A strange choice, one is impelled to say. For Pascal was not only a theologian, but also a master of the very first eminence in both the mathematical and the experimental researches of his time. Where shall we find a more conspicuous example of tireless curiosity united with extraordinary genius for pushing forward the frontiers of human knowledge? One recalls the treatise on conic sections, written before he was sixteen years old, which amazed and fascinated Descartes. One thinks of the invention of the hydraulic press, of those speculations so sound and so fruitful about the weight of the atmosphere, of the studies of the cycloid, of the calculus of probabilities, and one remembers with a sense of awe that all this was achieved by a man who died in his thirty-ninth year.

But Anatole France was far from challenging these titles to fame. On the contrary, he insists that there never was a genius more mighty than Pascal's.[19] And herein lies his ground of reproach against the dehumanizing effect of that religious dogma which perverted and corrupted such a mind. Against that Nature which Pascal's temperament should have disposed him to reverence, his Faith bade him declare war. Scrupulously exact in his physical researches, he forgot every obligation of veracity when he was pamphleteering against the Jesuit Order. With the keenest sensitiveness to what distinguishes evidence from mere assumption in the field of experimental inquiry, he asked no questions and raised no doubts about such hearsay tales as might be used to abash an Escobar or a Sanchez. Even Voltaire, anti-Jesuit as he was, had felt constrained to protest against a method of attack in which the extravagances of a few Spanish or Flem-

[19] *La Vie Littéraire,* IV, p. 216 sqq.

ish Jesuits were attributed wholesale to the entire Society, and in which what might equally have been urged against Dominicans or Franciscans was fastened upon the Jesuits alone. A characteristic instance, in Anatole France's view, of what Christian dogma has so often made of the intellectual virtues of mankind, even in those for whom everywhere else such virtues have a value that is paramount!

The picture of Pascal is completed by the addition of those hideous traits which he had in common with the ascetics of a far earlier time. Here in the France of Louis XIV was a man of science who on religious grounds lived in filth, allowed no sweeping of his room, rebuked as "sensuality" the most casual remark about a palatable dish or the most innocent compliment to a woman's beauty, gave alms for the sole purpose of storing up personal merit in Heaven, and rejoiced in the deaths of his own relatives provided only their deaths were Christian. His was a mind visited by no doubts, a theism which rested avowedly on the subjugation of intellect to faith, a mental arrangement in which the sanctuary of belief was guarded from profanation by a barrier across which the spirit of reasoning was forbidden to pass. Very typical was his way with anxious inquirers. They would visit him with their problems and difficulties, and for such colloquy he always took the precaution of wearing under his clothes a girdle of iron furnished with spikes whose points were directed inwards. "At each argument put forward by his opponent, he dug the points into his flesh. By this means he avoided all danger, and served his neighbour without fear of harming himself." [20]

Was he to blame for this? It was not reasonable. But for Anatole France it was on that account just the more intensely Christian.

[20] *ibid.*, p. 222.

II

He was much interested in the so-called "philosophic" theologians. Under the stress of criticism, certain champions of the Church, he said, had attempted to re-interpret into something more or less credible what was in essence—as Tacitus had described it—just *prava superstitio*. What simpletons they were in failing to see how rationalism, even ventured in homoeopathic doses, must prepare the way for unbelief! A "First Cause"—to that far distant and unimportant abyss had abbé Gassendi relegated God,[21] even as genial abbés of the nineteenth century had a theoretic belief in Hell, with the tacit understanding that the place of doom has no inhabitants.[22] Anatole France had heard seminary lecturers demonstrating religion as "natural", but he plainly agreed with his own Brotteaux that the human institution nearest to the ways of Nature is the guillotine, and that anyone of humane instincts must rather regard morality as a resolute enterprise by mankind against that "divine" order of the world which is nothing but useless carnage or the blind play of opposing forces.[23] The philosophic God that created such a universe must have been more malignant than most men, for even the Bastille was a merciful place when compared with the theological forecast for the damned, and those who mixed piety with regicide had killed lesser tyrants in order to re-establish one *beaucoup plus tyrannique et féroce*.[24] What a sorry tale was the history of metaphysic, not much better in our day than in the time of the old uproar about Nominalism and Realism, when the protest of common

21 *La Révolte des Anges*, XXI.

22 Cf. *Anatole France en Pantoufles*, p. 237.

23 *Les Dieux ont Soif*, p. 88.

24 *ibid.*, pp. 86, 87.

sense was condemned by the Council of Soissons! [25] Yet the theologians were still framing their futile apologetic, still working at the solution, dissolution and resolution of the Absolute, still determining the Indeterminate and defining the Infinite. The great philosophic systems were of historic interest, but only as psychic documents, to cast light upon different stages through which the human mind had passed, though they cast no light whatever upon the nature of things.[26] They might be likened to those combinations of cards with which old women tell fortunes.[27] Books on metaphysics belonged to the literature of fiction, more diverting than most novels, but not a whit more authoritative.[28] Our author's own creed seems to be embodied in the remark that this world is like the tragedy of a first-class poet, that the cast includes all sorts of people, and that one must be content to play one's rôle.[29]

He had a special word to say about that variety of philosophic theologians known as the Catholic Modernists. Theirs was a movement which Anatole France had observed from its inception. He had seen the issue of the encyclical *Quanta cura*, and—after another forty years had passed—the papal anathematizing of modern science in the famous document *Pascendi gregis*. Of the two sorts of creed he obviously preferred, on the whole, the orthodox Catholicism to the Modernist innovations, just as he preferred the rigorous mediæval Church to the compromise effected by Reformers. Speaking of Coignard, he says:

[25] *La Révolte des Anges,* XX.
[26] *Le Jardin d'Epicure,* p. 104.
[27] *ibid.,* p. 70.
[28] *ibid.,* p. 91.
[29] *Thaïs,* p. 193.

> I do not share his religious beliefs, and am of opinion that they deceived him, as they have deceived—for their good or ill—so many generations of men. But it looks as if the old errors were less vexatious than the new, and as if—since we are bound to go wrong—it were best to hold by illusions that have lost their sparkle.[30]

He liked a political order that had become inefficient through antiquity, and dreaded a new one that might be taken for a time as serious or imperative. So too he thought it best that men should stick to the Nicene creed which all would repeat but few would believe, rather than that they should construct a fresh set of formulas on whose consequences there might be a disposition to insist. The old religion, said M. Bergeret, had in the course of centuries become rolled smooth like a pebble, with all the points blunted. But a new one would have its points still sharp. Framed with an attempt at exactitude, it would act at first with "inconvenient austerity and painful accuracy." Even intolerance rubbed smooth was better than charity with a fresh edge to it.[31] Hence, if he had to make his choice, Anatole France would prefer the simple *curé* who still stood by the orthodox Church enthroned among the seven hills, the Church whose influence, in a modern atmosphere, would soon be shrivelled into harmlessness. He would avoid the real, though passing, risk of the politic *professeur* from the Sorbonne, who keeps a watchful eye upon "the modern man with his modern mind",[32] and who may reinvigorate for a time much of the dulled superstition by dexterous compromises with the spirit of the age.

30 Preface to *Les Opinions de M. Jérôme Coignard.*

31 *Le Mannequin d'Osier,* XV.

32 The phrase is Father Ronald Knox's. Cf. *A Spiritual Æneid.*

And he had a further reason for his preference. At heart Anatole France thought the unbending supernaturalism of the past was less incoherent, less of an internal contradiction, than any of those later substitutes which were neither rationalism nor irrationalism, but a fraudulent mixture of the two. With Huxley, and Auguste Comte, and Lord Morley, and many others, he could see no intellectual resting-place for any man between complete denial and absolute surrender to religious "authority." Rome they knew, and atheism they knew, but what was this wretched hybrid in which "private judgment" was allowed—under the precaution that it should not go too far? Cardinal Newman would have agreed with him, and made common cause again "liberal" Christianity. So true is it that spiritual misfortune, like other kinds of misfortune, can make strange bedfellows.

III

There is much in all this that is suggestive of Voltaire. But like Renan, to whom such books as *Micromegas* or *Le Huron* were always distasteful, Anatole France was saved by his genial humour from a quite Voltairean harshness. In his finer mood, at all events, he had no impulse to smash the idol in full view of the worshippers and to exult in their dismay.[33] He held that the Christian creed, being in its very essence Unreason, cannot be rationalized into anything really true or valuable. But he often felt that the consoling though baseless beliefs, the buoyant and yet deceptive hopes, should be treated by disillusioned men with a tender forbearance. "Truth", says M. Safrac in *La Fille de*

[33] Cf. especially his compliments to Renan for *la douceur de sa maturité* and for *le respect des illusions consolantes, une disposition naturelle à comprendre, à aimer les erreurs et les faiblesses des simples.* ("Vers les Temps Meilleurs," II, pp. 356.)

Lilith, "is like the sun. It needs the eye of the eagle to gaze upon it." And the eagle eye is not common among human searchers. Hence that curious judgment of abbé Coignard, that the two best friends of suffering humanity were Epicurus and St. Francis of Assisi; the one had delivered the soul from empty fears and taught it to seek only such happiness as its miserable nature and feeble powers admit, while the other had shown how by internal vision and in the depths of an enchanted solitude the utmost attainable ecstasy may be enjoyed for a time. "Both were helpful, one to destroy illusions that deceive, the other to create illusions from which one does not wake."[34] It is like the mood of Mr. Thomas Hardy, who suggests that Tennyson was more musical than honest in his advice "Leave thou thy sister while she prays",[35] but who has been moved to write also those pathetic lines called *The Problem:*

> Shall we conceal the Case, or tell it,
>   We who believe the evidence?
> Here and there the watchtowers knell it
>   With a sullen significance,
> Heard of the few who listen intently
>   And carry an eagerly upstrained sense.
>
> Hearts that are happiest hold not by it,
>   Why not let then the old view reign?
> Since there is peace in it, why decry it?
>   Since there is comfort, why disdain?
> Heed not the pigment the while that the painting
>   Determines humanity's joy or pain.[36]

Anatole France indeed speaks with some disgust of those who would suppress intellectual truth lest communicating it

34 *Les Opinions de M. Jérôme Coignard*, p. 8.

35 *Tess*, chap. xxvii.

36 *Poems of the Past and the Present.*

might *inquiéter dans sa conscience un berger sur la montagne, un matelot sur la mer.*[37] But in so far as the Church acts as a soothing analgesic, he finds it often tolerable and sometimes admirable.

He saw much advantage in keeping mankind in a comfortable simplicity, and judged that Church doctrine had its usefulness in this respect. The question seems occasionally to have occurred to him, not regarding the Church in France but regarding that in other places, whether a State-controlled worship is not best with this in view. For example, in his picture of Pontius Pilate taking the waters for gout in his old age at a health resort, there is a scene where the talk comes round to that outburst of religious voluntarism which had produced such disorders at Jerusalem. A "Galilean thaumaturge" had been crucified there a generation previously, and a friend asks Pilate about the circumstances of this event. But, ransack his memory as he will, the ex-Governor of Judæa cannot recall the thing. It must have been one among the many uproars of "enthusiasm" that had to be checked in the interests of the *pax Romana.*[38] The author's sympathies are fairly clear in this piece, as in the remark of the *préfet* Lucius Aurelius Cotta in *Thaïs* that all gods are divine in their own way, but that for himself he cherished respect for *un culte désormais impérial.*[39]

Much of this satire is perhaps partly to be understood in view of Anatole France's religious environment in the Catholic Paris of his earlier years. It was the Paris of incessant legends, of Louis Veuillot and his ultramontane diatribes in *L'Univers*, of abbé Gaume and his writings about the manifold potentialities of holy water, of the *Syl-*

[37] *Vers les Temps Meilleurs,* II, p. 39.
[38] *L'Étui de Nacre.*
[39] *Thaïs,* pp. 159, 160.

labus Errorum defended in a hundred pulpits. M. Paul Sabatier records how in the cathedral of Besançon a preacher had explained the Franco-Prussian War as God's judgment upon the nation which had harboured the writer of the *Vie de Jésus*.[40] In 1897, when a fire broke out in a cinema theatre at which one hundred persons lost their lives, Père Ollivier declared in his funeral sermon at Notre Dame that herein was a clearly discernible stroke by the arm of Providence at a sin-laden city.[41] Père Ollivier was no ignorant monk of the Middle Ages. He was the priest chosen to speak for the National Church about a recent calamity just thirty years ago, in the hearing of official delegates from the Powers of Europe. As late as 1908, when Messina was overwhelmed by an earthquake, it was pointed out in the Catholic magazine *L'Univers* that the Most High had thus taken vengeance for the publication of certain impious verses in a comic paper.[42] All this recalls the satiric passage in *Candide*, which makes the University of Coimbra give official explanation of a like horror in Lisbon as due to insufficient zeal in rooting out heresy. Was it, then, sheer burlesque when Anatole France made abbé Lapetite account for earthquakes and plagues as due to the need that God should from time to time remind humanity of His existence? [43]

When he speaks about "the Church", he means of course the Church of Rome. But only a very self-conscious Protestant or Modernist will dismiss the ridicule contained in these books as directed at the narrowness of Roman orthodoxy alone. The writer was well aware of the forms which Christian dogma had taken in other countries and in other Churches.

40 P. Sabatier: *L'Orientation Religieuse de la France Actuelle,* chap. iii.

41 F. Lawton: *The Third French Republic,* p. 172.

42 P. Sabatier: *L'Orientation Religieuse,* chap. iii.

43 *La Révolte des Anges,* VIII.

He regarded these as not more defensible, but rather as essentially less defensible than the creed of the Catholic seminary or the Notre Dame pulpit.

IV

As one reflects upon this varied arraignment of the Christian view of the world, it seems important to separate those points which must be seriously discussed from those others which are merely amusing or ingenious irrelevance. If we knew the course of Anatole France's thought only through his books, we should often have to wonder how far he was just working up some old legend into a diverting tale, and did not mean even to suggest a serious argument. He had extraordinary talent for this. His success in constructing such pieces—finely chiselled and glittering like diamonds—has gone far to illustrate the judgment that the short *conte* is as much a French monopoly as claret or sardines. But his conversations, so faithfully recorded by men who knew him well, enable us to see that in some at least of these burlesque tales he believed a real argument to be latent.

In the first place, there is a very obvious "playing to the gallery" in his constant citation of pagan or mediæval parallels to the Christian faith and practice of to-day. It may be assumed that Anatole France was not indicting simply the ludicrous and ignorant travesties of French rural superstition. Things done and things believed in a Breton village of our own time are often beyond caricature by any parallel with ancient propitiations of the underworld or mediæval manipulation of the saints. It is indeed hard to say of any superstitious practice that it is wholly obsolete, in the sense that no survival remotely like it can be found anywhere.

The antiquarian will find those old records and quaint *vestigia* well nigh inexhaustible, and out of this material the story-teller with a gift for the picturesque can entertain his readers without limit.

There is another field, too, which no humorist has yet fully worked, in those futile applications of the "Design Argument" by apologetic writers of comparatively recent date who have examined everything with a firm resolve that it shall yield up its "purpose." Paley was rich in such products of misapplied subtlety. Süssmilch, who was one of the authorities cited by Malthus a hundred years ago, explained in his *Göttliche Ordnung* how divine foresight had stopped the growth of trees lest they should inconvenience mankind by pushing their branches into the sky! If anyone found an intellectual stumbling-block in the immense stretch of life which was ascribed to the antediluvians, the same ingenious critic could point out how the earth was then almost empty, how the enormous families of a single parent provided a quick method by which it might be filled up, and how—as population increased—the divine watchfulness was shown in curtailing that span of days by which the contrary danger might have been incurred. When scarcity of food was regarded as a divine warning to a king who had denied the pope, the argument was scarcely better than that of him who said in Butler's *Way of All Flesh* that God must disapprove of intellectual research because He had attached such slight material rewards to its pursuit,[44] or that of the clergyman in Galt's *Annals of the Parish* who expected the Napoleonic wars to be long continued because male births were so much in excess of female, and herein was a sure sign that Providence had bloody work in view.[45] One recalls, too, the defence

[44] *Way of All Flesh*, p. 370.

[45] *Annals of the Parish*, pp. 72, 73.

of cock-fighting based on the indubitable final cause for which these birds were equipped with spurs.

But the Design Argument may be valid, and a providential order of the world may be objective fact, though in a dark age the ways of God are ridiculously misconceived, and though the theological heirs of an eighteenth century tradition may burlesque the purposes of Providence as foolishly as the *philosophes* burlesqued the purposes of the State. Nothing could be easier than to suggest, particularly in a work of fiction, that mediæval and modern apologists represent just different stages of a single monstrous enterprise, that the latter differ from the former only in an increased cunning, the use of calculated vagueness, and an avoidance of those particular cases which lend themselves to ready or immediate experimental disproof. But a comic history of science might be written in the same way, presenting the scientific men of our own time as lineal successors of those who used to cast horoscopes or search for the elixir of life, and dexterously suggesting that so far as their essential character is concerned, the astronomers and chemists of today are no more than astrologers and alchemists in disguise. It may be freely admitted, too, that in much of what he has to say against orthodox Catholicism our novelist will enlist the sympathies of not a few Christian believers who have been reared under the influence of Geneva or Lambeth.

Again, is it really true that religious beliefs are always made less secure in proportion as they are "rationalized"? One must distinguish between two senses in which a belief may be called secure. It may be strong in the sense of keeping its hold over the unintelligent. Or it may be strong in the sense of intrinsic credibility for persons who can think.

In the matter of ecclesiastical tactics, it may be that Anatole France is perfectly right. The creed of the Church, descending from a pre-scientific Age, is full of dogma by which the modern mind is offended. Just so far, then, as one is encouraged to criticize, to sift, to accept or reject by the criterion of rationality, a disturbing force has been introduced. For the average mind it is hard to distinguish between the selection of doctrines by reason and the selection by caprice. Thus "heresy" was well named. It was αἵρεσις—the choosing for one's self—and as such it was banned, for the process once begun it was not easy to determine a limit. Among the quarrels of rival Modernists, the simple French peasant was naturally perplexed. He had lost the only authority he knew, and the authoritativeness of "developed spiritual intelligence" was a conception too subtle for him. So the encyclical *Pascendi gregis*, forbidding the whole perilous adventure, was well contrived—like its predecessor, the *Quanta cura*—for ensuring ecclesiastical safety. As mass-psychologists, the advisers of Pius X had little to learn from any one.

It was the jest of Matthew Arnold that some of his friends were unable to believe in Elijah's ascent to heaven in a chariot of fire, but would have found it credible that he had ascended in a hansom cab. Such whittling down of "the supernatural", he argued, was surely foolish, for a small miracle was not more credible than a large one. In truth "small" and "large" had no meaning in such reference. In like manner one has heard it contended that there is far too much fuss about creeds and their revision, because he who can say "I believe in God" has taken that first step of faith which makes all remaining steps simple. Thus if, by chance, the framers of the Thirty-Nine Articles had framed three hundred and ninety instead, the "evidence"—such as it is—would have been subjected to no additional strain.

And yet, when one is neither purveying jest nor devising

tactics, but reasoning with care, one sees how the case for what is called Liberal Christianity is not much affected by Anatole France's humorous analogies. Most of us have long given up the idea that our universe can be emptied of mystery. We have watched too long the melancholy procession of persons who were sure that it could—the Deists, the Encyclopædists, the Hegelians, the Positivists, the National Secular Society—for whom the veil of the Temple was to be rent from top to bottom, and that within a quite measurable period. They have passed, as Burke said of that group of them he knew, to "the vault of all the Capulets." Nor does it seem reasonable to conclude that because some things must remain indefinitely unintelligible, therefore there is nothing that can be known for certain. What the Liberal Christian of our time contends is easy enough to state. He accepts as a fact the limitations of human knowledge, not because such limitation is authoritatively revealed, but because it is made obvious by the prolonged disillusioning and discomfiture of those who fought their battle for ultimate knowledge in vain. In this, at least, our sceptical novelist should be the last to disagree. The Liberal Christian, however, stands very firmly indeed by those value-judgments of good and evil of which he feels intuitively sure,—as sure, for example, as of the law of universal causation. For neither kind of belief can he offer reasons, but neither can he doubt. Each is, in its sphere, the basis from which reasoning begins, and hence no reasoning can lead up to it. As a rational person, then, the Liberal Christian is a man who has had to choose among world theories of which none has been demonstrated, but in each of which there remains an element of inscrutable mystery, and who has made his personal venture upon that one with which his intuitive certainties about life and conduct are least difficult to reconcile. This he thinks he has found in that particular view of the universe which is called Christian.

Whether he is right or wrong in this conclusion, is not the point just now at issue. The matter at issue is whether Anatole France is justified in likening him to the passive recipient of dogmas on authority, and in arguing that he is less consistent than his religious predecessor in that he has mingled reason with faith. Our Liberal Christian has reached his belief, or his quasi-belief, quite independently of all supposed external direction, and of all outer authority whether in Bible or in Church. Towards every account of what is "taught" he holds himself free to take that attitude which seems best to him, and in no case will he take an attitude of blind submissiveness. Accepting, as on the whole the most credible view, that one which has come down through the Christian Ages, he feels certain that it has in the process become much entangled with myth and fable. These entanglements he is resolved to escape, so far as he can, and aided by that same reflective intelligence which conducted him to the point of belief which he has so far reached. Is he, for example, really inconsistent in believing—if he thinks he has found evidence for it—that there was a unique revelation of God in the Person of Christ, without believing at the same time that miracles are wrought once a week at the altar?[46] May he not accept the view that in some special sense the Bible contains "The Word of God", without being forced to defend the arithmetic of the *Book of Numbers?* May he not bow before the inscrutable ways of a Power which neither he nor anyone else can "explain", though all men must recognize its working, without being ready to pretend that such satisfying explanation is at the disposal of the devout who consult "the Church" as an oracle?

[46] One recalls how John Wesley said that to reject witchcraft meant rejecting Christianity!

He suspects, indeed, that the ultimate truth about the structure of things would have many a surprise for every sort of dogmatist, scientific no less than theological. However shrill be the note of confidence in which Secularism proclaims its complete satisfaction, he knows that this too is an idle tale. But among mysteries he is entitled to choose. His acceptance of those which are on the whole least improbable is no good reason why he should accept at the same time such as are demonstrably false.

* * *

Moreover, if inconsistency there be, it does not lie with the Liberal Christian any more than with most of our contemporary Agnostics. As a rule, they have a quite definite theory of the values of life, and a quite definite conviction about the goal of human endeavour. Yet if they are thoroughgoing in their contention that nothing whatever can be known, it is hard to see how this intricate problem of values is to be solved objectively, though for every other sort of problem our so-called knowledge is irredeemably subjective. In this respect Anatole France is indeed free from such reproach. He has made it very clear that for him at least all assurance about the goal of life has become extremely precarious when separated from that conviction about the order of the world in which it historically took its rise. But he has vindicated his consistency at a price which very many of his admirers are reluctant to see him pay. When he declares himself an unbeliever in morals no less than an unbeliever in dogma, they set their wits at work to disguise or explain away this quite logical upshot of his thought.

In his humanism he persuaded himself that he was anti-Christian, and there are good grounds to think that herein he was mistaken. But in his attitude to what Dean Inge would call "the absolute values" he made no mistake in judging himself anti-Christian through and through. For amid the fields of possible controversy as to what the Christian ethic implies, there is at least no room for doubt that it means a tremendous emphasizing of the significance of the individual and his conduct. This is what Anatole France, theoretically at all events, repudiated as absurd. No thinker had less right than he to charge Émile Zola with having "denied the ideal of man." For in none more than in Anatole France was there a persistent and mocking ridicule of the behaviour of the human race as without serious consequence, as mattering not a pebble's weight for those who could see the universe steadily and see it whole.

It was on this ground that he so commended astronomical studies for the relief they gave to a mind which Christian superstition might terrify into remorse. He felt, with Shelley,

> It is the dark idolatry of self
> Which, when our thoughts and actions once are gone,
> Demands that man should weep and bleed and groan.[47]

Nor would he agree that the intensified valuation of human conduct, though historically arising in a myth about future worlds, is now justified on a surer ground. It was to be dismissed, he thought, with the outworn folly from which it had sprung. To the reader's intense amazement, he once declared Charles Baudelaire "a very Christian poet", one "whose morality differs very little from that of the theologians." [48] And why? Not because Baudelaire reprobated moral evil, for he rather rejoiced in it. His essentially Chris-

[47] *Revolt of Islam,* VIII.
[48] *La Vie Littéraire,* III, p. 21.

tian view was shown, for this critic, in that he thought evil was a momentous affair; "These things are for him of importance; they are sins, and there is something monstrous in any sin, however small."[49] Again and again Anatole France returns to this idea, pointing out how the first charm of the Christian message lay in its assurance that there was a tragic grandeur about man's misdeeds, that his soul was of value sufficient for seven devils to seize it, and that the conflict was watched with tense celestial anxiety.[50] Quite plainly he shared the view of his own Coignard, that a woman of impregnable virtue must be one who enormously exaggerates the interest taken in her person by God and the angels.[51]

That was his prevailing mood, and it would be hard indeed to imagine a temper of mind more completely contrasted with the Christian. But there were intervals when he thought differently. Sometimes he reflected how an indictment might be framed against science not less than against religion. Naturalism, he said, had taken from man all that was beautiful as well as all of which one might be proud, reducing the "soul" to a machine which ought not even to know that it was mechanical, yet somehow continued to protest.[52] He thought with Byron of the creature "half dust, half deity, alike unfit to sink or soar." And Anatole France would pursue the implications of this still further; for the mystery of things, however he might deride it, would not quite let him go. Nature, he pointed out, had created evil, while man had created good—a limited good, but man's peculiar work.[53] With the decay of religious belief a dark-

49 *loc. cit.*

50 *ibid.*, p. 122.

51 *La Rôtisserie,* chap. iv.

52 *La Vie Littéraire,* IV, pp. 45, 6.

53 *Le Jardin d'Epicure.*

ness had descended upon the whole drama, for the suffering and sorrow that used to be in a fashion explicable through Providence had become no more than "odious jests, ill-omened and farcical impertinences." [54] And the consequence was already revealing itself. Nowhere but in religion had man ever found any account of why he was in the world and what he had come there to do. But where is he now? All Faith was blotted out. And together with Faith and Hope, man was losing Charity.[55] The only resource left was to give up thinking altogether, if one were not to appreciate with too great keenness the tragic absurdity of living.[56] "If you could read in my soul", he once said to M. Brousson, "you would be terrified . . . I have never been happy for one day, not for a single hour."

And in one of those bursts of tenderness to which his mind was always susceptible, Anatole France would return in thought to St. Francis of Assisi, or to that early Franciscan hymn-writer who had made even the *Dies Irae* so redolent of compassion:

Qui Mariam absolvisti
Qui latronem exaudisti
Mihi quoque spem dedisti.

With what moving effect, he exclaimed, did those words ring out on the voices of a choir, before a catafalque surrounded with tapers, in some draped church, at the obsequies of one whom men had admired or envied! For himself, he had never heard that thirteenth strophe of the old Franciscan hymn without feeling "shaken by a religious tremor." [57] It was by such reverence to suffering that the Gospel had reigned

54 *ibid.*, p. 49.
55 *La Vie Littéraire,* III, p. 9.
56 *Le Jardin d'Epicure,* p. 48.
57 *La Vie Littéraire,* II, p. 9.

for two thousand years.[58] Whatever might have been her blemishes of another kind, the Church had at least humiliated those happy people whom the world chose to call just, and had reminded the best of men how great is their own need to crave forgiveness. For the moment, that Lucretian idea about the lulling of the mind through astronomy seems to have receded into the background of his thought. The Christian morality, said this neo-pagan, seemed to him infinitely wise and infinitely sweet, never wholly prevailing against the violences of the spirit and the pride of the flesh, but sometimes spreading its divine peace over hearts that were tired, and teaching all the sons of men to judge not that they be not judged.

A strange mood for Anatole France, and one to rouse strange questionings about whether such an emotional attitude can indeed find justification apart from that view of man and the world which he had been at so great pains to destroy. And it seldom endured for long. He often thought of Mary of Magdala, but by turns in the most opposite ways. Roused to protest against a righteousness that knew no mercy, he declared of Alexandre Dumas and his new gospel of relentless punishment that he had "revoked the Magdalen's pardon." [59] But at another moment, with the same figure before his imagination, his sympathy is with the Roman lady of fashion who objects: *Je ne veux pas d'une religion qui dérange les coiffures.*[60]

Like Matthew Arnold, and many another, he was "wandering between two worlds, one dead, the other powerless to be born." [61]

[58] *ibid,* I, p. 335.
[59] *ibid.,* II, p. 1.
[60] *Loeta Acilia.*
[61] M. Arnold: *On the Grande Chartreuse.*

CHAPTER XI

CLERICALISM AND CHASTITY

If we may treat as useful the design to make superstition ridiculous in the eyes of men given to pleasure . . . if the affectation of austerity in manners, if the excessive value attached to purity only serves the hypocrites who by putting on the easy mask of chastity can dispense with all virtues . . . if, by accustoming men to treat as so many crimes faults from which honourable and conscientious persons are not exempt, we extend over the purest souls the power of that dangerous caste which to rule and disturb the earth has constituted itself the interpreter of heavenly justice,—then we shall see in the author of the *Pucelle* no more than a foe to hypocrisy and superstition.

CONDORCET

Even though a gifted man like M. Renan may be so carried away by the tide of opinion in France, where he lives, as to say that Nature cares nothing about chastity, and to see with amused indulgence the worship of the great goddess Lubricity, let us stand fast and say that her worship is against Nature—human nature—and that it is ruin. . . . The Eternal has attached to certain moral causes the safety or ruin of States, and the present popular literature of France is a sign that she has a most dangerous moral disease.

MATTHEW ARNOLD

Whether any particular nation or city is superior to another in "the domestic virtues" must always be hard to decide. But that the bookstores, music-halls and cafés of Paris are exceptional in their *pornographie*, no visitor can feel any doubt. Under the Second Empire prosecutions were entered against Flaubert for *Madame Bovary* and against

Dumas for *La Dame aux Camélias.* What special depth of eroticism would be sufficient to rouse a public prosecutor under the Third Republic, one finds it hard to guess. The valiant crusade of M. Bérenger for "the decency of the streets" is said to have effected some improvement. In that case, the visitor of to-day must strain his imagination to picture the state of things before that reforming Senator took up his task.

The single, ever-enduring butt in a Paris theatre of our time is the husband or wife who betrays some lingering scruple against adultery. It is the promise of *gravures très risquées,* advertised without the least pretence of art, that lures young adolescence to countless picture shops. Novelists, having exhausted their invention in contemporary salaciousness, have turned to the classical world as to a fresh field, and offer "studies of antiquity" whose character everyone can predict. The whole pornographic flood is, indeed, "explained" by various considerations which are supposed to excuse it. Parisians declare very vociferously that it is meant for visitors from abroad, and that the native *père de famille* remains a watchful guardian of Pierre and Marguerite. Such interpretation of foreign taste may perhaps be as shrewd from the point of view of trade as it is uncomplimentary in international judgment. But it is hard to believe that the whole immense volume of comic papers, for example, should be produced winter and summer for the entertainment of tourists alone. And if it is no more than what Americans would call "vigorous tourist policy", one feels that the Parisian householder is running great risks with the morals of his Marguerite and his Pierre. Patriotic devotion to municipal business has involved great family sacrifice. At all events, the superficial appearance of life in the French capital is rather singular in its need for such copious explaining to all who view it under a conventional prejudice against the obscene.

In this respect Anatole France was a child of his city. Whether it is a mitigation or an aggravation of the lubricious that it should be presented with *finesse* rather than with *brutalité,* whether the subtly suggestive or the candidly indecent is more open to blame, is a point we may well debate. Burke thought that under the old *régime* vice itself had lost half its evil by losing all its grossness. But a book like *Histoire Comique* differs only in method from a paper like *Sans Gêne* or *Le Sourire.* It is incomparably more skilful, but in this particular aspect its purpose and its appeal are just the same. *Le Lys Rouge* closely resembles the familiar tale to be bought at a kiosk on the boulevards. Referring to such work, a recent biographer has said that "Anatole France deals rather frankly with questions of sex." One is surprised that the same biographer should describe the one novel in which such frankness has no place as "a conscious bid for popularity." Popular literature in France involves no reticence in such a field, as our novelist was soon to show.

I

Curiously enough, he once appeared as a stern critic of pornography. Zola's *La Terre* came into his hands for review, and Anatole France wrote about it in language that might have come from a Puritan. For once, as Disraeli would have said, he was "on the side of the angels."

La Terre was a novel on French village life. It describes many a rustic scene,—the haymaking and the harvest, the cottage meal and the alehouse festivity, the moralizing of the *curé* and the rude jesting of peasants. The book derives its title from its author's purpose of depicting men and women who live close to Mother Earth, and in fidelity to his spirit of realism Zola drew such figures very differently from either Wordsworth in *The Excursion* or Burns in *The Cottar's Saturday Night.* Whatever English or Scottish peasants might be, those in France—as this realist saw them—were not like that, and he was determined to present them as they were. So he gave his readers a very coarse book. All that gift of lurid imagination which made the Zola of *Germinal* so effective as a portrayer of life in a Belgian colliery town was turned to work upon a French peasantry which he believed to be gross in feeling and almost destitute of morals. *La Terre* is a novel which British critics have stigmatized as the nadir of realism—of the sort Aristotle would have condemned in his terse Greek way as simply *μιαρόν.*

But why was Anatole France so much enraged by it? Not, one may safely guess, because he regarded it as a provocative to esteem lightly the domestic virtues which lie at the basis of civilization. He himself esteemed those virtues very lightly indeed. He was the sort of man who confides to an intimate friend that there is no such thing as chastity, though there are many hypocrites who pretend it.[1] To him the ancient conception of a virtuous woman was something at which the modern world has very properly agreed to laugh. A manifesto by five leading French critics had denounced *La Terre* for descending "to the very depths of uncleanness", and Anatole France was quick to point out that two at least of these rigorous moralists had no right to cast the first stone. In his merry mood he said that they perpetrated upon their spiritual father the sin of Ham against Noah. They had advised the public to condemn *La Terre,* but not to waste such righteous indignation in a fusillade against "the sincere books of to-morrow"—a hint which drew the

[1] Cf. *Anatole France en Pantoufles,* p. 77.

characteristically Francian retort that these two gentlemen had evidently some volumes in the press, and that the ingenuousness of their recommendation was as interesting as its astuteness.[2]

But he had his own quarrel with *La Terre*, on æsthetic rather than ethical grounds. Zola, he argued, was at fault, not because he was immoral, but because he was gross. Such pictures, for example, as that of an aged peasant violated by her grandson were past all bearing. The prolix obscenity of those villagers was not redeemed by artfulness of innuendo —of the sort, we may suppose, that marks the conversation in *La Rôtisserie de la Reine Pedauque*. Whether the passage about a summer excursion in *Les Dieux ont Soif* is more elegant than a picture in *La Terre*, may occur to some readers as at least arguable. But Anatole France had not yet written in such a strain, and what affected him about *La Terre* was that there was no touch of "the grace of things." The features of country life were everywhere described in that novel "by some ugly name." And he thought it a grim comment on public taste that this sort of wallowing in the drab had brought Zola so great a literary vogue. Never before in literature, he exclaimed, had the ideal of man been so shockingly denied. In a paragraph of remarkable eloquence, weakened in its effect only by the reader's knowledge that the thought which appears to give it such power was not in the mind of the man who wrote it, Anatole France sums up his case against his victim:

> There is in all of us, in the small as well as in the great, in the humble as well as in the lofty, an instinct of the beautiful, a desire for all that adorns and beautifies, and this—spread throughout the world—makes the charm of life. M. Zola does not know it. Desire and modesty are sometimes charmingly blended in human

[2] *La Vie Littéraire,* I, p. 227.

> souls. M. Zola does not know it. There are on earth magnificent forms and noble thoughts. M. Zola does not know it. Even many weaknesses, many errors, and many faults have a touching beauty of their own. Grief is sacred. The sanctity of tears is at the base of all religions. Misery should suffice to make a man august in the eyes of men. M. Zola does not know it. He does not know that the graces are seemly, that philosophic irony is indulgent and gentle, and that human things inspire only two feelings in well-regulated minds, admiration or pity. M. Zola is entitled to the deepest pity.[3]

Even when he had written this, he had not yet finished with Zola's faults. He returns to the psychological dissection in his later review of *Le Rêve*. This had been announced by the publishers as a "chaste" novel, composed expressly to be "put into the hands of all women, and even of young girls." But, asks the merciless critic, could not a writer be modest without publishing his resolve in the newspapers? If he meant to espouse decorum, why celebrate the mystic alliance with so much noise and uproar? Must Saint Joseph's lily become in his hands an instrument for advertisement? There was some credit indeed in the change, for the purity of this novelist had been bought dear, paid for with all his talent, of which one did not find a trace in the three hundred pages of *Le Rêve*. But, for his own part, the critic would prefer a less noisy chastity; and of the two, he would choose M. Zola on all fours rather than M. Zola winged. For the natural had an inimitable charm, and no man could please when he had become no longer himself.[4]

All this is very illuminating. It should be read in the light of passages in M. Brousson's book, especially the two choice sections which describe the great æsthete's adventures first in a public park after dusk in Paris, and afterwards when on holiday in Tours. The reader may be left to judge

[3] *La Vie Littéraire,* I, p. 236, sqq.

[4] *ibid.,* II, p. 285, sqq.

whether the ways of those rustics at a haymaking in *La Terre* have anything to lose by comparison with the forms of amusement chosen by this venerable member of *L'Académie française.*

II

What Anatole France really believed about this matter is abundantly clear. He regarded the popular idea about chastity as having two sources, one derived from the State and the other from the Church. This so-called virtue, he said, was made sacred in pagan Rome, where for reasons of public policy marriage was built up like aqueducts and drains, by men who were supreme alike as lawyers and as masons.[5] In so far, then, as we share the Roman conception of the value of the State, we shall be disposed to guard marriage as it was guarded under such laws, for they were contrived with great skill for their purpose. But in so far as we are anarchic individualists, like Anatole France himself, this instrument of policy will be abandoned with the end it was meant to serve.

It has, however, he points out, another and a more powerful protection. Chastity as revered by most people who still undertake its defence is a survival of mediævalism. The superstitious guard it with a terrified solicitude. Ultimately its root is in that denial of "Nature" upon which the Christian priesthood must for ever insist, just because without it the Church would lose its *raison d'être.* For the Church as an institution could stand only so long as men could be made to believe in an essential antagonism between body and mind, only so long as they could be deluded with a theological figment about "souls" which had to be "saved" by the immolation of the flesh and the subjugating of all fleshly appetite.

[5] *ibid.,* II, p. 7.

At all costs there must be maintained what is described by Dr. Trublet in *Histoire Comique* as "that deplorable misunderstanding which, eighteen centuries ago, put humanity on bad terms with Nature."[6] Even as the early ascetics had fasted in some cases to death, even as scourgings and self-macerations had been accounted meritorious in the sight of God, even as virginity had for centuries been held to be the highest attainment in the life of holiness, so there was still in the minds of the devout a barrier against the natural in sex relationship. This barrier, he thought, must be cleared away, and Free Love must be restored to the place from which superstition had deposed it.

With this in view, Anatole France draws one scene after another in which the inhibitions of Christian morality are presented as no less grotesque than the veto which mediæval dogma had laid upon the free exercise of the intellect. He searched the *Lives of the Saints* for material about those visions in which the monastic cell was invaded by gay temptresses from a pagan world, and in which the exercises of piety were for ever being disturbed by the demon of concupiscence. In picture after picture of *Le Puits de Sainte-Claire* he has used the penitential records to show how ludicrous and how futile was this spiritual warfare, to what lengths of absurdity men and women were driven under priestly deceit, and how—as George Meredith would say—Nature avenges herself on those who would suppress her by constantly reappearing "not with her best side uppermost." The monk in *Thaïs* went out to evangelize the courtesan, but the enterprise ended, to the novelist's complete satisfaction, with the courtesan's seduction of the monk.

To those who are in earnest about the difficulties of this question in the modern world, such pictures from the Middle

[6] *Histoire Comique,* p. 7.

Ages have not much more interest than the corresponding pictures of mediæval resistance to the advance of knowledge and research. The inference that a Christian of to-day should be either a severe ascetic or a narrow dogmatist, because his spiritual predecessors had this character, involves an extraordinary limiting of the sphere of progress. But Anatole France has many a picture intended to drive home his "Immoralism" from the experiences of the present.

On this matter it is not of his so-called "frankness" that any critic, except a prude, will complain. The deepest and most powerful instinct of mankind cannot have its nature too faithfully analyzed or its workings too candidly shown. But psychological analysis in this field is not just another name for pornography. Those physical impulses which underlie the institution of the brothel and the *maison de convenance* are indeed treated in Anatole France's books with a skill that might be envied by the tired artists of many an illustrated Parisian weekly. It is a melancholy fact that the temptations of youth in *La Rôtisserie*, the conflicts of lust among the middle-aged in *Le Lys Rouge*, and senile passion in *Jérôme Coignard* are drawn from life. To catch an erring spouse "in flagrante delicto" was an exploit of M. Bergeret, as it has been an exploit of petitioners in the Divorce Court ever since divorce trials began to be held, and the record may well be imitated from that of many a trial *à huis clos* to which prurient youth sought admission in vain. But is the depicting of all this to be called a frank treatment of questions of sex? Only in the sense in which we may apply such description to the work of Herondas, or Apuleius, or Aristophanes. Nowhere else, perhaps, are we made so acutely conscious as in this aspect of his writing that Anatole France belongs to a world which modern civilization in its higher features has outgrown.

Whether it has been outgrown in practice, is not our problem. Nothing can be more sterile than an argument as to the moral superiority of the conduct in one age over that in another. But though we may be no more just, no more merciful, no more benevolent than the men of old, we do not doubt that we have truer theoretic conceptions of justice, of mercy, of benevolence. In the Great War we destroyed life on a scale which makes Julius Caesar's Gallic campaigns seem a trifle; but we are sure that our ideas of the justification for taking life are better than Julius Caesar's. The men of the eighteenth century may have had feelings as charitable as our own; but if their provision of public charities were copied by any nation of to-day, we should not hesitate to brand it as callous and inhuman. In like manner, no amount of evidence that western mankind is in practice "as polygamous as the Turks" can refute the general view that in the West the idea of monogamy represents a distinct and unquestionable advance.

Further and still less agreeable light is cast upon this aspect of our novelist's mind by certain sections of that extraordinary volume, *Anatole France en Pantoufles*, which M. Jean Jacques Brousson, "his secretary and intimate friend for eight years", has lately published. On the title page this is called "A Boswellian Record." As professing to contain the daily talk of an eminent man, reported by a very uncritical listener, it well deserves the name. In other respects, it is more Rabelaisian than Boswellian. With what purpose, and with what degree of fidelity to fact, M. Brousson has included in his otherwise very valuable work this collection of facetious obscenities, it is idle to guess, at least without some further knowledge of the compiler. But his book will long serve, in this respect, to darken the fame of the man it undertakes to reveal. Caliban reproached Prospero for having taught him language, so that he knew how to curse, and it is indeed a sort of moral Caliban—fertile of wit and nimble of tongue—that we have to contemplate as he mocks the finer feelings of mankind in *Anatole France en Pantoufles.*

If we may trust M. Brousson's portrait, we shall no longer be able to regard his hero as one "whose Muse was wanton, but whose life was pure." What is there drawn is the likeness of a cultivated satyr, a mind copious and picturesque, but turning ever to the salacious as a needle to the pole. Carlyle once said of Diderot's *Les Bijoux Indiscrets* that if any man, even a reviewer, must open it again, he should bathe himself in running water, put on change of raiment, and be unclean until the even.[7] And there are indeed products of Anatole France's pen which make one feel that such thorough disinfecting would not be out of place after a perusal. Often as one reads, there comes back to mind that terrific phrase of St. Augustine, uttered in a mood of self-reproach like that of Bunyan or Tolstoy: "infernal vapours which arise out of the corrupt depths of concupiscence." Anatole France once ventured to quote that, describing it as a thoroughly moral but very ungraceful reflection.[8] He has done more to illustrate it than to criticize it. And M. Brousson's account is of his disposition in old age, so that our novelist could not even have said, with his own Coignard, that he had smuggled virtue into himself through the breaches made in his constitution by suffering and by advancing years.[9] One hopes that his "secretary and intimate friend" may have mistaken an occasional lapse for a persisting temperament. But that such an error was possible at all casts most unwelcome light upon Anatole France.

[7] *Miscellanies,* Essay on Diderot.

[8] *La Vie Littéraire,* I, pp. 86, 87.

[9] *La Rôtisserie,* xvi.

How could such a man treat "questions of sex"? There is no real treatment of such questions which is not at the same time a treatment of human love; and of what is meant by love—except as physical attraction—he has shown only the dimmest idea. One might pursue many a reflection on this matter, regarding the French novel in general, and the ways of French life which it is bound to portray. The typical love story of an English novelist could not well have arisen in a land where, for example, the common preliminaries of a middle-class marriage are so exceedingly prosaic. It is hard to convey to the Parisian parent just what is thought by observers across the channel about the use of those family negotiators passing between the prospective bridegroom and the prospective bride, about bargaining for a *dot,* about the few weeks or few days judged sufficient for the lady to become acquainted with her future husband, and about the knowledge of each other's qualities that is formed for the most part on someone else's report. Parallels from Hindu practice suggest themselves, and the analogy of the aged προμνηστηρίαι of the Attic period going from house to house in pursuit of their trade.[10] It is true that chaperonage is maintained with a strictness beyond all that ever entered into the mind of a mid-Victorian parent, and one is not surprised that it should be so. Where no reliance can be placed upon the normal guarantees that prevail in another land, it is natural that precautions elsewhere unnecessary should be provided.

A love story, written amid such surroundings, must be expected to be different from the kind of novel that the English reader knows. What Anatole France understood by a *roman d'amour* may be seen in such books as *Le Lys Rouge* or *His-*

[10] Cf. e. g. Aristophanes, *Clouds,* 41; Plato, *Theaetetus,* 149 D.

toire Comique. They are pictures of "love" about which it is insufficient to say that they show no capacity for their subject. They are conclusive proof of incapacity. They deal with their subject in no sense other than that which suits the business of a French railway book-stall. In truth hardly any other great artist of our time could be named from whom this grand *motif* is so conspicuously absent. He might have said of it, as Laplace said of God, that he found "no need for that hypothesis." When the Archbishop of Buenos Aires laid his lecturing tour under the ban of the Church, and when in consequence no women were present in halls where Anatole France spoke, the action was dismissed with a raising of the eyelid and a shrug of the shoulders as a typical case of priestly intolerance. But it may well have had a better ground. The essentially pagan character of a novel like *Thaïs* lay far less in its disparagement of Christian dogma than in its exaltation of pre-Christian animalism. Those Greek artists whom the writer so loved set him here their least fortunate pattern. For seldom indeed until the Alexandrian period do we find in Greek literature any genuine portrayal of what the modern world calls love. But neither do we find in the same literature what the modern world calls a novel,—and the coincidence is significant.

III

Yet the connection which Anatole France found between Christian belief and the ideal of chastity is by no means groundless.

Among those who are concerned for that ideal it is safe to say that a large number find its only authoritative standard in their religion. For example, if they spoke their mind with complete candour, they would acknowledge that apart from the New Testament and its interpretation by the Church they can see no reason whatever for opposing a change under which marriage would be made dissoluble at will. It is religion, and religion alone, in their view which has ordained that this particular contract shall be raised above those common sense qualifications by which every other contract is revocable. For them chastity is indeed among the "theological virtues", and unchastity is among the theological sins. What such people infer from such premises will depend, of course, upon what they think of theology.

Many of them are in a position very like that of those men of the Renaissance who held to the doctrine of a "twofold truth." Thinkers such as Pomponazzi, Pierre Charron, or Montaigne, used to press their intellectual speculations to that point at which the veto of "Faith" forbade any further advance. So with a profound salaam to Authority, they were careful to indicate whither the argument would otherwise lead, but declined to follow it into those seas over which they acknowledged that the Church alone had a reliable chart. One is often puzzled to guess how far they seriously believed that they ought to stop at such theological boundaries, and how far their precaution was no more than a counsel of prudence in a dangerous Age. Whether Galileo really said *e pur se muove* or not, we feel certain that such muttered apology to a Reason whose fetters he dared not unloose was quite after the mood of many an impatient investigator under those popes so ironically called the Innocents.

But this idea of a twofold truth is so obviously accepted by many honest though dull folk of our own time that we cannot refuse to believe in the honesty of bygone thinkers like Sir Thomas Browne. There are passages in the *Religio Medici* which, if they had been written—as they might have been—by Anatole France, would leave us in no doubt of what was in the author's mind. If he had said, for example, like Sir Thomas Browne, that he could accept the story of Eve's being framed out of the rib of Adam without raising any difficulty about who would arise with that rib at the Resurrection, or the story of Lazarus without being troubled by the problem where his soul waited in that interval of three days and whether his heir-at-law who had hurriedly entered into his inheritance would have been justified in retaining it after the reappearance of the testator, it would have been perfectly obvious that Anatole France was jesting. But there is no reason to suspect a jest in the case of Sir Thomas Browne. For him the spheres of knowledge and faith were quite distinct. He said himself, and multitudes could still say with him, "Where the Scripture is silent, the Church is my text; where that speaks, 'tis my comment; where there is a joint silence of both, I borrow not the rules of my religion from Rome or Geneva, but from the dictates of my own reason." [11]

But we are far from having exhausted, and sometimes we have not even suggested, the true explanation of the tenacity of a belief or a practice when we have mentioned the grounds which its devotees can assign upon demand. The reason why a devout man like Sir Thomas Browne acted as he did was often, so far as he knew or could explain, just some injunction from his Church. But what of the reason why he bowed to that Church and accepted its injunctions? If the ultra Protestant is ready with a glib answer about superstition and fear, what account will he give of the source

[11] *Religio Medici,* Sect. III.

of his own attitude to the Bible? In the one case as in the other, it is the inner response to an ideal of life which gives the authority its binding force. The Christian insistence on chastity, however futile and absurd may be the theoretic defence of it which is often erected against attack, has its ultimate basis in the Christian conception of the family. And it is because, like so many other ultimate foundations upon which conduct rests, this one is unconsciously accepted by so many who could neither define nor justify it, that it is at once so easy to make it appear illogical and so difficult to reason it away. Why, then, it is fair to ask, did a mind so alert as that of our novelist adopt towards it an attitude so singular?

To suppose that in the rich and varied nature of Anatole France there was no appreciation at all of a love other than sensual appetite would indeed explain his *pornographie.* But perhaps this may be explained without an hypothesis quite so violent. If he himself associated chastity with clericalism, his admirers cannot complain when a critic tries the assumption that in anti-clericalism this strange campaign for unchastity may have had its impulse. And there are historic parallels which are at least suggestive.

A century and a half ago, the pamphleteering which paved the way for the great Revolution was, in one of its aspects, deliberately planned to weaken the Church by deriding that family virtue for which the Church was specially solicitous. Satire in an earlier Age had delighted to depict the hypocritical monk or *curé*, who affected to be austere beyond others, but who was in truth a secret libertine, and who turned even the Confessional into an instrument of his passions. But the satire of the Encyclopædists rested on the frank acknowledgment that the clergy were Puritanic, and it appealed rather to the resentment of those who chafed under such restraint. Voltaire mocked Joan of Arc, partly because she was typical of the Dark Ages, but also because she had become a national symbol of virgin honour.[12] Those readers, probably very few, who still go through the dull indecencies of Diderot in *Jacques le Fataliste*, can have no doubt that here was far less a novel than an anti-clerical pamphlet. Never was there a more shameless attempt to exploit human vices for the injury of the Church which forbade them. An atmosphere was to be created whose mephitic vapours might stifle the voice of the priest, and even Condorcet, in a shameful paragraph, declared that so desirable an end justified a means otherwise so questionable. Those who think that dishonest casuistry has been a sin peculiar to churchmen would do well to read his argument with care, that they may extend their censures to another quarter.

It was a casuistical performance that shocked even so vehement an anti-clerical as the late Lord Morley. The Voltairean school, he remarked, had poured constant derision upon the practice of sexual continence, and had done so because this was so sacred in the eyes of the Church. In Lord Morley's view there was indeed good ground for regarding chastity in its origin as due to ascetic misunderstandings and a myth about the inherent evil of matter. But the virtue that thus began had long vindicated its worth by better reasons, and the men of the Encyclopædic group were quite unaware of the anthropological facts that might have lent some colour of justice to their attack. It was enough for them that family virtues were guarded by "the Infamous." So they urged the "disastrous sophism" that these were, as

[12] Cf. the remark of Anatole France, recorded by M. Brousson: "Au xviii e siècle elle semble si burlesque avec son pucelage, que Voltaire la blasonne en petits vers burlesques." (*Anatole France en Pantoufles*, p. 187.)

a rule, even an impediment to the happiness of mankind. "It might be necessary", exclaims this critic, "to pull down the Church. But the worst Church that has ever prostituted the name and the idea of religion cannot be so disastrous to society as a gospel that systematically relaxes self-control as being an unmeaning curtailment of happiness." [13]

Thus the literary tradition to which Anatole France belongs is obvious, and he has numerous imitators who follow him to the best of their limited endowment. Parisian writers have indeed recently done themselves grave injustice before the world in their half-insane desire to flout the clergy. They do not really hate the Church because she exalts the chaste, but they have worked themselves into a mood of hatred towards the chaste because they look upon the unchaste as more effective allies against the Church. A like policy has been again and again ascribed to those expert psychologists who of late years in Russia have been breaking the bonds of ancient superstition. It may seem harsh to compare Anatole France with the Moscow anti-clericals who think the spell of the ikon may be counteracted by the lure of Free Love. But the auxiliary invoked against the priesthood is much the same in both cases. For a time it may have an ignoble success. Yet in the end this is poor strategy, because it implies such deep disgrace to the cause it would advance, and so dangerous a compliment to the cause it would destroy. It is worthy of the caricaturists of Christmas or Easter celebrations at Leningrad. But it is not worthy of Anatole France.

IV

That the mediæval valuation of chastity was rooted in a contempt for the flesh which was then judged Christian, just

[13] J. Morley: *Voltaire*, p. 141.

as neglect of cleanliness, the cult of poverty, and the hatred of knowledge sprang from a spirit of self-denial which was also judged Christian, is not to the point. Scorn for the "Dark" Ages, which our sons of the Renaissance everywhere else exhibit, seems curiously associated with the assumption that in respect of the real meaning of Christianity those Ages were not dark, but rather a time of insight which the Modernist theologians have lost. When one reflects that the true import of a system so complex has caused such difference of opinion among thinkers of our time presumably honest and apparently not altogether stupid, it is amazing to hear that for guidance upon what it meant we must turn to the period in which the light of the ancient world had been extinguished and the light of modern science had not yet dawned.

But dismissing this evidence from mediæval practice as no more than a polemical artifice which can hardly have imposed upon the quick-witted writers who used it, one can see how the veneration of chastity among the devout did in truth result from a habit of mind which was in essence Christian. Not in contempt for the body, as the Saints of the Desert so foolishly thought, but rather in respect for the body did Christian σωφροσύνη finds its justification. What is called "illicit love" was indeed often represented as a disgraceful yielding to that human nature which ought to be despised and suppressed. But a more genuine sense of what human nature is and may become has revealed the unnatural character of that vagrant passion which would corrupt all of the sweeter relationships of life, and the essential inhumanity towards women with which it has defiled every great populous centre in our time.

It is true that those to whom such phenomena of the modern world seem horrible are persons who—on some ground—

have accepted the idea of man as potentially noble and of his actions as by no means insignificant. To Anatole France this seemed mere human vanity, the self-exaltation of men who longed to "adorn their faults with the thunders of Heaven and the tears of the angels." They liked to be assured that in a higher world their lightest act or thought was of importance, especially as nothing they said or did was of any obvious importance here and now. Finding no satisfaction or encouragement in "the only life of which we are sure", they demanded a great place for their sins in the administration of another life of which they flattered themselves that they were the partakers. What specially charmed our novelist in the moral attitudes of the later Renan was that he asked so little from human nature, because he did not believe human nature to be capable of much. It needs no argument to show that herein, more than in any possible controversy about the "miraculous", Anatole France has declared war on the Christian conception of mankind.

Of this crucial contrast the treatment of sex problems is but an instance. Those who have been most insistent on the chaste ideal have also been sympathetic to many another attitude towards life in which a sense of special human worth has seemed to involve the practice of a specially human self-control. With some of these attitudes Anatole France found himself in accord, and from time to time he even recognized that they were most genuinely expressed in some hymn of Christian devotion. He did not, for example, suggest that the vast and quite new impulse of benevolence toward mankind as such, which historically began with the Christian charities and was historically determined by the Christian valuation of life, is to be abjured by those who know its "superstitious" origin. But for some reason he insisted that the one virtue of chastity, surely not less human in the highest sense in which that word can be used, should be dropped in deference to an enlightenment about the primitive asceticism which once burlesqued its demands. As a controversialist for the anti-clericals, he was unfortunate in the selection of a field on which to meet the enemy. For accepting and even demanding such an issue on which to fight, the Church is much more beholden to him than the phalanx of *libres penseurs*. Often indeed have the theologians been challenged to defend old dogmas about whose ground they had many a misgiving. But here at least, unless the whole spiritual progress of Europe has been a delusion, they may take up the gauge with a real joy of battle.

V

Once again we have to face the difficult question how far a thinker's *morale* is determined or affected by his speculative opinions. It is a point which Anatole France himself once discussed with considerable care. Reviewing *Le Disciple*, by Paul Bourget, he found grave fault with Brunetière for arguing that the crimes which the youth in that novel had committed sprang from the deterministic philosophy in which he had been brought up. Brunetière had held that any system of thought which results in moral enfeeblement is self-condemned. By its social consequences, he had said, a speculative doctrine must stand or fall. Ideas that were dangerous must necessarily be false, and in the end morality must be the judge of metaphysics.[14]

Anatole France could endorse no such view as that, and he had little trouble in representing it as absurd. Brunetière's rule, he complained, would obstruct all intellectual progress with the veto of social custom. Those widows in

[14] Cf. *La Vie Littéraire*, III, 54, sq.

Malabar who burned themselves on a husband's funeral pyre would be justified in the maintenance of an old tradition of their tribe, against the western reformers whose innovating thought was tribally dangerous. The barrier of custom would make it for ever impossible to rise from a lower to a higher morality. All modern conceptions of what is socially good had gone through an earlier stage in which they were subversive of the past, and there could be no more groundless confidence than that which would erect the conceptions of to-day into a system unchangeable for all time. What was at stake in such a controversy was nothing less than the honour of the human intellect. Thought of every sort must be permitted to expand freely, without continual pauses by the thinker to take ethical or theological bearings. Well had Renan said: *Il n'est pas permis au savant de s'occuper des consequences qui peuvent sortir de ses recherches.*[15] Let no man dare to incite against free intelligence "the little domestic gods that guard our homes."

Such comment seems trite and obvious enough. But, as became a writer for *Le Temps,* Anatole France proceeded to reassure his readers whom Paul Bourget's novel might have alarmed regarding the possible upshot of Darwinism. The consequences of Evolution, or any other doctrine, for practical conduct had been absurdly exaggerated. He pointed out that though limits should never be set to inquiry, there were limits in the very nature of man himself that were amply sufficient to protect us. Unfettered philosophy should, indeed, be monarch of the soul, but, like other monarchies, this one was sure to be exercised in conformity with a subject's "aspirations and necessities." Under all manner of speculative systems mankind had been tolerably faithful to those social rules without which it was impossible to live. If

[15] *Vers les Temps Meilleurs,* II, p. 39.

Moloch did not prevent the Phœnician mothers from feeding their babies, it was not to be feared that ideas leading to the destruction of the human race would emerge from the laboratory of a Parisian physiologist. What might indeed be destructive without limit and had shown such power to kill, times without number, in man's melancholy past, was the rigid adherence to some fanatical tradition, encrusted by time and consecrated by authority.[16]

All this is, of course, admirably said. The theologian and the moralist have ventured many a rash and indefensible inhibition, of which the exposure in days long gone by has often to be repeated in terms of the present. We have been warned in lines of unknown source, but no doubt produced by some laborious imitator of Pope, how

> Errors in the life breed errors in the brain,
> And these reciprocally those again.

Thus one's intellectual heresies were supposed to be due first to his low morality, and his morality in turn to be made yet lower as his heresies were nourished or expressed. But that line of Apologetic has become *démodé*. It has been given up, in the main, on account of embarrassment in the search for illustrations. There were too many cases of lofty-minded atheism which no apologist could explain away, and impeccable orthodoxy was too often found in men whose personal characters the apologist did not care to quote,—or to have quoted against him by some profane critic.

But among the consequences of this change in the methods of controversy one sees a most remarkable conclusion, now professed or at least assumed on many quite different sides. It is widely taken for granted that what a man believes about the origin and destiny of the race has nothing whatever to

[16] *La Vie Littéraire,* III, p. 70, sq.

do with his personal ἦθος. And this, when one reflects upon it, is seen to involve an extraordinary partitioning of the unity of human nature. The old theologians reached their strange doctrine because they enormously overestimated the influence of belief upon conduct. Their successors seem to assume that conduct is not influenced by belief at all. Surely the "honour of the human intellect", for which Anatole France was so rightly solicitous, is somewhat compromised when intellect is shown as thus wholly ineffective. Not a monarchy that is limited, but a monarchy reduced to some vain show of a Carolingian "king" is to be the rôle of divine reason. In its government, so-called, the reason is to be like Charles the Bald, Charles the Fat, Charles the Simple, while the true mayors of the palace are our obstinate and unreflective instincts! The intelligence that decides and the forces that drive are regarded as wholly separate. Apparently, though physiologists have no doubt that the brain is one system, it is possible and even natural—in Mr. Bernard Shaw's phrase—to "let not the right lobe of the brain know what the left lobe doeth." However strikingly some persons of our race may approach success in such an effort, one shrinks from accepting them as quite typical, and it seems time to protest that such a doctrine is still less credible than the one it has displaced. Our present-day contemners of the human intellect must be reminded that though others have erred in exaggerating the rationality of mankind, their error is not corrected by a frantic denial that man's character or will is determined by his reason in any degree whatever.

If there is force in this argument, it seems to follow that the peculiar intellectual condition known as complete Agnosticism cannot fail to have its corresponding condition of indecisive and vacillating will. Such correspondence will be most notable in those for whom intellectual activity is keenest, just as it may be almost unrecognizable in those who think least clearly and least systematically. Moreover, the long continued habit of treating rival beliefs or practices as just so much material for ludicrous and satiric presentation is equally suited to form a character for which no belief is stronger and no practice better than its contradictory. The service which the agile satirist can render to his Age is thus achieved at a considerable price.

There are those who persist in treating Anatole France as no mere man of letters, but as a sort of prophet, a serious thinker, with definite and valuable principles of his own. One is entitled to ask, then, just what these principles are. For example, as a devotee of "the Master" in this sense enters the polling-booth to cast his ballot, he does so with the knowledge that for whatever side he votes there is Francian authority to believe his enthusiasm for it to be absurd. As he enlists beneath the banner of a cause, he does so realizing that it makes no difference whether his cause is victorious or defeated. As he shapes his course in the common relations of private life, he is haunted by the recollection that where he has an impulse to set one ideal above another, it is his grotesque vanity about the significance of his own acts which makes him draw so groundless a distinction. That all this leads to moral enfeeblement, is plain enough.

* * *

On this general question there is a passage of extraodinary interest in Renan's *Souvenirs de Ma Jeunesse*. Looking back in his old age upon that shifting of beliefs which had marked his career, the great French leader of Freethought was struck by the persistence of his own modes of feeling and action, long after his abandonment of the creed under which these habits had been formed. Renan was well aware that this can be psychologically explained. He knew, for example, those virtues which had hardly appeared in the world until the Christian belief in immortality had given a new sacredness to life, and would have been the last to argue that he who has given up such eschatological expectations should abandon the benevolence which had been so initiated. He knew how virtues originating in one way may afterwards be justified in another. But he felt also how a rule of life with a definite and assignable ground in the past is by no means sure of continuing very long after that ground has been cut away. For it may turn out that the practice, though it may have reasons other than can be found in the ancient theory, often belongs to just the same habit of mind for which the theory has force. And he did not hesitate to place the maxims of the chaste in just this class.

For himself, he said, his effort had been to achieve logical symmetry, dropping only such "virtues" as derive all their binding force from the beliefs he had given up, and retaining only those that were at least equally reconcilable with the philosophic theories he had adopted. But the constraints of long-cemented psychological association had been too intense to be dissolved by the frigid demonstrations of logic. Late in life he found himself still determined by a faith that he no longer held. And he used to speculate about the question whether custom could thus prevail over argument indefinitely. Not for ever, he thought, could man live on "the shadow of a shadow." "An immense moral debasement will set in as soon as religion disappears." If some priest had written that, our *libres penseurs* would have no difficulty in disposing of it. But coming from such a source, as the French say, it "gives one furiously to think." And one thinks about it all the more when one recalls some of those later books in which that subtle pathologist of the soul may be held to have corroborated his own prognosis. *The Priest of Nemi, Water of Youth, The Abbess of Jouarre*—from what subsequent morbid diathesis did these proceed, so different from *L'Avenir de la Science* or *Marc Aurèle?*

Twenty-three years ago, Anatole France unveiled the monument to Ernest Renan in a public square of his native Tréguier. Surmounting the bronze seated figure is a statue of Pallas Athene, and the orator so well selected for the occasion spoke of the goddess that Renan had come to worship. In beauty of conception and felicity of phrase that address has often been likened to *La Prière sur l'Acropole*—the language "fitting the thought without crease or wrinkle." But it was the achievement of Anatole France to bury Renan at least as much as to praise him. In his literary successor the spirit of the savant has indeed gone marching on, taking that definite turn to the left which the insight of the *Souvenirs* had so strikingly foreseen. The Catholic Bretons, by way of protest, have set up over against the Renan monument an image of Calvary. Which is the more truly emblematic of the course of mankind's advance, it is for the future to disclose.

PART IV

IN THE SHADOW OF THE GREAT WAR

CHAPTER XII

PAMPHLETEERING FOR THE ENTENTE POWERS

Walk along any street in Berlin, and you meet men in uniform, officers and privates, erect, decorated. The literature in the windows of the bookshops has for the most part a practical tendency. Even the furniture and ornaments are influenced by the new spirit. . . . On the clocks, where of old a knight in armour knelt and kissed his lady's finger-tips, Uhlans and Cuirassiers now stand in full uniform. Conical bullets hang as trinkets from watch-chains, and piled muskets form candelabra. The metal in fashion is iron. The word in fashion is also iron.

GEORG BRANDES

The monstrous vanity that was begotten by the easy victories of '70 and '71 has challenged the world, and Germany prepares to reap the harvest Bismarck sowed. That trampling, drilling foolery in the heart of Europe, that has arrested civilization and darkened the hopes of mankind for forty years. . . . To those who love peace there can be no other hope in the present conflict than the defeat, the utter discrediting of the German legend, the ending for good and all of the blood-and-iron superstition, of Krupp, flag-waving Teutonic Kiplingism, and all that criminal sham efficiency that centres in Berlin.

H. G. WELLS

In the first few weeks of 1914 Anatole France was correcting proof of *La Révolte des Anges.* It was destined to be his last novel, the climax of the long series in which he arraigned dogma as the enemy of progress and the priest as the enemy of man. This time he pictured the historic feud as taking its rise in that noble insurrection of the angels so falsely called "fallen", who were the pioneers of all intellectual curiosity, initiating that scientific quest which faith might temporarily hinder but could not permanently defeat.

It is obvious that his weird tale was suggested by the opening books of *Paradise Lost.* But Milton's rebel angels had been ambitious for themselves alone, while those of the Francian fancy are moved by compassion for mankind. They are indignant at Him who made such a sorry world, kept its inhabitants in such prolonged distress, withheld from them the keys of knowledge, and profited by an ignorance which He deliberately deepens through His pretended "revelation." In such a plot there is plainly room for what Anatole France has elsewhere called the varieties of an audacious blasphemy.[1] Such chances are used to the full. The whole story of a malignant Providence has to be retold, with many a lurid picture of the spirit of freedom and justice in hopeless struggle against divine repression. Not without a piquant humour are the scenes in which the angels ransack a library by night, giving special attention to the theological shelves, that they may discern in greater detail just how our poor race has been misled.[2] And when the celestial visitants come closer to the human victims they mean to rescue, it is not hard to guess how such a novelist will illustrate the old scripture about the sons of God looking upon the daughters of men.

In 1909 the late Professor T. M. Kettle wrote in *The Fortnightly Review* about "The Fatigue of Anatole France." Readers of *La Révolte des Anges* will feel that our versatile author was indeed showing signs of strain. For there was nothing fresh, nothing more than a re-spinning of very old threads, in that fantastic romance. As in Mr. H. G. Wells's book, *The Secret Places of the Heart,* we have a piece made up out of spiritual materials used often already. And one

[1] *La Vie Littéraire,* IV, p. 7.

[2] *La Révolte des Anges,* chap. x.

is tempted to say of such a novel that there should be exceptions to even a brilliant writer's rule, *Quot anni tot libelli.*

But there is a special reason for recalling this otherwise unimportant addition to the bibliography of Anatole France. It closes with some curious paragraphs about the futile character of all war. The angelic champions about to storm Heaven hear a report that the Archangel Michael has given a large order for thunderbolts and arrows. They are urged to meet this by procuring "fifty thousand more electrophores", but hesitate to do so because it is from an electric firm that the advice comes, and they wonder whether they are not being tricked in the interest of high finance! One of them points out that in a chemical laboratory rather than in munition works the great weapon of the future must be sought. Another declares that the idea of waging war at all can nowadays enter the brain only of "a sottish bourgeois or a belated Romantic." And in the end Satan himself refuses to lead the attack, for he has seen in a dream that at best such a triumph can be no more than transient. Though the Enemy should be vanquished, he would revive again:

> Comrades, no,—we will not conquer the heavens. . . . War engenders war, and victory defeat. God conquered will become Satan; Satan conquering will become God.[3]

Reviewers were still discussing the merits and faults of this book when the German army crossed the frontier of Luxembourg.

I

To Anatole France the events of August 4, 1914, came with the suddenness of an earthquake. He had indeed felt misgivings about what might happen.[4] One who was present

[3] *La Révolte des Anges,* chap. xxxv.

[4] Cf. especially Preface to the *Vie de Jeanne d'Arc,* 1909.

at the reception in his honour held at the Savoy Hotel on his visit to London in December, 1913, can recall a sentence repeated several times in his speech "with strange insistency": *Travaillons de concert à la paix du monde.*[5] But the catastrophe when it took place was none the less a shock to him. From the world as he had intellectually construed it, certain things had fallen out, and into the picture certain quite unexpected things had entered.

He had borne his part, within the preceding years, in many a discussion of the German peril. It had been his favourite thesis that no such peril existed, except in the crafty imagination of those who could profit by inventing a scare, and in the terrified minds of those who were misled. He talked thus even in the exciting days of the crisis about Agadir in 1911. At that time his chief alarm was for the bellicose temper that was plainly rising among the English. "There is no doubt", he said, "that England is brave, and perhaps she does not fear a war for herself. But I am sure that she fears it still less for France." [6] And one can understand how suspicious he felt of the propagandism in his own country.

The men who declared Prussia to be a menace both real and imminent were precisely of the class which, in other matters, he had seen most reason to distrust. He had come to know them in the Dreyfus affair. When they spoke in 1911 about official and confidential information which, in the public interest, it was impossible to disclose, but upon which it was very essential to act, a satiric smile would come upon Anatole France's face. He seemed to remember having heard just those words before, and from just the same source. To his mind the credit of the Ministry of War had

[5] J. L. May: *Anatole France, the Man and his Work,* p. 100.
[6] P. Gsell: *Opinions of Anatole France,* p. 201.

become bankrupt, and the value of its appeals had sunk like the value of a debased coinage. In the field of secret diplomacy—where the "man in the street" must take so much upon the word of experts—he was not disposed to take the word of those particular experts very far. So he had bidden his countrymen to receive with the proverbial grain of salt what was urged about a need for "preparedness." There was in truth, he said, no national emergency, no international conflict to be apprehended. Germany had, no doubt, the best armies in the world. But she seemed to share this fame with France and with every other nation, for in the estimate of their War Offices they were all alike supreme in fitness for battle. Germany had indeed something more than the rest, in "the corporal Hohenzollern, the corporal Lohengrin", who during fifteen years in the purple had been contriving war to the utmost of his ability.[7] But that ability had been proved small, and the failure of William II's violent purpose was proof sufficient that the thing had become at last impossible. The comity of nations was in sight, and the international proletariat would block the path of the war-makers. European peace was secure with the Social Democrats across the Rhine.

Such was the ripe counsel of this literary sage. How much security was to be found in those Social Democrats across the Rhine, all men were soon to be made aware.

II

So great was our novelist's influence over the public that when the war broke out there was considerable anxiety regarding the position he would take. Forty-four years before, as an unknown youth of twenty-six, he had been extremely apathetic towards the German menace, and had

[7] *Vers les Temps Meilleurs,* III, p. 30.

responded with reluctance to the call of Napoleon III. Like another young man of letters—just six months his junior, but engaged on the other side—he was no national enthusiast. In 1870, Friedrich Nietzsche was in the German ambulance corps, while Anatole France was with the French infantry. In later years this conscript of the Second Empire had many a droll tale to tell of his adventures in the field—how he carried with him a copy of the *Æneid* for furtive reading when he had a chance; how when his battalion commander was killed, he and his friends dispensed themselves from further duty for the day; how they always took good care to give the German shells a wide berth; how some of their comrades, who had been incautious enough to get wounded, made a bayonet charge at these "safety-first" men. But he explains that their indignant comrades were tired, for they had been actually fighting, while the cunning youths had husbanded their strength, and in this instance the race was to the swift! On the way back to Paris, Anatole France and his friends pillaged a bakery. "Such was our conduct. I do not boast of it. No, I do not. But I love truth, and must do her homage." In all conscience, the story was as unlike that of Leonidas and his three hundred as it is possible to imagine. Is it any wonder that Gambetta summed up thus the reason for the premature surrender of Paris during the siege: *C'était le cœur qui leur manquait?*

It was to such scenes that the mind of Anatole France constantly recurred when he was asked what he thought of war and of the virtues characteristic of a soldier. For "cowardice" on the field he could find many an excuse. He hated those national animosities which divide men who ought to be brought together by a common humanity. There were indeed momentous differences, he used to say,—differences in great ideas and great feelings, which set one country in contrast with another. And the defence of a native land in peril was fit to elicit the most passionate devotion. But intermingled with such thoughts was another, best put in his own words: "A country is not just a collection of radiant ideas. It is also the business address of a host of financial enterprises, of which many have little to recommend them." One thinks of the munition firms of Paris in the closing years of Napoleon III.

During the forty-four years that had intervened, Anatole France had apparently been becoming a pacifist radical of the most pronounced sort, deploring the fact that no one was against war, except a few intellectuals like himself, who were quite unable to move the public mind. Even in August, 1914, he did not at once revoke the creed he had so long preached. His first letter to the press was not reassuring to French patriotism. It seemed like the familiar, hesitating voice of one of those "brittle intellectuals who crack beneath a strain." [8] His countrymen became impatient with talk about moderation. But the logic of events acted upon him fast. One morning Anatole France presented himself at the War Office, and asked to be furnished with a rifle. He was seventy years of age. Referred to the medical examiner for report, he was not accepted as a recruit. But his proposal was quickly announced, and he was told to use instead that pen which he knew how to make mightier than many swords.

Then began that terrific series of pamphlets, in which he won his repute as the most powerful propagandist in Europe for the cause of the Entente. The more notable of them were afterwards collected in a volume entitled *Sur la Voie Glorieuse*. He dedicated this to Albert, King of the Belgians,—that model king who had shown himself equally deaf to the promises and to the threats of the enemy, drawing

[8] *The Years Between*, Rudyard Kipling.

the sword for a conflict in which he would share every hardship and every risk of the common soldier, taking his place as indeed *un des plus doux pasteurs des peuples.*[9]

Of the short pieces that follow, some are addressed to newspapers; some are in the form of letters to personal friends, but obviously designed for publication; some are general appeals to the soldiers at the front or the French people at home, provoked by some special occasion such as Christmas, the New Year, or an outrage of exceptional grossness by the German troops. They have passed into that "war literature" most of which has now no more than an historic interest. But these particular letters have an interest of their own, indicating the development of a singular personality. There is indeed nothing remarkable about them, except that perfect aptness of phrase and that unusual gift of illustration which all readers of Anatole France's books had long learned to expect. The pervading thought is common to all the propagandist journalism of the Entente Powers during that fearful period. But it is worth while to notice how, at least for a time, this novelist—so divorced in general from prevalent ways of thinking about society and about patriotism—was caught up in the current of the national temper.

In these pieces, he nowhere argues. There is no reasoned statement of a case. Anatole France assumes that the question of "war guilt" is *une chose jugée.* Sometimes he specifies purposes to be kept in view: the winning back of Alsace-Lorraine, the revival of Poland, the restoration of Schleswig to Denmark as of Trieste and Trente to Italy. But it is never upon the spirit of a narrow Nationalism that he seeks to play. His appeal is always to the sense of justice, to the love of public law as contrasted with the claims of "the

[9] Dedication of *Sur la Voie Glorieuse.*

stronger." If he calls for the defence of any country, it is because that country deserves defence. French civilization, he said, was threatened, and it was thus fitting to dwell upon what that civilization had meant to the general wellbeing of mankind. The Hun was a barbarian, as ever, acting on a plan of calculated *Shrecklichkeit*. He was sparing neither the works of art nor the structures dedicated to charity: *Pour moi, je ne cesserai d'élever ma faible voix contre les barbares qui déchirent la belle robe de pierre dont nos aïeux ont paré la France.*

Let Frenchmen think of their smiling fertile land, their august cities on the banks of rivers graced by monuments of old, their palaces, their museums, their hospitals—all that constituted the beauty of French life. Poison gases were being tried for the first time, at the behest of a science which was prostituting itself to the vilest end. Before long it might be expected that there would be not only chemical but bacteriological warfare, and that the German pathologist would show how to turn loose from the cultures in his laboratory a still unconjectured horror. Woe to those who should dare to suggest a peace until Teutonic militarism should have been destroyed from top to bottom. Woe to those who could pretend neutrality in a crisis such as this for all that made life worth living. By the tombs of their fathers and by the cradles of their children let French soldiers swear to persevere to the very end.

Those who, in any country, took part in the construction of such appeals will realize how difficult it was to vary the form of this constant message. But Anatole France's hand would indeed have lost its cunning if it had not been equal to such a task. At Christmas, 1914, he wrote about the events which that season commemorates, characteristically pointing out how it had a place in pagan no less than in Christian times, and how the worshippers of Adonis or Mithra could see at that period of the year the incipient return of Providence to revivify the fields, just as the watchers at Bethlehem saw in their own way *la renaissance du Dieu.* It may be doubted whether this line of reflection would have helped a Yuletide letter in England, but our novelist knew his own audience. And he goes on to speak in terms that would have emotional effect anywhere. He pictures the Christmas family table, the reunion of the household, for which at this festival of December, 1914, there would be many a vacant seat:

> Combien de vieillards et de femmes, cette année, seuls avec les petits, à la table trop grande, mangeront leur pain mouillé de leurs larmes. Et pendant ce temps, combien de jeunes hommes, sous la lune froide, au fracas des obus, songeront dans la tranchée à ceux qui, demeurés dans la maison, pensent à eux et qui, cette nuit, allument tout de même la grosse buche, font tout de même griller le boudin, car les usages anciens doivent être toujours suivis.

Falling back upon the ancient world for a parallel, he compared the resistance of the Entente armies on the western front to the stand made by the allied Greeks against Persia. A very suggestive piece is that entitled *D'après Hérodote.* It is a dialogue supposed to have taken place between Xerxes and his confidential adviser, Demaratus, the exiled Lacedæmonian.

The Persian monarch, we are told, under pretext of a quarrel with one small State, was advancing in B. C. 480 to the conquest of Europe. Invoking confidently the aid of his gods, in command of two million Orientals, and caring not at all for the "contemptible little army" under Leonidas, he asks Demaratus what can possibly be in the minds of those three hundred Spartans who, on the very eve of their destruction, were reported to be holding athletic sports in the narrow pass of Thermopylæ. Demaratus replies that it is ever the custom of his countrymen to go forward even against incredible odds in a spirit of gaiety, that in their code of discipline no account is taken of peril, and that theirs is that peculiar sort of courage which belongs to free men knowing no fear except the fear of proving recreant to their patriotic duties. Xerxes is depending on the rumoured dissensions among the Greeks themselves, upon their notorious political disputes and factions. His adviser bids him put such a thought out of his mind:

> Mais ces dissensions ont cessé à ton approche, o Roi. Les chefs de l'aristocratie ont été rappelés dans leur patrie, et ils la gouvernent aujourd'hui de concert avec les amis du peuple.

The picture ends with the escape of Xerxes back to Asia in a fisherman's boat: *L'Europe cessa d'entendre une menace insolente, et ne craignit plus de subir le joug des Barbares.* The moral was not hard to draw.

Another comparison, out of many, will serve to illustrate his method further. It was on Bastille Day, 14th July, 1915, that *Le Petit Parisien* published our novelist's open letter "to the soldiers of France." It recalled to mind how, one hundred and twenty-six years earlier, the workpeople of Paris had won for freedom a victory that had resounded through the world. Armed with pikes, disregarding a deadly fire from the garrison, to the beating of drums and the ringing of the tocsin, they had swept down the Faubourg Saint-Antoine and made an end of the Bastille. That fortress of the tyrant had been overturned by men who were resolved to acknowledge no obedience save obedience to the sovereignty of law. It was the authentic soul of France that blazed forth amid those flames. And the lovers of freedom in every land had exulted at the sight.

That sight was being renewed when July 14, 1915 had

broken "in a dawn of blood and glory." It was the soul of the free that was once again doing battle with merciless Force. "The Fatherland! Liberty! Beloved children of France, these are the sacred treasures committed to your keeping. For their sakes you endure without complaint prolonged fatigue and constant danger. For their sakes you will conquer. And you, women, children, old men, strew with flowers and foliage all the roads of France. Our soldiers will return triumphant."

III

Those warlike appeals are by no means so remote from the whole spirit of Anatole France's earlier work as at first sight they may appear. It is true that for long years back he had been earnestly and even fiercely pacifist. But it is a mistake to think that in the issue of *Sur la Voie Glorieuse* he was "simply repudiating all the professions of a lifetime." In his lifetime Anatole France had professed so many and such varied opinions that it would have been hard to construct a pamphlet which should repudiate any of them without confirming some others. The legend that likens him to Tolstoy as an apostle of peace at any price is one circulated by readers who have seen his work only in selected parts. Those pacifist newspapers which love to quote things he wrote in *L'Humanité* are careful to avoid quotation of other things he had previously written in *Le Temps.*

In his youth he had "devoured with passionate eagerness" de Vigny's *Servitude et Grandeur Militaires.*[10] In middle life he had deplored those degenerate days of Athens when the troubles of the philosophic temper began to agitate the descendants of the soldiers of Marathon.[11] He had spoken

10 *La Vie en Fleur,* p. 160.

11 *La Vie Littéraire,* II, p. 188.

of the army of France as a sacred ark which critics should touch, if they touched it at all, with reverence. He had described the iron rule under which the soldier lived as "an imperious necessity", and had blamed those who pled for more intelligence in military circles. This was a mistake, he said, because men who by the nature of their occupation could have no will of their own were rightly guarded from the disturbing perils of thought. If there was anywhere a sacred thing in human society at all, it was the organization of the national forces. When that disrespectful book, *Cavalier Miserey,* had been ordered by an irate colonel to be burned on the barracks dungheap, and imprisonment was decreed for any soldier who might be found with a copy of it in his possession, Anatole France so far overcame his zeal for free thought as to remark that he would rather have written the order, inelegant as it was, than have written so shocking a book.[12]

But the classical passage for his views at this time was the famous paragraph in which he disavowed the desire that war should ever cease. The military virtues, he said, were at the basis of the whole social fabric. It was war that had created them, and it was through war alone that they could be preserved. Here, in truth, had been the most powerful agent of civilization and progress. If it was not humane, it was undeniably human, and man's essentially violent nature must be accepted as a fact which no "reforming" could alter. "The soldier", he exclaimed, "is a necessity, and of all things which the Fates have entailed upon society the most constant and the most imperious is war." [13] Those to whom the sword had given power had been, as history showed, just those by whom power could most worthily be

[12] *ibid.*, I, p. 83.
[13] Cf. J. L. May, *Anatole France, the Man and his Work,* p. 72, sq.

wielded. Pacifists were pursuing a chimera, and it was a chimera fraught with social danger. One is not surprised, then, that when Anatole France took a leading part in opposing the three years' military service Act, this journalistic pronouncement of his past rather puzzled such onlookers as remembered it. The passage might almost have come from Bernhardi's *Deutschland und der nächste Krieg.*

* * *

Despite his temperamental internationalism, Anatole France felt that civilization had many a grievance in the past against Imperial Germany. Hospitable as he was to many a racial difference, he could not help disliking those peculiarities which the *régime* of Bismarck had made so characteristic of life across the Rhine. Reviewing Madame de Gronsart's *Life* of the great prince, he had dwelt upon that scene when, towards the end, the creator of Imperial Germany had mused before the fire in his study upon all that he had achieved. Someone suggested to him that he had "made a great nation." But Bismarck was melancholy, and, says Anatole France, "I congratulate him upon it." For he thought of the calamities he had caused:

> But for me, three great wars would not have taken place; eighty thousand men would not have perished; fathers, mothers, brothers, sisters, widows, would not have been plunged into mourning. I have settled all that with my Creator; but I have gained little or no joy from all my work.

"Never", says Anatole France, "was Prince Bismarck so great as upon that evening." [14]

But Bismarck had left an enduring stamp upon the people whose ideals he had so shaped. In a most diverting passage

[14] *La Vie Littéraire,* I, p. 144.

of M. Brousson's book [15] there is a picture drawn by Anatole France of the life of Berlin, a city where he could find not one original building, whilst the palaces, museums and churches were like a caricature of those in Paris. Like everyone else who has not been Teutonized, he thought the efficiency and order of the place were bought dear at the expense of the freedom and small amenities of social intercourse. When he went there, an old man of great fame, "heavy attentions" were showered upon him. But his years did not save him from being pushed off the pavement "by some brute going on his way with the blind obstinacy of a cannon-ball." And it was explained to him that it was he who should apologize for the collision, because notices everywhere made it plain that people going in different directions must use different pavements. As one might expect, the things *verboten* were too numerous for his patience. What, he asked, was to happen to a lunatic, a lover, or a poet in the midst of all those notice-boards? Kind Berliners replied that such disorderly folk were taken to the police-station and fined or sent to jail.

One day Anatole France had committed the offence of leaving a newspaper on a bench in the Tiergarten, and a terrific storm was raised by the constable on duty. He was excused, however, in the end as a Frenchman from whom such heedlessness was to be expected. And of course he found the manners of the Prussian officer insufferable. The proprietor of a *café* turned him out when he asked for beer in a place sacred to men of military rank. He noticed how these social leaders used to hustle everyone else in a street car, and reflected with national pride how such rudeness would be resented in *la belle France*. One day he watched the ceremony of changing guard at the Palace. Rain was

[15] *Anatole France en Pantoufles*, p. 258 sq.

descending in torrents, but the guard marched past impeccably, whilst the soldiers' boots crashed on the ground "so that the water spouted up from the asphalt to join that in the heavens." The drum-major moved like an automaton, throwing his stick towards the angry skies, and receiving it as it came back to his streaming hands like a well-trained bird. Anatole France offered a little prayer:

> Lord, if you exist, send a cold in the head to this excessively superb drum-major. Make him sneeze on parade, and let this presumptuous mortal receive the heavy knob of his stick in his massive face.

Thus the whole surroundings of Berlin used to annoy this child of freedom and personal initiative. But he recognized the strength of the system. One day he saw a group of soldiers in undress on their way to enjoy the "Sunday stew"—a great, appetizing dish which one of them bore aloft on a stretcher. All of a sudden a lanky officer appeared, down went the stew, and the whole group began the goosestep till sparks flew from the paving-stones under the nails of their boots. "Now I am alarmed", said Anatole France to Madame by his side: "if there is a war with Germany, we are lost." And why? "Do you think that any soldiers could be found in France who would drop a 'stew' like that to salute the Archangel Michael himself, with his wings of gold?"

It was against all which this typified in a national purpose and national ideals that the resentment of a lifetime burst forth in those war pamphlets by Anatole France. Even as the Tsar had killed Tsarism, so, he said, the German *Kriegsherren*, having first killed peace, were going on to kill war. They had taken out of it all its chivalry. They were like Trinco in *L'Ile des Pingouins*, whose statue commemorated the warrior who had conquered half the known world, planting his flag amid the icebergs of the Pole and the burning sands of Africa, and who at the time of his fall had left in Penguinia only the hunchbacks and the cripples. But the Penguins reflected that he had given them "glory", and that "glory never costs too much." [16]

It is superfluous to recall now any further details of that subtle propagandism, whose motto was *Debout pour la dernière guerre.* With a heavy heart, Anatole France decided that there was no choice possible save to rouse his nation to the utmost, in the hope that this might be indeed the last time for so desperate a necessity. They were magnificent appeals, couched in terms of psychological effectiveness which no other surpassed and which few could rival. Yet one feels that for him there must have been a measure of constraint and embarrassment in framing such calls to enthusiasm and sacrifice.

* * *

For the sluggish and the apathetic had an obvious reply in language which this apostle of the strenuous life had so often used before. He was appealing to men to lay down their lives, because they believed in something more valuable than the personal life, and he could not well accept the excuse upon which he had so frequently insisted: that the man willing to die for what he believes must have a very exaggerated estimate of the value of his own opinions.[17] He was asking for unlimited personal sacrifice that French civilization might be made safe, and had he not prescribed it as a philosophic task to show men how "their weak and silly nature has never constructed or imagined anything worth the trouble of attacking or defending very briskly"? "If men knew", said Coignard, "the crudity and weakness of their greatest

16 *L'Ile des Pingouins,* IV, ii.

17 Cf. e. g., *La Vie Littéraire,* III, p. 31. The dictum is borrowed from Montaigne, who in turn seems to have borrowed it from Rabelais.

works, such as their laws and their empires, they would fight only in fun or in play, like children building sand-castles by the sea." [18] Our prophet was extolling the glory of an eternal cause as contrasted with the selfish ease of the present hour, and might have been reminded of his indulgent mood towards those eighteenth century ladies who "for the sake of greater certainty secured their happiness in this world." For the time he was as confident of the righteousness of the Allied cause as those ladies professed to be of the eternal values, and a time was coming when he would once more be as sceptical of his earthly purpose as they could be of a heavenly one. So it was difficult to argue that a recreant to one faith while it lasted was wise, while a recreant to another—at least equally uncertain—was to be reproached. As Anatole France wrote *Sur la Voie Glorieuse*, he must surely have remembered his old contention that the soldier has no impulse to courage higher than the impulse which comes from fear, that the Franco-Russian entente was a mere electioneering bait thrown by politicians in distress, and that the three years' military service law was no better than a dodge to keep the proletariat occupied and obedient. A philosophic Epicurean is indeed rather hampered when he has to rouse an enthusiasm he had himself tried to kill. Many a morning, as he sat at his desk during those four years, Anatole France must have recalled with some satisfaction that most people read novels for their ephemeral entertainment only.

But before many more years had passed, it was his Epicurean nonchalance that he was most pleased to remember, and his absent-minded zeal that he was most desirous to forget.[19]

[18] *Les Opinions de M. Jérome Coignard,* Preface.

[19] Cf. especially what he wrote and published a year before his death: "I even suffered myself to make little speeches to the soldiers, living and dead, and I regret it as the worst action of my life" (*Under the Rose,* chap. ix., M. Corday).

CHAPTER XIII

A REVERSION TO TYPE

War is not, and never can be, a mere passionless discharge of painful duty. It is in its essence, and it is a main condition of its success, to kindle into fierce exercise among great masses of men the destructive and combative passions—passions as fierce and as malevolent as that with which the hound hunts the fox to its death or the tiger springs upon its prey. . . . It would be difficult to conceive a disposition more remote from the morals of ordinary life, not to speak of Christian ideals, than that with which the soldiers most animated with the fire and passion that lead to victory rush forward to bayonet the foe.

LECKY

Where the spirit of the Western nationalism prevails, the whole people is being taught from boyhood to foster hatreds and ambitions by all kinds of means, by the manufacture of half-truths and untruths in history, by persistent misrepresentation of other races and the culture of unfavourable sentiments towards them, by setting up memorials of events very often false which for the sake of humanity should be speedily forgotten, thus continually brewing evil menace towards neighbours and nations other than their own. . . . This is poisoning the very fountain-head of humanity. . . . We can take anything else from the hands of science, but not this elixir of moral death.

RABINDRANATH TAGORE

The glow of Anatole France's war enthusiasm became heavily overcast as he watched the transactions at Versailles in the first months of 1919. Before long he was telling the world that the only hope for Europe was in the great awakening of Russia, that Russia could be saved only through

Bolshevism, and that British and French parliamentarians were far inferior to Lenin or Krassin! [1]

I

At Versailles, he said, the fine promise of better days had vanished. The most horrible of all wars had been followed by a treaty which was no treaty of peace, but just a prolongation of the strife.[2] A complete downfall of Europe was inevitable unless and until the spirit of reason should be imported into its councils, and of this spirit he could see no sign. Such was the strain in which he spoke at Stockholm when, in 1921, he went there to receive the Nobel Prize in recognition of his long and distinguished services to literature. The decision of that international tribunal, so well known for its impartiality, gratified him much. With apparent disregard of all that he had said against the purpose of the *Académie française*, here at least he acknowledged that there was such a thing as "objective" literary criticism.

But his mind was much occupied at the moment with the tragic circumstances of the world. Like so many others, Anatole France had indulged the hope of a world made new through the Great War. What he saw—or thought he saw—at Versailles was something hideously familiar, the "green baize table" of the diplomats, round which men had taken their seats in just the old spirit, to devise tricks and territorial balances of the sort that had so often bred wars in the past. America had refused to enter the League:—so much for parliamentary and democratic institutions! Had not the satire on "New Atlantis" in *L'Ile des Pingouins* been

[1] Cf. interview with Anatole France related by Mr. Pitts Sanborn in the New York *Nation,* Nov. 5, 1924. The interview book place in August, 1920.

[2] Cf. J. L. May, *Anatole France, the Man and his Work,* p. 108.

well conceived? [3] Were not the guides of a parliamentary republic just as quick as the guides of a monarchy to wage war? Their problem was to calculate how much the thing would cost, and what was the chance of a residual profit when the audit should be made, for the lives to be expended must be provided for in the dollar-appropriation. So the spirit of Woodrow Wilson's Fourteen Points, as Carlyle said of the spirit of Christianity, had been found "inexecutable." [4] M. Clémenceau had demanded, amid the plaudits of his countrymen, that France should have her "natural" frontier re-established on the banks of the Rhine. Mr. Lloyd George had won an election on talk about hanging the Kaiser and making Germany pay the whole cost from August, 1914, on both sides. The practical men had mocked as doctrinaires those who dared to suggest that this war, being unlike other wars, should be terminated in a temper of generosity such as had never been shown before. All over Europe was resounding the old accursed motto, *vae victis.*

Thus for Anatole France the period that followed the Treaty of Versailles was a period of exceptional sadness. His intellectual vigour was undiminished, but he had not the heart to write another novel. The last decade of his life added nothing to his literary achievement, except those two fascinating little books of reminiscence called *Le Petit Pierre* and *La Vie en Fleur*. On the contemporary situation he had relapsed into an almost silent despair, for he felt that he had been cajoled and misled. The thing in which he had taken part had proved to be just an international scramble

[3] Cf. *L'Ile des Pingouins,* III: "What? You an industrial people, and engaged in all these wars!" "Certainly", answered the interpreter; "these are industrial wars. People who have neither commerce nor industry are not obliged to make war, but a business people is forced to adopt a policy of conquest!"

[4] Carlyle, *Historical Sketches.*

of the old sort, lasting until one side had been worn out, and leading to just the old sort of "Peace"—nothing more than an armistice, an interval until the combatants, rearranged perhaps in different groups, should be ready to fight again. Nothing of a fundamental character had been done, or seemed capable of being done, to prevent a ghastly repetition of the whole. He had himself actually preached a "holy war,"—as if any war could be holy, and as if he had not a hundred times, in days gone by, expounded a truth which in the hour of crisis he so lamentably failed to remember.

One can understand his feeling so. In a very penetrating passage of *The Map of Life,* Lecky has laid down in his more prosaic way what Anatole France has so often set forth with picturesque metaphor, and what perhaps sums up most clearly the mood in which he watched the Europe of 1919. The orthodox view of war, said Lecky, was that herein is a fearful choice, not to be refused when circumstances demand it, but to be accepted with full knowledge that it is just the lesser of two evils. Yet it was plain that war could never be undertaken in such a spirit with the least chance of success. No side could win if it relied solely on armies moved by a pure and noble purpose. They had to be roused to the temper of the jungle, and that temper would not abate when the need for it had passed away. Thus the actual destruction, suffering and horrors of the battlefield or the desolated home were by no means the whole of the price that had to be paid. Still graver and much more lasting was the lowered *morale,* the weakened sense of the sanctity of life, the readiness on other occasions for the arbitrament of force, which a returned soldier was likely to bring into the normal affairs of the place where he lived.

There was no such thing possible as a "war to end war." [5]

Anatole France had often spoken in a like strain in the years before 1914. And though, carried away by the enthusiasm of the time, he issued the appeal *Debout pour la dernière guerre,* he was to revert quickly to his earlier mood. In 1920 he was sharing front-page distinction in radical journals with such caustic writers as Mr. Bertrand Russell and Mr. Bernard Shaw, or with such farsighted men of affairs as Senator LaFollette and Mr. Henry Ford. Some of his pacifist manifestos, issued in his period of reaction from the Treaty of Versailles, lend themselves to ridicule. For instance, his tremendous onslaught on the impropriety of sailor caps for small boys and toy rifles for the Christmas tree will long be remembered by those French school-teachers who listened to him in the Congress at Tours. They must have reflected with remorse how, thinking no evil, they had often allowed their pupils to read war poems in their lesson books, and how they had failed as child-psychologists to caution parents against the grim suggestiveness of many a household practice at Yuletide. At all events, that address to the Teachers' Institute supplied material exactly to the taste of the American radical journals which quoted it in prominent type from the report in *L'Humanité.* But a graver consequence of the doings at Versailles was that disgust with the older European diplomatists which turned the mind of Anatole France to Russia. There at least a new experiment was being tried. Whilst the representatives of other peoples were still tinkering with methods of tried and proved sterility, the Soviet leaders were making proof of a method which might be better and which at all events could scarcely be worse. Our novelist's attention became fascinated by Moscow.

5 W. E. H. Lecky: *The Map of Life,* p. 87.

II

That interest, for him, was by no means entirely new. He had long been not only in sympathy, but in intimate personal contact with Russian revolutionaries. At the time of the 1905 agitation for a Duma, his house in Paris had been a sort of rendezvous for strange shaggy visitors, whom his housekeeper suspected of carrying bombs, and whose topcoats she wanted to throw into the street because they were "full of fleas." M. Gsell used to find him closeted in his library with some refugee sociologist from the land of the knout, or some press correspondent from St. Petersburg who was on a lecture tour, explaining to French audiences how horrible a thing was Tsarism.[6]

Anatole France was chief orator at many a protest meeting, held in Paris in 1905, to denounce the Romanoffs and the Grand Dukes. Some of his speeches have been preserved, and their most interesting feature for readers to-day is just that in which they so closely resemble a speech by Lenin or Trotsky. There is much about the world-execration which would fall upon the accursed head of Nicholas II, much about the inhumanity of the Tsarist police, much about those coming avengers who would yet spring from the blood-stained ice of the Neva.[7] No doubt many an English man of letters would have spoken similarly at such a time, and to many—who did not say so with equal explicitness—the news of another assassination of a Grand Duke did not seem like news of a murder. But in Anatole France there was none of that "British Menshevism" which Lenin so disliked in a speech by Mr. Ramsay MacDonald.

Those addresses of 1905 and 1906 would indeed, fourteen

[6] *Opinions of Anatole France* (Translation by Ernest Boyd), p. 219, sq.
[7] *Vers les Temps Meilleurs,* III, 10.

or fifteen years later, have won rapturous applause at a meeting of the Petrograd or Moscow Soviet. "Self-government" of the parliamentary type was not emphasized, but rather the inevitableness of the Social Revolution, the opportunity of the proletariat, the need to be class-conscious and to stir up the class-struggle. Neither British nor French institutions were held up as a pattern. In the very spirit of Karl Marx, the scenes being enacted in Russia were presented as simply an example of what must come all over Europe. The speaker's own countrymen were bidden to see the case of Russian workers as one in which they must themselves sooner or later be involved. For disguise it as one might under the formulas of a nominal republicanism, the same antagonists—they were told—were confronting one another in Moscow and in Paris alike. French grievances, the speaker said, were indeed as yet light comedy when compared with the sombre Russian drama. But it was on the banks of the Neva, the Vistula, and the Volga that the fate of the future Europe was being settled. On December 16, 1905, Anatole France declared that the forces of reaction and oppression were at that very moment preparing in Paris "*un petit tsarisme et un petit tsar*," "*un tsarisme et un tsar proportionnés à la médiocrité bourgeoise.*"[8] The reference seems to have been to M. Doumer and his projected candidature for the presidency. He was to be carried into office *sur le dos des gens de bourse, aux acclamations des syndicats jaunes.* Again and again our critic returns to the horror of the Franco-Russian alliance, an alliance not between peoples, but between autocrats open and autocrats disguised.

How Lenin would have applauded the passage in which he described the fall of Delcassé from the generous, or at

8 *ibid.*, III, pp. 51, 52.

least the innocent, mood of the youth who got off the train at the gare de Lyon long years before—young, eager, with his pockets full of manuscripts in prose and verse! [9] He was not bad in those days, rather *un bon petit diable de radical* —but he lived to conclude the Russian alliance in the Quai d'Orsay! And how was he won over? The Tsar Nicholas II one evening gave him "a big cigar" after dinner.[10] Such a cigar was always in his mouth, and the memory of the imperial condescension was always with him, hiding from his view the miseries and crimes of Tsarist government. A strange French Minister of Foreign Affairs,—not much altered from the days of Louis XV. One might think that Delcassé had been nursed on the knees of Madame de Pompadour. And how delighted Lenin would have been at the declaration that it was just the same arrogance of rank, just the same greedy imperialism, just the same brutality of *la haute finance*, which made the bourgeois politicians so complaisant to one another in all the oppressed countries of the continent!

With tremendous energy Anatole France used to urge that workers everywhere must unite in an international understanding, because there was already an international understanding among their natural enemies,—the alliance of armies, priests, financiers, which held the toiling masses everywhere in its grip. Not until there was a proletarian revolt against the whole "military caste" could there be any real hope. Men like Ferry, Dupuy, Méline, might affect the trappings of republicanism, but they were in truth heart and soul with the Grand Dukes in a purpose of tyranny that knew no national boundaries. Had not the first president of the so-called French Republic used the troops van-

[9] *ibid.,* III, p. 19.
[10] *ibid.,* III, p. 18.

quished at Metz and Sedan for a wholesale massacre of thirty thousand unarmed "proletarians"? [11] Cursed be the *entente* in which, behind closed doors, the ministers of democracy had involved the French people with that Russian oppressor.

In those days Father Gapon used to call at the Villa Saïd, where he once described Nicholas II as "a tiger athirst for human blood." It was a curious view, surely, of the well-meaning architect of the Hague Tribunal, and Anatole France was by no means sure of Father Gapon's sincerity. One remembers how that priest managed to disappear from the working-class demonstration he headed, just at the right moment to escape the fire of machine-guns, and how the revolutionaries themselves killed him as a traitor. But in general our novelist at that time felt very doubtful about the prospects of a Russian rising. He suspected that there was not enough of the spirit of liberty in those long enslaved people to make them willing for such tremendous risks in such a cause. It occurred to him, as a matter of general experience, that zeal for complete emancipation is commonly found only in those who are already in a measure free. For example, the Vendeans and Bretons, who had in truth most wrong to endure under the Bourbon yoke, had acquired so much of the slave mind that they fought against those whom a taste of happier conditions had made eager to advance still further. Anatole France would point out, too, how in his own country the most obstinate opponents of Socialism are now just the peasants who suffer most from the bourgeoisie, whilst its most ardent champions are the miners whose discipline has already secured a great part of what Socialism has to offer. And he would ask his Russian friends whether Tolstoyan doctrines had not confirmed those moujiks—naturally so mystical—in a quietism which would never "re-

[11] *ibid.*, III, p. 13.

sist evil." Surely Tolstoy had taught the oppressed peasant to content himself with "bleating"?

One interview, recorded by M. Gsell, is of particular interest.[12] His Russian visitors on that afternoon were assuring Anatole France that the moujik had been thoroughly roused at last, and that no one was likely to be deterred by the idealism of the seer of Yasnaya Polyana. What they really wanted was help in preventing a French loan to the Tsarist government, until such time as a liberal Constitution should be put into force. One of the group, "a young Slav with high cheekbones", broke into the conversation to say that there was nothing in the idea of a voluntary abdication by the Tsar. Only violence would serve, and there would be a great deal of bloodshed. But it would be worth while. "This young man", said Anatole France to the rest, "is, one can see, a full-blooded revolutionary. If necessary, he would throw bombs." The young Slav, with a smile, took from his pocket two steel tubes, remarking that so long as these remained separate there was nothing to fear, but that when screwed together they would blow up the house. "Do not screw them, please", said his host. And he at once launched into a homily on the need to use other means so long as possible. "Remember this; homicidal justice, even when administered by a people struggling for freedom, can never be anything but a wretched substitute. It is not good to quench with blood the thirst of the gods." But when the editor of the *Guerre Sociale* introduced to him "Boris Savinkov, assassin", he declared himself delighted to make such an acquaintance, and asked "Whom has he assassinated?" "The Minister Plevhe and the Grand Duke Sergius", was the reply. "Big game", said Anatole France.

He plainly held, however, that one element essential to

[12] *Opinions of Anatole France*, p. 227, sq.

justify a rising must be its reasonable prospect of success. And he looked forward to the effect of a successful Social Revolution anywhere as inspiring a like movement everywhere. For instance, he used to say, a Russian victory for the proletariat would give a great impetus to Socialism among the French. What hampered the collectivists in cities like Bordeaux was their shocking indifference to "general ideas", and the Parisian workman was not a reader. Our novelist had been told by the secretary of the Electricians' Union that pamphlets about the Socialist cause had no interest for his group, who could understand no kind of literature other than the *Adventures of Sherlock Holmes*! To Sir Arthur Conan Doyle this may not seem to indicate a low degree of intelligence. But it filled Anatole France with despair.

III

His Socialistic development had a curious history. French Socialism, as it is now understood, dates from about the time of his own birth. Anatole France was an infant a few months old on that memorable day when a young man of German-Hebrew descent and with a consuming intellectual industry—Karl Marx by name—was expelled from Paris by order of the government of Guizot. The attention of the police had been aroused by those strange all-night conferences with the revolutionary publicist, Pierre Proudhon, the radical apostate from the world of business, Friedrich Engels, and the fierce young poet Heine. On a hint from the Prussian authorities, the adviser of Louis Philippe had driven Karl Marx—like so many other dangerous exiles before and since—to seek an asylum first in Brussels and next in London. Guizot was not mistaken in his diagnosis of peril. Those were the days when Louis Blanc had begun to denounce the competitive system in industry, to demand the institution of national workshops by which private enterprise would be gradually superseded, to talk about the *droit au travail*, and to argue that under a true social order the remuneration of all men would be made equal. Disturbing formulae were being concocted and launched. "The State", said Louis Blanc, "should be the banker of the poor." "Property", said Pierre Proudhon, "is theft, and God is evil." Such a book as the *Système des contradictions économiques* showed that in France, unlike England, the economists were to be met on their own ground, and such schemes as that of Proudhon for a tax of thirty-three per cent on interest and rent showed that the spirit of 1848 was far from being harmlessly speculative.

In 1847 appeared the famous "Communist Manifesto", drawn up by Marx and Engels,—the first historic document from an international combination of workmen, with its motto that was yet to mean so much: "Proletarians of the world, unite." Some of the changes for which it called, like many of the points in "The People's Charter" a few years earlier in England, have since been enacted without any of the disasters so confidently foreseen at that time. It demanded, for example, a progressive or graduated income tax, free education for all children in public schools, and the abolition of child labour in factories. But it likewise proposed to abolish all property in land, to terminate all rights of inheritance, to make all men equally liable to labour, and to centralize in the hands of the State all means of communication and transport. The heart and essence of the movement was, however, its international aspect, its appeal to the "proletarians" of all countries to come together in a spirit of class-consciousness and ready for the class-war against those international capitalists who were their natural enemies.

How far this tide of feeling would have moved, if the policy of Louis Napoleon had not combatted it with the immense strength of a revived national prosperity, it is impossible to guess. Before long the imperial provision of remunerative employment for all on great public works had taken the force out of insurgent plotting, and the native resentment of the French peasant proprietor against a nationalization of land left the Socialists of the capital without support in the country districts. Under the Second Empire the revolutionaries made far less progress than they would have been certain to make if the policy of the House of Orleans had been continued. It was the Emperor's success in supplying jobs, far more than his measures of repression towards trade-unionism, that secured the ten years of tranquillity with which his reign began. Discontent ceased at all events to be vocal as the vast wealth of the Orleanist dynasty was applied to public charities, as loan funds became established, as hospitals were founded at the expense of the State, as wholesome tenements were substituted for the long familiar slums. Napoleon's projects for *extinction du paupérisme* threw into the shade those of .Louis Blanc for *organization du travail.* For the thrifty French workman felt that however a leader of democratic revolt might theorize for a Utopia, it was wiser to follow the autocrat who seemed not only willing but able—in the terse American phase—to "deliver the goods."

There is no evidence that Anatole France in those days, or for long afterwards, took any great interest in the nascent Socialism of which he heard chiefly from across the Rhine. Like Renan, he was rather alarmed at the perils of "culture" in the rude hands of democracy—those perils portrayed in

L'Avenir de la Science. Whether he would have been prepared to avow himself, like Renan, "on the whole a supporter of the House of Orleans", there is nothing to show. But his habitual way of writing about the French Revolution of 1793 and about the Commune of 1871 proves that he was far from being enthusiastic for abstract phrases regarding Liberty, Equality, and Fraternity. Quite in a different vein did he conceive such paragraphs as that in *Sylvestre Bonnard* about the revolutionary misunderstandings of the past, about the pseudo-history of empires "from Noah to Charlemagne", about the long procession of ambitious princes, greedy prelates, virtuous citizens, philosophic poets, "and other personages who had no real existence outside the novels of Marmontel." [13] In those days his mood was that of the intellectual Epicurean, for whom it was hard to be sure whether the myths of religion or the myths of democracy were the more absurd. And with an impartial pen he wrote caricatures of both.

It was in the early years of the twentieth century that he proclaimed himself a Socialist. The cause which operated most powerfully in deciding him seems to have been his growing conviction that the ever present peril of a European war could be best counteracted by fostering the movement for an international understanding among the working classes. It was for such understanding that Karl Marx had pled so earnestly more than thirty years before. Anatole France was working as a publisher's assistant in Paris at the time when *Das Kapital* first appeared; and when in 1872 that disquieting work was translated into French, he was too much occupied with his youthful efforts at Parnassian verse on subjects of pagan antiquity to give much thought

[13] *Sylvestre Bonnard,* II, iv.

to this announcement of a "class-struggle." But much had happened in the years between 1872 and 1900. There had been a monstrous growth of armaments. There had been the Dreyfus case. And there had been the rise to fame of Jean Jaurès.

It was the influence of that extraordinary Socialist leader which gave to Socialism in general so tremendous a grip upon the men who had signed "La Protestation des Intellectuels" in the Dreyfus affair. M. Guérard, who was living in Paris at the time, has testified to the wave of excitement which Jaurès stirred, especially among the students of the capital.[14] While the adherents of Church, Army, nobility, high finance, were allied together against the revisionists, it was the Socialist leader who proclaimed that, Socialism being synonymous with justice, every member of his party must make the cause of Dreyfus his own. Men like Zola and de Pressensé were swept into the stream, accepting many an item in the Socialist programme which they had previously disliked, because it contained—or they thought it contained—a root principle of humanity which was to be found nowhere else. And in politics, as Anatole France said to Mr. May, you must choose one side or the other.

From that date began his fierce propagandism for the group so generally stigmatized as "the enemies of social order." The longer he thought about it, the more convinced he became that the Dreyfus case belonged to a class, and that it was but symptomatic of a general principle whose applications were without limit. There must be a vast shifting of the centre of gravity of power,—a great dethroning and a great establishing. And the means to this must lie in fostering the radical school known as *universités populaires.* So

[14] A. L. Guérard: *French Civilization in the Nineteenth Century,* p. 208.

Anatole France, leaving his "Tower of Ivory", as Plato said the philosopher must re-enter the cave, mounted the public platform.

Whatever his subject in the addresses he then delivered, there was sure to be something said about the imminence and urgency of the Social Revolution. Like the Hyde Park orator, he preached ever "divine discontent", bidding the proletariat to that most attractive exercise: *réfléchir à la place des privilégiés.*[15] For instance, as a guest of the "Society for Portuguese Studies", on the occasion of the jubilee of Theophilo Braga, he might surely have thought this particular appeal inopportune in his speech. But it was no more to be omitted than John Wesley could omit a Scripture text or the late Frederic Harrison could omit a reference to Auguste Comte. Anatole France began by dwelling, naturally enough, upon the internationalism of all true literature. He spoke of the Provençal and Italian elements which could be discerned at the basis of Portuguese poetry, of the philosophy and the song passing from people to people whose minds no geographic distance could separate and whose thoughts must overleap every national frontier. But, like every other, this reminiscent mood must lead to the persisting moral. Before he ended his speech, he had to remind his audience that the "proletarians" of Europe must interchange their reflections on life and work, not less than the products of their soil or the manufactures of their industry. They must be partners in their deepest projects, their most intimate hopes and fears, the aspirations of their hearts as well as the fruit of their brains. And why? Because only thus would the ancient rivalries of princes give place to "the union of all who toil." [16]

[15] *Vers les Temps Meilleurs,* I, p. 20.
[16] *ibid.,* III, p. 90.

Somewhat monotonously, but for the light of the ever vivid metaphor and the thrill of the apt phrase, the same idea recurs at a celebration in honour of Diderot or Victor Hugo, and at a funeral eulogium on Pierre Lafitte or Émile Zola. The thing most notable about the founder of the *Encyclopédie* was, we learn, his exaltation of manual work, so long held in contempt by all the aristocracies—military, civil or religious. He had been *un grand serviteur du peuple, un défenseur du prolétariat.*[17] Victor Hugo was to be remembered, not for the huge array of volumes he had placed on our shelves, or for that body of thought *à la fois éclatante et fumeuse, abondante, contradictoire, énorme et vague comme la pensée des foules:* [18] but it was he who, as a member of the Assembly, had fought the Falloux Law which handed over the charge of public instruction to a priesthood. The great idea of Pierre Lafitte, proclaimed so often in his long "apostolate", had been the vital need for bringing together into fighting alliance the thinkers and the proletarians, that "union of a great thought and a great force." And what of Émile Zola? His greatness had lain in his capacity of righteous hate,—hate for "an idle and a frivolous society", for "an aristocracy low and noxious", the hate that made him so mighty a champion against the giant evil of his time, *la puissance de l'argent.*[19]

How far Anatole France was prepared to support the more revolutionary projects of Labour, became obvious about 1906 when he gave his benediction to "Syndicalism." *Syndicat* is just the French word for "trade-union", and as so understood it may mean nothing very dangerous. The alliance of workmen engaged in a single trade to protect

17 *ibid.,* I, p. 48.
18 *ibid.,* I, p. 62.
19 *ibid.,* II, p. 9.

their common interests by collective bargaining had indeed long been discountenanced and even forbidden. But as a policy, after severe repression under the Second Empire, it was tolerated in the last six years of Napoleon III, and it was even favoured under the Third Republic during the administration of Waldeck-Rousseau. It quickly revealed a character that was very remote from the purely economic and non-political attitude with which it began. Syndicalism became the creed of those who trust to what is called in England "direct action", despise the slow and cautious methods of parliamentary pressure, value above all else the weapon of the strike.

In the early months of 1906 the menace to public order had become very grave indeed, for the institution of the *Syndicat* had found a place among employees of the State. There was a postmen's strike, a general railroad strike, a rebellion among the vinegrowers of the South. Nor was it difficult to show that the administration of the civil service had itself been corrupted by that very political intrigue to which employees were expected to rise superior. Appointments and promotions were known to depend far less on individual merit than on skill in the lobbying of deputies or senators. But it was by no means the "reactionaries" alone who were here at fault. During the years after the Dreyfus agitation, the sins of the old *régime* were copied rather than repented by the radicals. Wholesale displacing of civil servants in favour of men who could be trusted to share the politics of the party in power, persistent espionage in the army, the promotion or punishment of railroad men for their views—known or suspected—on clericalism or Freethought, made it appear impossible that the employees of the State should show a virtue from which their employer was to be freed. The non-political character of a civil service can be demanded only on condition that the methods an official is prohibited from using shall not be used against him.

While the turmoil was brewing, Anatole France addressed a body of school-teachers who were asserting the *droit syndical des instituteurs*. He urged the need for co-operation of brain workers with hand workers, *ceux qui tiennent la plume et ceux qui manient la pioche.*[20] It was intolerable, he said, that nomination and dismissal of teachers should be a matter of political bargain. Nor could such grievances be adjusted by any method other than that which had been used in the common combinations of Labour. There must be collective bargaining between teachers' delegates and their official chiefs. The profession must become class-conscious, as a branch of the *Confédération Général du Travail.* It was idle to pretend that State employees should be excluded from any right which was granted to employees of a private business, and the teacher's conscience could be trusted to make no use of a strike which would imperil the welfare of the children of the proletariat:

> Instituteurs, ce sera votre éternel honneur d'avoir pris la plus grande part à cet harmonieux effort, d'avoir organisé le prolétariat de l'école et d'avoir tendu la main au prolétariat des bureaux, des octrois, et des routes.[21]

It was while he was engaged on these very radical addresses that Anatole France was asked to be principal orator at the unveiling of a statue to Ernest Renan. Speaking on such an occasion and at such a time, he could scarcely omit all reference to the political and social opinions of his master, which everyone knew to have been far from Socialistic. But one passage in a book of Renan's pessimistic old

20 *ibid.,* III, p. 81.
21 *ibid.,* p. 82.

age lent itself to the dexterous purpose of his eulogist. It was from his study of *The Tempest*, where Caliban—with pointed ears and the skull of a gorilla—is likened to the ignorant proletariat, and Prospero to a cultured aristocrat, fit for rule, but dethroned by the mob. Renan deplored so premature an event. He would rather, he said, have seen the son of Sycorax with ears a little shortened and convolutions of the brain a little fuller before these responsibilities were assumed. But Anatole France reminded his audience how the book closed with the consoling reflection that culture today has less to lose at the hands of the Caliban in power than at the hands of Prospero as he would be restored. For Prospero was being manipulated by agents the most dangerous of all. It was better far to take risks with democracy than to see the legitimate prince re-enthroned *par les jésuites et les zouaves pontificaux*. Under the circumstances, well had Renan exclaimed, *Gardons Caliban.*[22]

This was not very radiant encouragement for the proletariat. But it was the best thing Anatole France could quote to them from such a source.

III

His sympathy with the Moscow Internationale was thus no mere consequence of disappointment with the Treaty of Versailles. After all, the "Big Four" had acted only as he expected such men always to act, for they had been bred in a diplomatic tradition which they could not break. If for a moment he had hoped better things from them, he quickly saw, or thought he saw, that his hope had been foolish, and he reverted to his earlier mood.

For at least fifteen years, Anatole France had been

[22] *ibid.*, III, p. 47.

arguing that war can never be abolished and at best can only be interrupted by a "treaty." To his mind the real source of war lay in "Nationalism", and of this the diplomatist was a representative. The only possible remedy for war must thus be found in the destruction of Nationalism, and hence in the superseding of those agents whose business it had been to keep that evil spirit at a white heat. All else was but palliative, temporary, a treating of symptoms instead of rooting out the disease. And if Nationalism was thus to be overcome, it must be by the substitution of an enthusiasm very different. Nowhere else could this be sought with such hopefulness as in the organizing of an "international proletariat." The only public leaders who seemed to appreciate such an idea were the Bolsheviks.

Thus while fully expecting that the Bolsheviks would perpetrate many an outrage, comparable for a time even with the outrages of the old *régime*, Anatole France thought they were at least worth a trial for the sake of the essential soundness of the principle they had embraced. And he was attracted to them by their resolute attack upon traditions. For instance, he thought about traditional dogmas regarding crime and punishment, contracts, the State, patriotism, as he thought about the traditional dogmas of religion. He knew the part the Greek Orthodox Church had played as a constant ally of Tsarism, and thus he heard with a thrill of delight how the walls of Moscow were placarded with the motto: "Religion is a drug for the workers." Many a gay mocker, aristocrat or bourgeois, who had been delighted to hear Anatole France burlesque the creeds, began to listen with a clouded brow when he applied just the same kind of solvent to "loyalty." But whatever force the argument had in the one case, it had also in the other. It was in a publishing house, as proof-reader of theological works, that Pierre

Proudhon had learned to be an atheist. And Anatole France lost his orthodox economics as he mixed with men who "viewed Property with a sort of religious terror such as the moon inspires in dogs." [23]

Turning, as ever, to the soliloquies of Coignard for light on his attitude to the social order, one realizes how he found a *prava origo* for many a revered custom of "the social heritage." That reflective abbé living in the eighteenth century, when in France as in England theft was still a capital offence, used to point out how easily one is reconciled to such barbarities as are habitual, even as the gentle Seneca was not much disturbed by the crucifixion of slaves.[24] Yet, could anything be more ridiculous than the idea of punishment as a retribution for crime? It sprang from the myth about Free Will, which science had long ago exploded. For who could be sure of the motives of conduct? Who could devise an accurate scale to determine what penalty was the "equivalent" of this or that piece of wrongdoing? It was time, Coignard thought, to abandon the pretence that justice as commonly administered means anything more than a device to secure men in their possessions, "to which they are naturally attached."

But the question then arises: What are legitimate "possessions"? The abbé recalled how Ulpian had laid down the principle that a man should be guaranteed in the tenure of "what belongs to him." There was little enlightenment in that, for it was no more than the substitution of another phrase. By what criterion could we say what it is that "belongs" to a man, in any sense other than "the fruit of inherited or recent rapine"? [25] In the modern world men, as

[23] *L'Orme du Mail,* XVII.

[24] *Les Opinions de M. Jérôme Coignard,* XX.

[25] *loc. cit.*

Coignard saw them, were engaged on a vast game with one another,—a game which had rules descending from a remote past, a game in which they were not at liberty to take or refuse a hand at pleasure. We must all play it, and the courts were custodians of its rules. It was indeed always possible to raise the previous question whether such a sport should be maintained at all. But so long as it was maintained, its terms must be preserved, and to raise that "previous question" was treated as a breach of the greatest rule of all: namely, that no such query should be put by anyone.

Anatole France clearly felt, with Coignard, that in current systems of law throughout western Europe there had been preserved many an old prejudice which had long faded from both the manners and the minds of men. Judges, as the abbé saw them, were affecting a profound reverence for such antiquities, though knowing them to be barbarous, and they were professionally bound to do so. They had their written codes, under which it was necessary to proceed,—intricate and muddled beyond aught that anyone could discover in the *gramarye* of a wizard.[26] But the judge, says Coignard, is not invariably bad. He is only the agent of a ridiculous system: "For my own part, I know one magistrate who is an honest fellow enough." [27]

In a passage of *La Vie en Fleur* our novelist avowed that his views on the subject of property were not in agreement with those of his contemporaries, adding that in his early youth he had been "by no means a Proudhonian." Without inferring that he had afterwards become so, one may conjecture that he had moved in that direction. And the view of Proudhon was clear enough. *La propriété, c'est le vol.* One remembers how in *L'Ile des Pingouins* the origin of property

[26] *ibid.*, XXI.
[27] *loc. cit.*

in land had been traced to the self-assertion of the stronger, how Greatauk had felled another Penguin with his club that he might take possession of the parcel of ground his victim was cultivating, how this was the beginning of the noble house of "Greatauks, Dukes of the Skull", and how the astute thinker who managed to vindicate such rapine was known afterwards as the founder of civil law for Penguinia. The obvious upshot of such reasoning is that by "legitimate" rights of possession should be meant only such rights as it has been found socially advantageous for the State to recognize and enforce. And these have altered with the passage of time or the growth of knowledge. Lenin could have desired no better philosophic basis for innovation.

Thus Anatole France began to speculate upon possible developments of the Socialist State. He dreamed of a coming co-operation of workers, in which warfare—whether military or industrial—would be obsolete. It would take, he thought, a long time to achieve, for mankind emerged but slowly from barbarism. No one, says M. Bergeret, wants now to abolish armaments, except a few thinkers who are unable to make themselves heard,[28] and the day is yet far distant when pictures representing battle-scenes will be hidden out of sight "as exhibiting an immoral and shameful spectacle." [29] But one might hope that as men became less wretched they would be less ferocious, and in the yet unexhausted possibilities of electricity there was much to expect for lightening the lot of Labour. At the heart of this would be the co-operative principle, just as the obstacle to be overcome was the traditional competitive individualism. Such blessings would be shared, like the light and air which were enjoyed by all. For, as one of the Positivists had so well re-

28 *Le Mannequin d'Osier,* I.
29 *M. Bergeret à Paris,* p. 173.

marked, all property came from a social source, called into existence through the joint efforts of the whole community —a truly Marxian doctrine. As the monopolist rights of feudalism had passed away, so would the monopolies of our present industrial and bourgeois order. But it was idle to ask for predictions of the date. The process would be very gradual, like the changes in the earth's crust, and a prevision of what is coming was mercifully forbidden to man. "We must work at the future, like weavers who work at their tapestries, without seeing what they accomplish." [30]

More than once our novelist indulged in drawing a Wellsian Utopia. Fifteen years before the Russian Revolution, he had published a forecast of the Socialist future which, if it had appeared anonymously, in an English translation, would beyond doubt have been ascribed to the writer of *The Time Machine* or *In the Days of the Comet.*

The book is called *Sur la Pierre Blanche.* A few reflective Frenchmen, sitting round the table of a *café* in Rome, talk about the possibility of guessing the trend of social development from a study of the past. Monarchy had gone, and the feudal system. What about the coming fate of the capitalistic order? One of them argues that at all events war is plainly becoming obsolete, because the divisive forces that have hitherto caused it are becoming lost in the economic bonds by which a world society is being knit together. There will be sporadic outbursts, he thinks, for some time to come. At that very moment Russians and Japanese were slaughtering each other in Manchuria and in Korea Bay. The delusion that it is advantageous to have colonies was not yet wholly exploded, and nations would continue for a time to fight for more territory abroad. But the integration

30 *ibid.*, p. 174.

of world society, though often delayed, could not be stopped.

The same night, one of the group continues his reflections in a dream. He dreams himself in the Paris of A. D. 2270. Science has made enormous strides, and life is regulated to the last degree of social organization. There are no trains, no automobiles, no vehicles of any kind, but the air is thick with birdlike and fishlike planes humming overhead. Where railroad notices had formerly appeared, there are balloon timetables, with a chart of the atmospheric currents. From tall poles are flying crimson oriflammes, bearing in letters of gold the words EUROPEAN CONFEDERATION. Official proclamations, in unfamiliar character and a language of which the observer can identify no more than certain words here and there, intimate that it is the year 220 of the Federation of Nations, and that it is time to celebrate the "Festival of the Earth." In his dream Hippolyte Dufresne questions people he meets regarding what has taken place, and is told of great changes from "The Closed Era." In a restaurant he is asked for his "voucher", and, being apparently unemployed, he is referred to the "delegate who hires journeymen." Those too weak to work must apply to "the delegate who attends to persons in need of succour." By some chance, it is to a bakery that he is assigned, despite his protest that he is quite ignorant of baking, for it is pointed out to him that bread is now made by machinery so simple in its terrific effectiveness that even a child can manage it.

It is co-operation that has done all this. What was in the Utopian dreamer's mind is clear enough.

IV

There is indeed much to amaze the reader in Anatole France's enthusiasm for the Russian Revolution. Were not the men who led it at least as hopeless doctrinaires with their "Dictatorship of the Proletariat" as those of a century and a half before, whom he satirized so fiercely for their "Rights of Man"? That he should have sympathized with even the most violent outburst against Tsarist government is intelligible enough. What is less intelligible is that he should have been so little impressed by the perils of a Revolution in which the leaders were men maddened by old personal wrongs, and the rank and file were so completely illiterate. Least intelligible of all is his belief that in the Lenin and Krassin methods there was something not merely justifiable, *faute de mieux*, for the special circumstances of Russia, but of constructive value as a pattern which the rest of Europe might imitate.

In no other aspect of his writings does he strike one as so abstracted a dreamer. A great deal which the event has revealed, and by which Anatole France had to confess himself disillusioned when it took place, was plain enough at the outset to men without a tithe of his ability. What seems to have attracted him most of all was the Soviet plan for cutting across all international frontiers, obliterating all the nationalisms of the past, and uniting the proletarians of all races in a bond of alliance against the anti-proletarians in each. This characteristically Marxian project was proclaimed and panegyrized by Anatole France in many a speech long before the Great War, so that the period of his national "patriotism" which began in 1914 seems to have been but an interlude between his earlier and his later moods. Speaking on 13th February, 1905, in the "Salle des Sociétés Savantes", with M. Paul Painlevé in the chair, he had commended that *grande parole socialiste:* "Proletarians of all countries, unite. The union of the workers will be the peace of the world." And he did not leave the maxim in harmless ambiguity. He explained with great explicitness just what he meant. At this hour, he exclaimed, upon the collapse of the old and outworn aristocracies, on the ruins of capitalistic society, arises the peace-loving and industrious proletariat, "which will be to-morrow the master of the world." [31]

Words, words, words! One recalls how that vigorous English Socialist, Mr. H. G. Wells, was driven almost distracted by the inquiries of Lenin when he met him in Petrograd, as to the probable date of the coming class-war in England, and as to the mystery of its long postponement. Idealistic as may have been the League of Nations, it was nothing to the fantastic dream of a proletariat internationalism which should arise at the call of a Russian dictator to an exhausted and war-weary world. And what of the manifold problems of finance which the Moscow experiment had raised? About an economic question Anatole France never professed to know anything at all, and yet how crucial was the economic difficulty! When he referred to finance, our novelist used to talk the language of the street in the rhetoric of the study, declaring that he knew how "money is the cause of all those ills which afflict our social order, a thing so cruel and whereof we are so proud." [32] As a child, he says, he was "ignorant of money matters." One is constrained to add that in this field even maturity had not brought any notable advance in his insight. Was he just wilfully paradoxical when he talked so? If there was a single item of political conviction to which he had been relatively faithful in the past, it was the belief that the worst peril of democracies lay in a tyrannical enlargement of State control and the suppressing of individual freedom. In 1905 he was able to say, without obvious ab-

[31] *Vers les Temps Meilleurs,* III, p. 22.

[32] *Le Petit Pierre,* VIII.

surdity, that the Russian proletarians were giving lessons to the world, even as the French proletarians of 1789 had given such lessons more than a hundred years before.[33] But with what appearance of truth could he declare that a model was being set in the Moscow of 1920? The most intense form of proletarian despotism that mankind had ever known was thus being commended by the prophet who had found oligarchic rule on the whole best because it at least "left people to themselves"! [34]

We are assured by M. Gustave Hervé that those who "know their Anatole France" will not be surprised at the sight of "this delightful sceptic" always taking the side of the Left. Like Mr. Bernard Shaw, he loved to *épater les bourgeois.* But it is hard to think that herein is the whole explanation. In such a crisis of public affairs, and when issuing not novels but appeals vibrant with a note of earnestness, Anatole France cannot have been merely posing, any more than he was merely posing in the four years that followed August, 1914. And he might well reply that since 1914, in a world turned upside down, the opinions of the most sagacious might be overturned too.

He felt about the Treaty of Versailles, as General Smuts seems now to feel about it, that it were well for that document to fall into "a merciful oblivion." And if he judged more favourably of the Bolsheviks than most other observers did, one reason at least is not far to seek. Bolshevism might be good or it might be bad, and no doubt Anatole France should have made up his mind on its intrinsic merits, apart from both the character of its assailants and the character of the arguments they used. But it was psychologically impossible for him to do this. Here was a new venture in gov-

33 *Vers les Temps Meilleurs,* III, p. 52.

34 Cf. Soliloquies of Bergeret and Coignard.

ernment, not necessarily evil just because it was new, yet denounced as evil by all the reactionaries in Europe, who seemed to assume that the system of the past must be held for ever sacrosanct. Of that system Anatole France thought that it had "sunk beneath the weight of its sins." And when he heard, for example, that the Bolsheviks had massacred four hundred officers of the Black Sea Fleet, there would come into his mind another massacre, when one thousand unarmed workmen had been mown down by machine-guns in Petrograd, and there had been scarce a quiver of disapproval among these zealots of justice.

In short, what he saw was the downfall of Tsarism, like the downfall of the Bourbons a century and a half before. Once again there must be the thunder of the tumbrils; once again the gods were athirst. And he had no belief in a "constitutional" movement. To Anatole France it seemed that there was as little hope in a Kerensky as he had found to lie in one cautious bourgeois "reformer" after another among the French. On the other hand, Lenin seemed to know that for a big change there must be big measures. Perhaps in England freedom could slowly broaden down from precedent to precedent. But waiting for this in Russia was too tedious, and the men who urged such waiting were the ineffective people whom all knew too well. Would that there was a like spirit of "Thorough" in Europe as a whole!

What could be thought, again, about the "reactionaries"? They argued as their predecessors had argued in the Paris of 1793. Hideous as had been the Place de la Guillotine, it served a purpose which could not have been served otherwise. The White Army, with the foreign gold that sustained it, was but a successor of the counter-revolutionaries subsidized by Pitt. And amid the inevitable excesses might not one say, as Coleridge had said of a like spectacle: "The sun was rising though ye hid his light"?

Such seems to have been the line of thought by which Anatole France approached the puzzle of Bolshevism. And no doubt he was much stimulated by the tone of the anti-Bolsheviks. Perhaps the tenure of private property in land, for example, should be maintained as socially expedient. Perhaps private trading cannot with social advantage be regulated or controlled. But that either of these usages should be erected into a dogma, exempt from all criticism or challenge, on no ground other than its traditional authoritativeness, seemed to our novelist as absurd as any article of an outworn creed. Other causes besides that of Tsarism were indeed collapsing in Russia, causes which quickly showed themselves to be essential, and have quickly been in a measure restored. But to speculate about these was not within the compass of Anatole France's mind, and the defenders of the *status quo* he knew to be for the most part deserving of no respect. The assailants of a principle are indeed not nearly so dangerous to it as those advocates whose defence makes it ridiculous. Probably British Communism, for example, owes more of its strength just now to critics like the Duke of Rutland and the Duke of Northumberland than to the "Red" orators in Hyde Park. For whatever the intrinsic demerits of a project, it has an immense advantage when its opponents use only such reasons as habitually attend upon the absurd.

It has often been pointed out that much of the speculative folly so rampant everywhere after October, 1918, sprang from "war psychosis". But a corresponding part of it sprang from what may equally well be called "anti-war psychosis." There was hysteria of both kinds. The cant of patriotism and the cant of anti-patriotism were alike in full efflorescence in those years which followed the Treaty of Versailles. If Anatole France was touched by the latter, he is not to be utterly contemned by those carried away by the former. For, on the whole, the latter is the more respectable and humane. The superstitions on which, to a great extent, the old *régime* had rested were such as our novelist could detect at a glance, because he was so constantly on the watch for stupid traditionalism, for the pretences of ancient prestige, for the self-seeking and the fraud of diplomatists with whom he was familiar. But the superstitions on which the Soviet experiment reposed were not similarly within his ken. About the vast and intricate conditions of international trade, he was at once as irritable as a Communist workman and as ignorant as a simple child. Thus around economic blunders and venomous invective he threw the halo of his own dazzling rhetoric.

For he was essentially a satirist. And it is the penalty of the satiric attitude of mind that such a thinker's influence upon his generation—still more, upon succeeding generations—must always fall far short of what his talents might lead one to expect. When Carlyle fulminated in *Latter Day Pamphlets*, displaying his rare powers of invective, the fascinations of his wit, his brilliant suggestiveness of analogy and parallel—"words and phrases infinitely picturesque and satiric, marvellous collocations and antitheses" [35]—he was discharging all this artillery for the most part in vain. His readers felt that, although Lord John Russell and Lord Palmerston might probably enough be wrong, they were not to be thus dismissed as either sheer scoundrels or hopeless imbeciles. Readers felt much the same about Anatole France's pictures of Delcassé, or Millerand, or Doumer.

[35] Morley, *Recollections*, I, p. 57.

They knew that the diplomats at Versailles in the first months of 1919 were facing a tremendous problem, and they were not prepared to see either mere stupidity or wilful selfishness in the defects of its provisional solution. By the mordant phrases in which these leaders were characterized from the Villa Saïd or La Bechellerie, they knew that French controversial literature was being enriched. But what they did not see was how a single controversy in French affairs was being illumined.

The diplomats were at Versailles not just to embrace all rival ideas at once, and "send them out for an airing." They were there to conclude a settlement, which the satirist might easily make to appear ridiculous, but upon which it was not probable that the satirist if he had been consulted could have improved. When M. Gustave Hervé remarked that he would prefer to follow a man like M. Clémenceau rather than a man like Anatole France, one enthusiast for "the Master" remarked that herein spoke the authentic voice of "Pecus." Perhaps experience had developed in Pecus a sort of bovine instinct that was not altogether astray. To the claim of the seer as a guide it was the obvious retort that this seer himself had explained how a profound reflectiveness makes men unfit for a practical undertaking, how all action results from a certain narrowness of outlook and a certain limited kind of thought, how he who speculates deeply has his energies so hampered at the outset that he must find reasons for coming to a stop at every move he takes. Pecus, blessed with the safeguards of a slow-moving mind, felt that such as Anatole France might be left to circulate epigrams on the Quai Voltaire, but that quite other persons should frame despatches at the Quai d'Orsay.

CHAPTER XIV

ANATOLE FRANCE IN PRIVATE LIFE

Paint me exactly as I am, with all my warts, humours and blemishes, or I will not pay you a farthing for your picture.

OLIVER CROMWELL

Though many a friend will give an idealized portrait, it is certainly juster to the dead that the selection and description should be carried out on the principle of illustrating good qualities at the cost of giving insufficient space to bad, than of illustrating faults in such lengthy detail as to leave little space for anything else. The latter method can give no real picture of those qualities but for which the biography should not be written at all. Neither course is satisfactory; but if omissions are to be called suppressions, and to be regarded as uncandid, it is hard to understand how a biography is more candid which is written on the principle of omitting nothing which tells against a man, than one which leaves nothing unsaid which would tell in his favour. Luckily the latter class is the more common.

WILFRID WARD

Thomas Carlyle once remarked that, with the exception of the Newgate Calendar, no printed record could be more melancholy than Biographies of Authors. It was a cynicism which his own literary executor was soon to illustrate. But the *Life* of Anatole France cannot be cited in further exemplification. Whatever our novelist might say, in an outburst of dyspeptic ill humour,[1] it was as one well pleased

[1] He was much troubled, for a time, with liver complaint. Cf. *The Opinions of Anatole France,* chap. vi, P. Gsell. One need not take seriously his statements to M. Brousson and M. Ségur that he had never since child-

with his own fortunes and with his rôle in the world that he looked out upon men and things. With an excellent physique, great material prosperity, and ever-increasing success at the sort of work he loved, what more could he desire? And, like his favourite hero Rabelais, he had too much of the comic spirit to be morose for long over a world that was out of joint. Of his personal characteristics, his writings are indeed both deliberately and incidentally eloquent. He might well have adopted the motto of Montaigne: *Je suis moy mêsme la matière de mon livre.* But much further light has been cast upon his temperament by the memoirs of those who were near him.

Threading one's way through memoirs is no easy task, and the memoirs of Anatole France are increasing month by month. Some of them read like a panegyric on a tombstone, for which it is understood that neither composer nor engraver has taken an oath of veracity. Others are more suggestive of a *chronique scandaleuse*, written on the acknowledged principle that in these days no biography can be attractive which is not in a measure disturbing. Perhaps about each kind one may fitly quote Sir Charles Wetherall's comment on Campbell's *Lives of the Chancellors*, that such a book was enough to add a new terror to death. As the memoirists grow in numbers, and as their strident disparagement of one another's trustworthiness continues to perplex as well as to amuse the general reader, the authentic likeness of Anatole France in private life becomes harder and harder to draw. But there are still some features, happily the more important, upon which those who knew him best have managed to agree.

hood been happy for an hour. (*Anatole France en Pantoufles,* p. 61; *Conversations avec Anatole France,* chap. xix.) It is not in such language that the really miserable express themselves.

I

He was a tireless worker, at first by necessity, afterwards by choice. Anatole France was not handicapped at the outset by that freedom from youthful struggle with circumstance which has spoiled so many careers. By birth a "son of the people", he had the bracing tonic of compulsion to hew his own way in the world of letters. He had, at the beginning, none of that prestige which Voltaire found surrounding those French writers under the monarchy whose names ended in *-ille* or *-oc*, and which still—under the Republic—gives an initial but injurious facility to authorship. Our diligent memoirists have betaken themselves to that little village in Anjou where Anatole France's grandfather worked at the shoe trade. They have ransacked the parish register of marriages and baptisms, and have discovered from some odd features of the record that our novelist's father at the age of twenty-one could neither read nor write. The family name was Thibault, but after the prevailing custom of Anjou he was familiarly called—or nicknamed—"France", an abbreviation of his Christian name, François. It seems remarkable that one who had reached manhood without being taught to read should not only have repaired this early defect, but should have taken up almost immediately afterwards the business of a bookseller. And it is still more remarkable that such a man should have become a writer of occasional book-notices or reviews, which he invariably signed "*France, libraire.*" Believers in the transmission of talent and of taste will see here a striking instance to quote. It was his father's nom-de-plume that our novelist accepted as his own name, and that of "Thibault" which was legally his has passed almost wholly out of sight.

He was brought up in narrow, but not exactly straitened,

circumstances. Anatole France never suffered that extreme hardship of which he has himself said that it does not purify but rather defiles. Sometimes he recalled, in later life, how his father had "cast off" the son who insisted on writing poetry. But we have no clue to what he meant by this strong expression, and it is clear that he was never driven to those distasteful preliminary occupations which want has so often thrust upon an aspiring author. At no time did he pursue any means of livelihood other than literary or quasi-literary work. There has been much conjecture regarding his sources of knowledge about that gay fashionable world which he depicted with such verisimilitude, and a lady belonging to the ranks of *ton* has lately undertaken to gratify public inquisitiveness on this matter. Whether she deserves the credit she claims for coaching the great author on subjects outside his ken, and whether the local colour of polite society in his descriptions was in truth borrowed from her, is a point which it seems impossible to determine. Andrew Carnegie used to say that the men who professed to have contributed to his initial success by carrying his bag to the Dunfermline railway-station when he was starting first for America had become past all counting. Moreover, he added, the truth was that he had carried his own bag! Perhaps Anatole France found that those powers of mind which were adequate in so many imaginative fields—more remote than Parisian fashionable life—were not sterile even there. And one recalls how Mr. H. G. Wells, with no recorded coaching from within the charmed circle, was able to describe Bladesover.

Though he dwelt so often and so rhetorically upon the imminence of "the class-struggle", it does not appear that he cherished any personal resentment against those more favoured by fortune. He was indeed always the intimate and sympathetic friend of persons in humble life. That ancestral shoemaker in the Thibault family never haunted the recollection of Anatole France, as a like grim spectre among the Merediths of the past was ever hidden out of sight by the author of *Evan Harrington.* With clerks and artisans, says M. Ségur, he was as much at home as with artists and men of letters.[2] But however strongly his feelings were enlisted on the side of those with whom fortune had been severe, nothing like class-hatred ever really poisoned his mind. He might pay his occasional compliments to Lenin and Krassin, and he might even share their feelings towards the bourgeoisie; but no one who felt as the Bolsheviks feel about the aristocratic tradition could have written as he did about Marie Bashkirtseff, or about *French Ladies of the Old Régime.* In the passing of that old *régime* Anatole France saw indeed a good deal to regret. As a boy he had listened in his father's bookshop to the talk of men who had heard the drums of Citoyen Santerre.[3] But in his later years he would point out to many a democratic enthusiast how the men of the *Encyclopédie* had enjoyed under the Bourbons a toleration such as the Third Republic would never grant to critics equally frank, how Voltaire during the Seven Years War had been the friend and guest of Frederick II, and how the monarchy of that time had shown him an indulgence which these apostles of freedom would never grant to M. Caillaux.[4] And the full-blooded Russian revolutionary, encouraged by news that the greatest living man of letters was his friend and ally, must have read with disgust such satires as that of the great French Revolution in *Les Dieux ont Soif*, that of the Commune in *Les Désirs de Jean Ser-*

[2] N. Ségur: *Conversations avec Anatole France,* I.

[3] M. Couchoud's Introduction to *Rambles with Anatole France* (Sándor Kémeri).

[4] M. Le Goff: *Anatole France at Home,* chap. iv.

vien, or that of insurgent movements as a whole in *L'Étui de Nacre*.[5]

But how could a writer of such historical imagination, combined with such artistic temperament, have written otherwise? As Anatole France looked out upon the historic emblems of the city he loved so well, there would come back with a rush to his mind all that civilization of which these had been the products, and he would exclaim with a sigh that "democracy can never produce an art." Across the dinner table he would jest with Jean Jaurès, whom he so much admired, about the probable outcome of that universal nationalization which fine pictures would have to share. He would insist that excellence is the very antithesis of the idea of equality, that nothing great can take root except by the predominance of the gifted and the capable, and that he was feeling just a little anxious about what would happen to things of the mind in the coming Socialistic State. "Eh, Jaurès, you will see to it that intellect, the finer minds, are properly housed and cared for in your future city, won't you? You will be sure to see to that?"[6] Though at times he might reflect that with fewer thinkers and fewer men of letters the world would perhaps be happier, he was haunted by the same query as troubled George Gissing: "What has a hungry Demos to do with art?"[7]

But in truth his comparative gentleness when he spoke of the old *régime* resulted less from his gratitude for the

[5] Cf. the remark to M. Le Goff: "The Revolution is vastly overrated, and fundamentally evil. . . . I have been accused of being severe and even unjust toward the great ancestors in *Les Dieux ont Soif*. . . . As a matter of fact, I spared them; they were worse." (*Anatole France at Home*, chap. vi.) Well, surely, did our novelist describe himself, in that appeal to American women in 1923, as an old man who had "espoused all the political illusions of his time." (*Under the Rose*, chap. ix.)

[6] N. Ségur: *Conversations avec Anatole France*, XIV.

[7] G. Gissing: *Demos*, p. 17.

treasures it had bequeathed, than from his sympathetic feeling towards all who must act as they have been endowed at birth and as they are compelled by their situation. Believing, with Mr. Thomas Hardy, that mankind is in the grip of that Immanent Will which

> works unconsciously, as heretofore,
> Eternal artistries in circumstance,[9]

he would not make discrimination in favour of the class in which he was himself born, against another class equally the plaything of fate. One cannot imagine the author of *Le Jardin d'Epicure* in any exultant mood over the doom of Nicholas II at the fortress of Ekaterinberg. He thought of the poor Tsar as he thought of Louis XVI or Marie Antoinette. And in that complaisant allowance which every sceptic must make for infirmities of character, he did not commit the common fault of excusing those vices whose lure he chanced to feel, while showing a Calvinistic austerity towards those by which he had never had a chance to be tempted. As a reformer of his time, he never failed in that "tolerant placidity" for which, as Walter Bagehot used to say, a reformer like Henry Brougham had no gift.

II

A man who has decided to earn his living by authorship must take note, more perhaps than any other, of the conditions of popularity and fame. The literary Stock Exchange, Anatole France has pointed out, has even more fluctuations than the financial one. But with the requisite initial impetus, particularly from the critics whose word is taken as

[8] T. Hardy: *The Dynasts*, I.

authoritative, a writer is soon "out of the reach of babbling tongues." [9] So he was extremely anxious to win his way into the *Académie française*, not because he had any real respect for that Association on its merits, but because its membership was a great passport to public deference. "If a man were to go to the Opera in bedroom slippers and a nightcap, instead of a dress coat and a top-hat, the caprice of 'one of the Forty' would be received with homage"! [10]

Anatole France's chance came in 1896. Fifteen years before, his *Le Crime de Sylvestre Bonnard* had been crowned by the Institut, and a great advance had thus been made upon that languid appreciation with which his earlier work had met. During the next decade his successive novels as well as his critical journalism had attracted an ever-widening circle, and so far, by chance perhaps as much as by contrivance, he had aroused little of that personal antagonism which was afterwards to mingle with panegyrics upon his genius. Not yet had any of those social and national crises occurred in which he was to be the centre of angry passions, patriotic or ecclesiastical. It was as the master of a delicate and nervous French style, with a rich imagination, ironic and meditative, but commonly making his cautious salaam to the powers that be, that he was urged by his friends to become a candidate for a vacant *fauteuil* at the Palais Mazarin. The vacancy had arisen through the death of Ferdinand de Lesseps, that brilliant pioneer whose achievements at Suez and Panama were so dimmed and clouded by the obloquy that fell upon him in his last years.

It was indeed for him a strange society whose membership Anatole France now sought,—a society he liked to describe

9 N. Ségur: *Conversations avec Anatole France,* XVIII.

10 J. J. Brousson: *Anatole France en Pantoufles,* p. 293.

as more Catholic than the pope and more royalist than the king.[11] In his fiercer moods he wondered why the Republic should tolerate its existence, why bishops and squires and generals—all enemies of the republican Constitution—should be permitted to dispense a vast annual budget for whose use they were accountable to no one. Most of its uncontrolled funds, he said, went to religious congregations, to disloyal groups, to "right-minded authors,—that is to say, authors without any mind." But there it stood, invulnerable, autonomous, and the politicians who should have restrained it would rather commit any sort of baseness to win admission to its ranks. A Frenchman might be President of the Republic, but was still unsatisfied until he had won an Academician's chair.[12]

Under such circumstances, it was to be expected that candidature would be a matter of intrigue—and the Forty were intriguers in the highest degree. If, exclaimed Anatole France, they had shown in their works an industry or a talent comparable to that which they brought to bear on an election, the ages of Augustus and Louis XIV would pale before that of the closing nineteenth century.[13] Still, he wanted very much—just like the politicians—to have this crown set upon his own professional brow. And if we may trust his own narrative, it was by singular strategy that he secured his place.

The Forty, whatever their politics or their faith, were at least of painful and obtrusive decorum,—like the electors to an All Souls Fellowship at Oxford, insisting on the test *bene natus, mediocriter doctus.* Against this radical applicant many things might be quoted. Had he not written *Les*

[11] *ibid.,* p. 231.
[12] *ibid.,* p. 144 sq.
[13] Cf. Brousson, p. 145.

Noces Corinthiennes, La Rôtisserie de la Reine Pédauque, Le Lys Rouge? But he had also written such blameless pieces as *Alfred de Vigny, Le Crime de Sylvestre Bonnard, Le Livre de Mon Ami, La Vie Littéraire.* There was a chance that these last might have caught the eye of the average Academician more than the flagitious works, and even that the superficial piety of *L'Étui de Nacre* might conceal from such dull wits the subtle derisiveness which underlay it. At all events, the thing was worth trying. M. Halévy drilled Anatole France in the part he must play as he canvassed for votes, trusting—as he had reason to trust—that most of his books had never been read by the electors whom they might well have shocked. He was bidden to be careful with his tongue, to speak in the right quarters about the surpassing genius of Victor Hugo, to disguise under a show of compliment his real opinions about Chateaubriand, to make judicious reference to the Comte de Chambord. M. Halévy did not like his proposed letter of candidature, rewrote it for him in more diplomatic tone, and in the draft which the candidate copied *verbatim* he was pleased to observe that there were "not more than three or four mistakes in French." [14] To add to the humour of the situation, it is recorded that he was chosen over the rival candidate, Ferdinand Fabre, mainly because Fabre was regarded as dangerously anti-clerical!

But the tact which secured his entrance was not enough to keep him there with any comfort, and he soon became an Academician only in name. There are merry tales, strewn through the memoirs, about the tricks he played on his colleagues, and about his ironic deportment to candidates soliciting his vote. He would talk to abbés and monsignori

[14] P. Gsell: *Opinions of Anatole France,* IV. Cf. *Anatole France en Pantoufles,* pp. 96, 7.

who acknowledged that they had not read his novels, assuring them that it was needless to apologize; he was equally to blame, for he had so far neglected to read their sermons or their decrees.[15] Sometimes the ecclesiastical candidate for election was a witty Modernist divine, like Monsignor Duchesne, whose satire on his credulous brethren was as subtle as that of Anatole France himself, and of whom our novelist would remark that his Catholicism and his archaeology dwelt together in his soul as mutual strangers. "The physical resemblance", he said, "between Monsignor Duchesne and Voltaire is striking. I conclude . . . that Voltaire was a holy man." One anecdote in particular, which admits of only veiled repetition, is concerned with a famous sitting of the Dictionary committee. Anatole France insisted that they should include among the varying senses of *anneau* that which is associated with the name of Hans Carvel![16] But few, it seems, of those lexicographers had sufficient acquaintance with the text of Rabelais to realize how they had been insulted. And those who had chosen this member as an alternative to the anti-clerical must have had a rude shock when, a few months after his *Discours de réception*, he published *Le Mannequin d'Osier*. In the storm that quickly arose between Dreyfusards and their opponents, Anatole France signified his anger by ceasing to attend at the Palais Mazarin, just as he returned his insignia of the Legion of Honour when Zola's name had been officially erased from the list.[17] That was a time when old friendships were being severed and new friendships were being formed. For the signatories to the *Protestation des Intellectuels* there was an end of intimacy with such men as Lemaître, Barrès,

[15] J. J. Brousson: *Anatole France en Pantoufles*, p. 226.

[16] P. Gsell, *Opinions of Anatole France*, III.

[17] *Anatole France en Pantoufles*, p. 139.

Coppée, Moréas, while there was a very novel *rapprochement* for the same group with Zola and Jaurès. Old barriers were taken down, but new barriers were set up.

III

The friendships lost were often more congenial than the friendships acquired. Charles Péguy, for instance, was not a satisfactory substitute for Jules Lemaître. But Anatole France was destined in any case to a spiritual isolation, for reasons far deeper than the Dreyfus incident. The *Protestation* was a symptom much more than a cause.

His biographers have dwelt upon his intellectual loneliness. Superior to the common illusions, he could not share those common joys which depend so largely upon illusion. It was not only, nor was it chiefly, from the "orthodox" that he had to dissent. At least one recent memoir shows how, as time went on, the glib secularist gospel roused in him a contempt he never felt for the message of the Ages of Faith. Though in the stress of an anti-clerical fight he might talk on a platform the optimism of *Vers les Temps Meilleurs*, one can see that in his intimate conversations he disavowed all belief in social progress. Again and again he would return to the mood of the singular passage written long before in *La Vie Littéraire*,—that passage about the desolating effect of Darwinian evolution for the great values of life, about the pathetic insignificance to which human ideals had been reduced by the syndicate of astronomers, biologists and chemists, about the futility of expecting a new ethic to arise out of science, and about the inevitable collapse of both hope and charity which must follow upon the collapse of faith. The society of the flippant who might jest about this was more tiresome to him by far than the society of the simpleminded who knew not what had taken place in the thought of Europe.

One is startled, for example, to meet with those reflections he confided to M. Ségur. He spoke of the strength that must have come to those who could really pray, of the depth of that solace which once resided in an Immortal Hope, of the new meaning that our troubled life would hold if it were any longer possible to lift up one's eyes to an answering gaze from on high. His interlocutor, in much surprise, asked whether he deplored the great change which science had brought. By no means, was the reply. No man loyal to truth could regret the journey that the race had made. None could wish to go back upon it. But it was idle to deceive one's self with the thought that Naturalism had taken nothing from man's dignity in the present, or had left unaffected his outlook for the future. The significant point was that Free Will had gone. We knew ourselves as but manifestations of chemical energy, with all our choices—the so-called good as well as the so-called evil—reduced to uncontrollable currents in the nervous system, and conscience—"which, after all, implies the idea of God"—analyzed away into the fitful glow of a few poor human embers, destined to quick extinction in the night of everlasting death.[18] The thing had to be faced. But nothing was gained by the pretence that the horizon had not been darkened.

How much there is of truth and force in such an estimate, this is not the place to discuss. Our present concern is the portraiture of Anatole France's mind, not to determine whether his case furnishes better ammunition for controversy to the devout or to the undevout. *Non nostri est tantas componere lites.*

[18] *Conversations avec Anatole France,* XVI.

From a psychological point of view, one can understand how it was the doom of such a spirit to realize with exceptional poignancy the tragic aspects of the human lot. His was the hypersensitiveness to suffering of any sort which made him avoid the streets in Naples where lambs were exposed with cut throats, because he could not forget "those dreadful rattles."[19] Deprived of the usual solace, Anatole France had more than his share of that sympathetic distress which for most men is assuaged either by dullness of imagination or by religious and quasi-religious hope. Sometimes he wished that his intelligence had been less active, less vivid in its grasp of things, less fertile in its lurid imagery, so that he might have been spared the pain which visits none but the deeply reflective. Oliver Wendell Holmes has said about religious melancholia that he could respect those who hold certain dogmas and go mad, but not those who hold the same dogmas and keep their wits.[20] What Holmes felt about the creed of the faithful, Anatole France seems to have felt about the creed of scientific secularism,—that the one refuge from what it involves must be found in an imagination sterile or inert.

There is no real ground to think that this was just a pose, just a *façon de parler* of a writer who knew himself brilliant. In his talk with intimate friends, much more than in his books, one can see the range and intensity of Anatole France's compassion. Those occasional outbursts of anger, strange in one so urbane by temperament, are outbursts not against the stupidity which he could always tolerate, but against the cruelty to which at no time, in no place, and from no man or group of men, would he give a moment's quarter. Feeling, like Mr. Thomas Hardy to whom his re-

19 Sándor Kémeri: *Rambles with Anatole France,* VIII.

20 *Autocrat of the Breakfast-Table.*

semblance is so close, that to be born is a palpable dilemma, and that for poor mankind the problem is no longer how to advance in life with glory but how to retreat from it without shame,[21] he could have no patience with anyone who would make a fellow-sufferer's lot even by a hairsbreadth less bearable than it is. It was his sense of pity, he told M. Ségur, that had made him join the Socialists.[22] Against the horrors he saw latent in the old European "Balance of Power", he turned to the promise of an international proletariat, as others have turned to the League of Nations, not perhaps with glowing confidence, but as a desperate resort, and sure that though it might make things no better it could not possibly make them worse. It was the haunting memory of what he had seen ten years before in Russia that made him rejoice when Tsarism was extinguished in blood. For he could never forget those interminable processions of the doomed, setting out under a brutal Cossack escort to tramp on foot to the Siberian mines,—aged people, women, little children, most of them destined to breathe their last unattended and practically unnoticed on the roadside.[23] To stop the social injustices at his own door he would at least never fail to raise his voice, powerless as he was to affect the grosser inhumanities of the diplomat. And Anatole France was ready for many a personal risk which is dexterously avoided by other men of letters, even in the cause they would like to promote by a vicarious sacrifice. His signature to the *Protestation des Intellectuels* was affixed just after he had been elected to the *Académie française*, and in full consciousness that he was ruining that social prestige which he had so

[21] T. Hardy: *The Return of the Native,* IV, i.

[22] *Conversations avec Anatole France,* XIX.

[23] *Anatole France at Home,* p. 68. It is interesting to learn that a statue has been erected to Anatole France in Moscow, side by side with one to Jaurès.

worked and even intrigued to attain. When he was within a week of his seventy-fifth birthday, he marched through the streets in a procession of working men, under *le drapeau rouge*, to protest against the acquittal of the assassin of Jaurès, though he knew that in the war psychosis of that tense time the jury which had voted acquittal had the applause of all the "patriots." And surely not because it was either congenial to his taste or a probable road to personal advancement did this fastidious littérateur betake himself on appeal to some grimy artisans' club, that he might help in an agitation for better safeguards against the perils of the industrial worker. It was his response to a personal entreaty from a miner with a bandaged arm! [24]

His reflectiveness, of course, became still more sombre during the Great War. A recent and an intensely interesting volume of memoirs [25] has propounded the theory that Anatole France turned pamphleteer for the Entente as a precaution for his own safety, that the fate of Jaurès seemed to him an ominous portent for radicals in general, and that he was terrified into making this gesture of appeasement to the French public by the stream of anonymous letters threatening his life which he so constantly received. In the first week after August 4, 1914, unfamiliar faces, it seems, were to be seen round the Villa Saïd, and many a spy made some pretext to call upon him. He fully expected that M. Caillaux would meet his doom by some bullet or some dagger on the street. "The fate of Caillaux awaits you", wrote one genial correspondent; "your place is in prison with all bad Frenchmen, and before the court-martial. You are a defeatist and traitor." It is the testimony of Madame France that letters of this sort preyed upon his mind, and that he be-

24 P. Gsell: *Opinions of Anatole France*, II.

25 M. Le Goff: *Anatole France at Home.*

came extremely careful of his public statements. His wife very naturally felt the nervous strain, suspected visitors, servants, even farmhands on the country estate. And some colour is lent to M. Le Goff's conjecture by the fact that Anatole France spoke afterwards in such regretful language of the patriotic appeals he had been forced to write, talking —as he said—in the tones of his housekeeper, of which he became thoroughly ashamed.

But perhaps those who experienced in that fierce time the alternations of enthusiasm and despair which the Great War occasioned will see no need to explain the altering moods of our novelist by so discreditable an hypothesis. In the Franco-Prussian War of 1870 there came into current use the phrase "false as a bulletin", and that persistent deluding of the French public with bowdlerized news was enough to shake the zeal of a critic far less suspicious than this one regarding the political and military administration at Paris. The press, he said, would lead one to believe that the long procession of victory was almost without the loss of a gun or a ship! [26] General Joffre had learned for the first time from *Le Petit Parisien* that he had won the Battle of the Marne.[27] M. Millerand, sitting at his desk, made cannons out of red pencil, and believed them ready for the front as soon as he had completed his memoranda. General Sarrail at Salonica was living the life of an oriental prince. The Russian commanders were sending in amazing reports of their prisoners, in which they must include not only the civilian populations, but also the asses, cats and dogs in the villages they "took." But in truth all military men were alike, Sarrail like all the others. Did he not know the breed? Even Alfred Dreyfus, when his friends were toiling day and night on his behalf,

[26] *ibid.*, II.
[27] *ibid.*, I.

had been too much the military man to approve of it, and if anyone else had been the victim he would assuredly have been with the persecuting gang![28] In this temper of growing disillusionment, to which publicists in all the allied countries could furnish many a parallel, Anatole France from time to time fiercely repented that he had ever had a hand in rousing war enthusiasm. But there is no ground to suppose that his zeal was not real while it lasted.

It was all the more likely to be real just because it was for him such a novelty. His was not the mechanical, and consequently fictitious, enthusiasm of "patriots" who rise to every national war summons whether right or wrong. To Anatole France, at least in those months after August, 1914, the World War was no mere episode, like others which had gone before and others which were sure to follow. It was Armageddon. *Debout pour la dernière guerre.* No hint of the mood of Colonel Repington's *Diaries* is to be found in his table-talk during that awful time,[29]—none of the cheerful optimism of those whose superficiality of mind is so great an aid to composure. He may have been childishly fanciful, but it was a fancifulness which did credit to his heart. And hence the shock when he was undeceived. For the war, as he watched it, became just like all other wars. He saw the desire that peace might be long deferred in order that certain firms

28 *ibid.,* III.

29 Cf., e. g., this entry in Colonel Repington's Diaries, under heading *The Outlook for 1916:* "Lunched in Belgrave Square. . . . The Princess very nicely dressed, and charming as usual. Mrs. Duggan was in the most attractive widow's weeds imaginable. Callaud of Paris makes a specialty of mourning for war widows apparently. These particular weeds included a very pretty hat in crape, with a veil hanging down behind. . . ." And again, under date September, 1917: "I said I saw no good reason why it (the war) should end until the Huns were more badly beaten . . . especially as so many people were growing rich by the war, the ladies liked being without their husbands, and all dreaded the settlement afterwards."

might get more orders for munitions. He saw others eager to "keep it going" until they should be more extensively decorated. He saw multitudes quite content with any state of things under which salaries and wages were so high. To him all this was not diverting; it was horrible. Sometimes he feared that his own reason would give way. An occasional fool would remind him how the battlefield is the great stimulus of heroic virtue, and in truth he had long before—in the piping times of peace—said something of the sort himself. But as the ghastly reality was appreciated, this piece of arm-chair moralizing was frozen upon his lips. He would turn upon such a comforter with the retort that by a like logic we should welcome croup, without which the altruistic energies of the nurse in a children's hospital might remain for ever unawakened.[30] And to the vindications of Providence by religious apologists he would respond—as was natural in a man of such opinions at such a time—with the profane rage of a sufferer who feels that he is being mocked.

* * *

In the same spirit he regarded those post-war statesmen who seemed set upon "balkanizing the centre of Europe",[31] and thus scattering the seeds of a more dreadful conflict yet to come. He had no patience with President Woodrow Wilson, passing and repassing between the Scriptures and the typewriter, mixing financial interests with Biblical problems, a man ignorant of European history, but seated in State at Versailles to measure out the rights of nations on scales and distribute justice by the milligram.[32] Still worse, in his view, was Mr. Lloyd George, using the Wilson vocabulary, but crafty rather than candid, reading the Bible and

30 *Under the Rose,* chap. ix.

31 *Anatole France at Home,* chap. xii.

32 *loc. cit.*

chanting the psalms while he filled his country's pockets. From the Poincaré escapade in the Ruhr he predicted calamities; it had been forced upon the premier by the *Action Française*, but, once begun, it would be carried out to the bitter end, because M. Poincaré was both too cold-hearted and too vain to give it up.[33] Lenin, on the other hand, was the most highly gifted man whom Russia had produced since Peter the Great. "I am proud that he speaks well of me."

But, on the whole, there was no other leader of the time upon whom Anatole France poured out such vials of wrath as upon M. Clémenceau. The rigour of the Clémenceau *régime* of suppression after 1918 was enough to stir every chord of resentment in this philosophic objector. In public he had to hold his peace. "I am going", he said, "to surround myself with silence." It was a new Reign of Terror. But to those intimates whom he could trust, Anatole France said what he thought. Naturally he interpreted the actors of the present in terms of his memory of their past, and in reminiscent mood he ever harked back to the part they had played in the decisive hour of the Dreyfus case.

For that case he always held to have been the great touchstone of character. He liked to quote how the Empress Eugénie had said to him, "I know military men, for I have seen them at close quarters, and hence believe them capable of anything." The poor Empress had desired to sign the *Protestation*, but, said our novelist, there were already enough difficulties in the way, and that one would have been insurmountable. How had M. Clémenceau acted at that time? He had been with the committee indeed—with Jaurès, de Pressensé, Briand—and he had shown a tremendous strength of will. But had he been disinterested? Zola had

[33] *ibid.*, chap. xiii.

been great, and Bernard Lazare had been sublime, but more and more had the conviction forced itself upon Anatole France that M. Clémenceau had been in the *Affaire* for pay![34] "He never willed anything that was not evil." Men showed at a crucial time just what they were—men, for instance, like M. Albert Thomas, whose joy on the night of the assassination of Jaurès it was impossible to mistake.[35] And M. Clémenceau had no heart. He would have millions massacred, if need be, to secure his own glory, in all that pitilessness and that insatiable thirst for personal honours which mark wicked men in their old age. In truth, the so-called "republican" leaders at Versailles had been planning a peace of such outrageous character as no King of France would have dared to conceive.[36]

How far these are fair estimates, it is not for a foreigner to judge. They are quoted simply as disclosures of the way in which the mind of Anatole France worked in the time of his "disillusionment."

IV

With what propriety, then, has he been called, by common consent, an "Epicurean"? The epithet still carries a certain flavour of reproach. Yet it was not unsuitable, as all can see who have escaped from the vulgar misunderstanding of what the school of Epicurus taught.

Anatole France loved and cultivated "pleasure", in the loftiest sense of that much abused word. There is a tale of a poor Russian student,[37] who came armed with a letter of introduction, and who expected to find this champion of the

[34] *ibid.,* chap. x.

[35] *loc. cit.*

[36] *ibid.,* chap. xii.

[37] P. Gsell: *Opinions of Anatole France,* chap. i.

destitute in such ascetic surroundings as would best harmonize with his creed. But what meant this great hall, the Persian china, the pottery from Rhodes, the consoles adorned with ancient statuettes, Italian pictures ranged on the staircase according to schools of art, the iridescent light falling through gold-spangled stained-glass windows? While the housekeeper was taking a message upstairs, the student fled in terror, and that introduction was never presented. In Russia it was no friend of the peasantry who lived in surroundings such as those.

No doubt the same sort of people who affected to see in Mr. Ramsay MacDonald's motor-car a crowning proof of "Socialist hypocrisy" will quote the house in Paris and the summer retreat called "La Bechellerie" as proof that Anatole France never meant what he said on a working-class platform. But those who think a little more clearly, and are not preparing pamphlets in aid of the Duke of Northumberland's campaign, will agree that a man may have genuine enthusiasm for the poor without rushing to the extravagances of a useless self-mortification. This enthusiast was fastidious, indeed, in many a personal habit, as the chefs of Italian hotels had cause to know when he declared a "hunger strike" against their preparations because the butter or the oil was not up to his standard.[38] And surely no man ever took more luxurious delight in those pictures which charm a discerning eye. But the Epicureanism of Anatole France was, first and foremost, an Epicureanism of the mind. He fairly revelled in the intellectual opulence of the past, dwelt ever in thought with the great masters of literature, science and art, felt himself heir to a spiritual legacy whose fruits within the span of a lifetime it was impossible for a single mind to enjoy or to exhaust. His surroundings were chosen

38 Sándor Kémeri: *Rambles with Anatole France,* chap. viii.

and disposed with the perfect taste of a connoisseur. In his great library, wrapped in those "silent orgies of meditation", he would never tire of rearranging and recombining the constituents of man's intellectual inheritance, living again with the Greeks of the Periclean Age, the Romans of the late republic and the early empire, the mediæval monks, the children of the Renaissance, the brilliant society of Louis Quatorze. A Greek play, a Horatian ode, a passage of torrential eloquence from Massillon, an exquisite paragraph from the prose of Bossuet—all alike ministered to that Sybaritism of the mind. They were his refuge in times of detachment from the pressure of contemporary horrors which he felt with such keenness. No doubt there are higher and nobler occupations than that of viewing as a detached spectator the successive failures of mankind as the great human enigma has been met by thinker after thinker anew. But to a man without the common consolations, who would deny a consolation so pure, so disinterested, enriching him and impoverishing no one else?

There is a social value, too, in this occupation of the detached thinker—a value which has seldom been so clearly put as in that tactful response which Anatole France made to a Socialist deputation pressing him once more to become a political candidate.[39] In declining the honour, he made it plain that he did so with no contemptuous thought of the political life as unworthy of him. For reformers fighting nightly in the conflicts of the Chamber he expressed profound admiration. Their talent, of which he felt himself wholly destitute, was his perpetual wonder. Some of them, he said, such as Guesde, were heroic champions of the poor against aristocrats and *bourgeoisie* alike. Others, such as

[39] Recorded by M. Gsell, *Opinions of Anatole France,* chap. xv.

Jaurès, had the still harder task of conciliating the social extremes, standing like a mediator in a violent industrial strike, "target for both the bullets of the police and the paving-stones of the mob." All honour to the strenuous politician, the man of affairs, the law-maker. In comparison with him, the speculative dreamer seemed impotent.

And yet, Anatole France reflected, there was a sense in which the speculative dreamer was indispensable to the man of action. Before a law could be formulated with any hope of success, the conduct it prescribed must have become established usage, for laws which attempted anything more than a sanction of custom must be for ever ineffective. And by whom, pray, were customs formed? In a sense by everybody, but very especially by "the dreamer." In the field of scientific progress, it was some frail bespectacled denizen of a laboratory who was found always to have changed the world. It was such as Copernicus and Darwin who had made it impossible for life any longer to be directed as it was directed in the Middle Ages. It was in the minds of the poets that the moral unity of a country was born, for it was they who both divined and formulated that common principle hidden under diversities of race and circumstance. In their retirement these recluses were forging the material which the leaders of action would have to use. And let their function, unnoticed though it was by the noisy herd, be appreciated as no mere self-centred amusement. "I do not know whether the men who *cut and polish ideas* have more merit than other mortals. At least, when they play their part well, they are entitled to some gratitude." [40]

[40] *loc. cit.*

V

Such are a few of the more profound and central qualities which one can discern in the private life of Anatole France. But perhaps it is worth while to notice qualities which we have no reason to believe thus central or profound, qualities which many a reader may find it hard to reconcile with the outline of the picture as it has so far been drawn. Every life is mixed, and that of Anatole France was perhaps more mixed than most others. The memoirists have been at our service to supply the fringe as well as the main texture of the fabric.

They have revealed him in a hundred situations where he was off his guard. He was a journalist, as we know, of rare power. But the story of his writing for the daily or weekly press has some quaint chapters. We watch him, for example, as a messenger calls at the Villa Saïd for his "copy", and when he seizes pen and scissors to extract and recombine from the current French newspapers what will pass muster—when enlivened by his own comments—for a specially contributed article in the *Neue Freie Presse* of Vienna. "We cut out the most striking paragraphs from the papers, and gut the leaders. 'What's the use of changing anything?' remarks Anatole France: 'it will only be spoiled in the translation.' "[41] But for such work he was to get eight hundred francs per article! No wonder he had a poor opinion of this fluent journalism of our time. As a rule he wrote with painful slowness, though on one memorable occasion his pen "simply ran over the paper", and the editorial office raised his salary for exhibition of a facile fire previously unsuspected. The truth was, as he afterwards confided to M. Brousson, that he had been dining well on the day be-

[41] *Anatole France en Pantoufles,* p. 320.

fore the article was due. Whatever new qualities his style revealed were just the result of intoxication! Here and there he lets us into the secrets of journalistic finesse. His correspondence with editors and publishers included, for example, a communication from Mr. Gordon Bennett to the effect that the *New York Herald* took pleasure in enclosing a cheque for his last manuscript, but unfortunately could not make use of it, because the American public would be annoyed by its disrespectful picture of St. Paul! [42]

Particularly interesting are the walks which these writers of memoirs invite us to take in his company. We go with him on his habitual saunter through the Paris streets in the twilight. The note of melancholy is often in his talk. His eye is caught, for instance, by the sight of a corpse washed up on a bank of the Seine, and he moralizes on those mocking comments by onlookers, so different from that reverential tone which the same people would adopt towards death when hallowed with the trappings of a funereal pomp. The cemetery had indeed always a certain attraction for him on his rambles. Sometimes it stirred him to reflect gravely and sadly: *Sunt lacrimae rerum, et mentem mortalia tangunt.* Sometimes, as in the churchyards of old Italian towns, where too much eloquence has found its way to the tombstone, he would conjecture that a widow's memorial to her departed spouse had been meant to serve also as a marriage advertisement.[43] We accompany him in his lighter mood on a tour of the bric-à-brac shops, and among the dealers in antiques —hear him bargaining for a curio, perhaps for its own sake, perhaps with keen eye to profit on a re-sale, ridiculing some "faked" reproduction, or bursting into raptures of delight over a genuine Venus or a real Tanagra vase. Not purely

[42] *ibid.*, pp. 219, 220.

[43] Sándor Kémeri: *Rambles with Anatole France,* chap. x.

or exclusively an artist was our Anatole France. He knew how to turn to advantage his exceptional skill in detecting the things of high saleable value to the collectors of two continents. Whether he had the same sensitiveness about profiteering in works of art as about other forms of profiteering, one sees some reason to doubt. For himself, at all events, he visited those musty stores that he might buy in the cheapest market to sell again in the dearest. And he knew well those Paris dealers in the antique who, like their London brethren described by Dickens, would take no pleasure in selling a thing if it was just what they represented it to be. *Caveat emptor.*[44]

No account of his private life can omit reference to his housekeeper, the "grim janitress" Joséphine. All who knew him are rich in anecdotes of this commanding personality, both in the home in Paris and in the country house in Touraine. Thinking, with considerable evidence, that except when at his desk he needed more than the shepherding of a child, Joséphine does her utmost with her wayward charge. She has to make certain that he has not forgotten to eat his breakfast, that he has at least taken the trouble to change into reputable attire before going to a fashionable luncheon, that he has some money in his pocket out of doors, his keys, his handkerchief—above all, his spectacles—and to endure even the savage retort that in her upbraiding she treats him as badly as she treats her mother tongue. With all her efforts, she cannot prevent him from being late for his appointments, from arriving to keep a dinner engagement only in time to find his host and his fellow-guests at dessert or sipping liqueur, and with no more substantial apology than that he had been distracted *en route* by the lure of a bookstall or a curio shop. But Joséphine just taps her fore-

[44] Cf. *David Copperfield,* chap. xxiii.

head significantly, to indicate to visitors how uncertain a guide for the movement of his limbs is the organ that resides in her master's skull. "A fine master, indeed", she exclaims, when driven past endurance: "if I were not here, he wouldn't be capable of so much as changing his pants." [45]

His domestic relations do not appear to have been very winsome. Anatole France was quite frank about his parents, from whom, he said, he had inherited an almost superstitious reverence for the aristocracy. But he was sure that the current tale about a bishop among the Thibaults of the past must be a myth, because if such distinguished kinship had existed, its obligations would beyond doubt have been impressed upon him from the first. Such merits as he had he traced to his mother, and of her he spoke in old age with an affection that had never waned. To his father's account he debited his faults. Even his mother did not quite escape his criticism, for the ardour of her tenderness had "literally poisoned" his life. Till he was thirty-five years old, she never went to bed at night before she had seen him come home: "Whether it was midnight or four in the morning, I would find her, candlestick in hand, waiting in implacable silence." There is an occasional ring of Ibsen or Mr. Bernard Shaw about some of our novelist's comments on those whom even the most satirically-minded son is wont to spare.

Nor did he shine in the conjugal relation. Anatole France's first marriage was unhappy, and he had his career of adventure in the Divorce Court. This is perhaps not unusual for literary men, and to Frenchmen it seems so common that any reference to it may call for Auguste Comte's phrase about *hypocrisie anglicane*. But perhaps even French men of letters, once they are freed from the inconvenient bond, do not often speak of a tie so easily dissolved as having

[45] *Anatole France en Pantoufles*, p. 12.

given them their "first real conception of hell." [46] In what light the divorced Madame France looked back upon the experience, I have no available reference to show. But the precautions our novelist took, long after his divorce, to make sure that his early spouse might not benefit in any respect from his decease indicate that the feud was never even nominally composed. There was one child of this unfortunate alliance, a daughter who became the wife of Ernest Renan's grandson. Her husband fell in the Great War, and the young widow died not long afterwards, leaving an only child who went to live with his maternal grandfather. Visitors to La Bechellerie say that for this boy the most tender affection was shown by Anatole France. And with his second wife, though it is clear that she had good ground for the jealousy of which her husband used to complain, there was never any open breach of that matrimonial understanding which, in the Parisian mind, is accounted normal.

* * *

He had to face the usual penalties of a writer who has become "lionized":—the photographer camping outside his hall-door for the chance of a snapshot, an endless stream of curious tourists, newspaper interviewers, ladies with a volume open at the fly-leaf and a stylographic pencil all in readiness that he might "write something witty" for them to treasure. His recorded wit on such occasions had many a subtle innuendo which escaped deletion only because its point was not realized. Less intelligible or excusable, perhaps, was the habitual fulsomeness of the compliments he would pay, to those he had never seen before and hoped he might never see again. Unlike most men of genius, but recalling a few cases such as Alexander Pope and Immanuel

[46] *ibid.*, p. 294.

Kant, he was rather vain of his personal appearance. One is amused to hear how he loved to have his portrait painted as often as possible, and how he would take endless pains to select the particular skull-cap that would suit the artist's colour-scheme! But he met bores with a resourceful ingenuity, and by methods which were at least effective for the safeguarding of his time. Authors innumerable used to send him their works, with a plea for a criticism, an appreciation, an autograph. They must now feel a wholesome chagrin at M. Brousson's account of that huge bathtub into which such parcels were indiscriminately emptied, to await the next visit of the second-hand bookseller who was under contract to buy them at "fifty francs a bathful." The vast pile of his correspondence, one hears, was habitually thrown into the fire unread. An occasional caller, who was in urgent need of a small loan, might be dismissed with a hundred-franc note, and a warning—shouted over the banister to Joséphine—not to admit him again because he had "a genius for 'touching.'" That inevitable crowd, with evangelical solicitude about the state of his soul, was treated in general with more leniency than one might have thought probable.

And, with all his fame, he had his reminder of the fickleness of public admiration. Within his own household, he once just managed to prevent a precious manuscript from being turned into jam-covers. And he resolved to refuse all further requests for his autograph on that painful afternoon when he found a copy of his *Thaïs*, first edition and duly autographed, but with most of the pages uncut, among the cookery books on the one-franc stall of a second-hand dealer.[47]

It is indeed a most diverting portrait that might be drawn from those materials which many memoirists have brought together. The eccentricities of genius are there in profusion,

[47] *ibid.*, p. 112.

and it is safe to assume that these *trivialia* about such a man will be acceptable to countless admirers. It was well known that medical students of Byron's day used to practise at the looking-glass in order to catch the Byronic scowl. Let us hope that Anatole France's inveterate habit of street-lounging will not provoke the same class to idleness, and that his constant chewing of candy will not be imitated with grave harm to their digestion. Among his hobbies, perhaps the oddest was that of attending a spiritualistic séance, but with what expectation it is hard to guess, for this hardened unbeliever used to report with apparent seriousness that he had never been convinced of a single abnormal "rapping"!

* * *

It was inevitable that a writer of such renown should be invited to undertake a transatlantic lecturing tour. What is really surprising is that Anatole France should have consented. But he was fond of travel abroad, though not fond of lecturing, and by some curious chance he found himself booked for such a trip in Brazil and the Argentine, where he spent the summer months of 1909. He undertook to speak on Rabelais. How poorly the promoters of the course had made their selection either of lecturer or of subject, became apparent as the series proceeded. Even his biographer is forced to admit that it was "but a qualified success."

Few subjects, indeed, could have been more congenial to Anatole France's taste, and there were few on which he had acquired more extensive information. In a corridor of his villa stood two models confronting each other, one of the statue of Joan of Arc, the other of the statue of Rabelais, and it was the second which appealed to him more. The priest of Meudon, he used to say, supplied the mirth which was a needful antidote to that "mystic, poisonous stuff" about the Maid of Orleans. His album, with elaborate paintings of Rabelais, his friends, and the places where he lived, was a treasure which Anatole France would clasp in his arms "like a beloved child." At one stage in the writing of the *Vie de Jeanne d'Arc* the author had almost resolved to give it up and "do a Rabelais instead." He naturally thought of himself as related to the life of his time after a manner not very different from the relation of the satirist of *Pantagruel* to the Middle Ages on which he could look back.

But the elusive wit which might trace so vividly such congruities for a French audience was not adapted to either the taste or the insight of an audience in Brazil or the Argentine. It was too recondite. It assumed a quickness of thought and a delicacy of appreciation which the hearers lacked. They were bored, as not a few—who are careful to disguise their impatience—are bored with a novel by George Meredith or a play by Mr. Bernard Shaw. And on the platform the lecturer had "no popular gifts." He read closely from manuscript. If he stopped to improvise, he was so fastidious in choice of just the right word that he began to stammer.[48] And his nasal intonation was far from pleasing. So Anatole France must be added to the growing list of those distinguished men from Europe who have crossed the Atlantic to meet eager audiences, but have left the audiences wondering what Europe saw in them to glorify. Mr. Shaw has not run the risk of such an experiment. Perhaps Dean Inge is just now best qualified to write an explanatory comment on the South American tour of Anatole France.

[48] I observe that this estimate is corroborated by a recent volume of memoirs. Mlle. Laprevotte assured M. Le Goff that his chief horror was that of addressing a popular audience. "He feels that his harmonious sentences are not suitable to a public that does not appreciate their beauty." (*Anatole France at Home*, chap. vii.)

VI

The very latest volumes of memoirs do not indeed add much to what we previously knew of him, though they furnish many a fresh example of the qualities so long familiar. It is interesting, however, to learn from M. Corday that even after he had completed *La Vie en Fleur* the aged novelist had still various literary projects in view, and that memoranda for future books have been found in his desk. These tentative drafts have been brought together and edited. From their contents one cannot regret that they were never finished.

They deal with such matters as metaphysics, old age, the promise of mankind's future,—and, of course, we have to hear again what he thought on the topic which always haunted him to little profit and less edification, the topic of "sex-modesty." Metaphysics, about which he plainly knew nothing at all, is burlesqued in a few paragraphs of the sort in which the ignorant delight. It is assumed to be a pseudo-inquiry, fostered by the theologians for the purpose of escaping the outcome of science by finding or inventing sources of knowledge which science cannot touch. Perhaps such a view is intelligible in one whose mind never developed on this subject since that period of his childhood in which the dominant Parisian philosopher was Victor Cousin. That had been a time in which the dissection of *Le vrai, le beau, le bon* attracted such multitudes of the devout as had never thronged a philosophical *conférence* since the great days of Abelard. But to confuse the Paris of Victor Cousin with the Paris of Bergson, Boutroux, Renouvier, Émile Durkheim, was odd indeed. Some of our English-speaking philosophers, too, will learn with intense amusement that their speculations are just suborned propaganda for a piety to which they have so far shown such scant respect. One recalls how George III hated "poets, atheists and metaphysicians", without—as Macaulay has remarked—drawing any fine distinction among the members of so miscellaneous a group.

Of deeper suggestiveness is the effort made by admiring friends to supplement and correct M. Brousson's picture of the Francian attitude to social morals. They write in an indignant mood, which does credit not only to their personal loyalty but to their good taste. One welcomes the assurance, so authoritatively given, that M. Brousson's portrayal erred by setting at the focus what was at most in the periphery, and that far too much emphasis was there laid on the darker aberrations of a fine character. But for this one feels it necessary to accept the later memoirists' assurance, rather than to learn from the revised picture which they have drawn. It cannot be said that this part of either M. Corday's or M. Ségur's work will alter in any material respect the impression left by *Anatole France en Pantoufles.*

On the contrary, they confirm that impression at many points. The hero in M. Ségur's book is met in very varied surroundings,—rambling through the stately alleys and historic apartments of Versailles, the centre of interest in a fashionable salon of the Avenue Hoche, at a "radical banquet" in a town of Brittany, or climbing the slope of the Athenian acropolis. But wherever he is, he talks exactly like the Anatole France of M. Brousson. In Versailles he is roused to reflective memory of Louis XIV, the glitter and hollowness of the *Grand Siècle,* the transformation effected by Rousseau and the Romanticists—deeper far than all that was done by Mirabeau or Robespierre—and that wonderful seventeenth century which, with all its faults, he honoured as the golden age alike of the manners and of the literature of France. In Brittany he talks, of course, about Renan, and derides once again that pathetic fancy which clung even to *le plus sage des hommes*—the faith in science as a deliverer of mankind, while science was in truth "but part of the Great Illusion." In the soirées of the Avenue Hoche his favourite subject is the ignoble character of virginity. To a group of ladies he expounds his familiar thesis about the origin of sexual taboo in a superstition which has now been outgrown, dwells in his sprightly style upon the religious value of the harlot as a lure to those sins of the flesh without which there would be no place for repentance, sets forth the promise of that coming time when priestly vetos will have ceased to impede the freedom of Nature, and lights up his discourse with many a lascivious anecdote—heard, it seems, by those Parisian ladies of to-day in a mood like that of the company in the *Decameron* or at the court of Queen Marguerite of Navarre. On the slope of the Athenian acropolis his musings are naturally of St. Paul, of the quick-witted audience which separated so fast when the Resurrection was named, of the ironic courtesy which promised to hear the apostle further at some subsequent time, and of those wise and gracious divinities of Greece for whom, alas, the missionary of the Gentiles managed to substitute "the ancient Iahweh and the young sad-faced Adonis of Palestine." [49] As Anatole France once said of a passage in a novel by Zola: *Il n'y a pas besoin d'être catholique ni chrétien pour sentir l'inconvenance de ce procédé.*[50]

The austere moral critic will perhaps dismiss very abruptly indeed a character marked by traits of which these are a sample. Throughout the foregoing pages they have been neither minimized nor extenuated, but treated as definite

[49] N. Ségur: *Conversations avec Anatole France,* chap. ii.
[50] *La Vie Littéraire,* I, p. 233.

blemishes upon a career otherwise admirable and at times heroic. In the jocosity of some Francian devotees they have indeed been singled out as points of special distinction, tokens of a straightforwardness which compares very favourably with British or American conventionalism. No attempt will here be made to argue with those who judge so, for British and American conventionalism in such matters can dispense with either argument or apology. But a plea may fitly be urged against that wholesale condemnation of Anatole France which certain stern moralists have ventured, upon this ground alone.

In the complex web of character many a strand may appear for which logic can discover no place. But the psychologists know well what the logicians refuse to understand, —that human nature cannot be reduced to a single formula, and that a man is not necessarily a hypocrite because strange eruptions from "the subconscious" defile the current of his will at its best. One should not lightly disparage, on the basis of an infirmity which may have been in great measure physical, a character which gave such notable proof of some of the highest human virtues,—passionate love of truth so far as truth was seen, courage that never faltered in the service of a noble but unpopular cause, intense sympathy with those to whom fate and circumstance had been harsh, a hatred at all times of injustice and cruelty, a compassion that knew no limits of race or class. Anatole France was a man of the best eighteenth century type, born perhaps out of due time, carrying over into the twentieth century the same merits and faults which characterized a Voltaire, a Diderot, a Goethe. If one feels that the special qualities both for good and for evil which the eighteenth century displayed would be anachronisms to-day, it is but fair to remember that they were not anachronisms in Anatole France, for he lived apart from the chief spiritual influences of his time, and the intellectual climate with which his rich imagination surrounded him in his study was the intellectual climate of a century and a half before. If he had not the special virtues of his own Age, he was in remarkable degree free from his Age's more sordid and unlovely faults. What his hand, holding a pen, found to do, he did with his might. And his powers were on so vast a scale that his worst literary exploits strike one by the magnitude of their grossness, while their really exceptional feature is in truth the magnitude of their skill. There is a peculiar risk, and in consequence there should be a peculiar allowance, for men of superlative gifts. Nothing else is quite so perilous as ingenuity when it has missed its direction. So with a charitable mind, of which Anatole France at least set the constant pattern, we may well think of himself. Long ago George Eliot crystallized, in one of her unforgettable paragraphs, the principle by which such criticism should be tempered:

> It is apparently too often a congenial task to write severe words about the transgressions committed by men of genius, especially when the censor has the advantage of being himself a man of no genius, so that those transgressions seem to him quite gratuitous. . . . His indignation is not mitigated by any knowledge of the temptation that lies in transcendent power. . . . We make ourselves over-zealous agents of heaven, and demand that our brother should bring usurious interest for his Five Talents, forgetting that it is less easy to manage five talents than two.

CHAPTER XV

ANATOLE FRANCE AND HIS LITERARY KINSMEN

As though there were a metempsychosis, and the soul of one man passed into another, opinions do find—after several revolutions—men and minds like those that first begat them.

SIR THOMAS BROWNE

Some day, no doubt, an aspirant to the Doctorate at an American university will execute a thesis in which Anatole France's varying opinions on politics and the social order will be exhibited as just successive stages in an exquisite evolution of the spirit. The ground plan for what is sure to be described as "a piece of admirable research" may be sketched by almost anyone, however subtle must be the mind that is competent to carry it out. First, attention will be drawn to the apparent sharpness of conflict among Anatole France's different social doctrines, so that the magnitude of the candidate's undertaking may be duly appreciated by his examiner. Next, there will be a chronological table of the various books, carefully annotated with memoranda of the special public situation in which each was composed. Finally, it will be shown how each separate opinion was but "one facet of the diamond", "a moment in a great symmetrical whole", and how with the comprehensiveness of genius the thought was ever moving through paths, at first sight very devious, to the grand synthetic unity in which all were included. Such Hegelian interpretation, carried out with the laborious ingenuity of a harmonizer of the Gospels, will no doubt merit a Doctor's degree, as claims for such honour are now judged. For Henry Sidgwick's disquieting question still remains neglected,—the question how one is to distinguish those contradictions which may be taken as evidence of error from those other contradictions that are the token of a higher truth.

With due respect for the zeal of these post-graduate investigators, no attempt will here be made to anticipate their detailed results. It is indeed easy to show, as Mr. W. L. George and others have shown, that even the most enthusiastic of Anatole France's political tractates have an occasional note of cynicism, and that even the most cynical of his satires is not wholly free from a tinge of hope. With a measure of success the search has been made for intervening links, by which the transit from assertion to denial of one and the same doctrine may be represented as not altogether abrupt. Assiduous unifiers are welcome to all the encouragement they can extract from the "evidence" so patiently collected. But they must surely have noticed with dismay the passage in *La Vie Littéraire* which proves that Anatole France at least was no friend to their undertaking. Not by this method did he account for his own apparent changefulness.

A vast country, he said, must have diverse climates, and in like manner an expanded mind must have many a contradiction.[1] Travellers in the territory of the Unknown, where no man could pretend to have a reliable chart, were entitled to choose by turn every route strewn with flowers and every path whose leafy elms lent enchantment to the view; for, though it might be necessary to return upon one's tracks, there was none the less a joy in such pleasant ram-

[1] *La Vie Littéraire*, II, Preface.

bling. No man could be infallible, but the inconsistent had a chance of being right sometimes, while the logically coherent might well be always wrong. That was an excellent rule of Lemaître, to reconcile hostile ideas by embracing them all simultaneously, and—having done this—to "send them out for an airing." [2]

These are, perhaps, as Burke would have said,[3] rather similitudes to illustrate and adorn than analogies from which to reason. And at all events they warn us not to look for close reasoning in Anatole France. So long as we think of him as a pictorial mocker of human foibles, it is impossible to deny him a place with the very highest of his own craft. And his craft was far from that of trivial persiflage. When one realizes the vast effectiveness of the mocker in making mankind aware of the absurd and chimerical in its own projects, in exposing what is contradictory in some facile scheme for human improvement, in stinging the dull into alertness or shaming the impostor into silence, one must acknowledge the great social value of what George Meredith has called "the comic spirit."

To recognize this in writers of a time long past is easy enough. It is harder to admit it in writers of one's own time, who must necessarily wound many a favourite prejudice or deride many a pet enterprise of the critic who appraises them. Coleridge once declared that Rabelais was among the deepest as well as the boldest thinkers of his age, and that a treatise might be written in praise of the moral elevation of Gargantua or Panagruel,—a treatise which "would make the Church stare and the conventicle groan, and yet would be truth and nothing but truth." But it is safe to guess

2 *ibid.*, p. 174. Cf. "Le Génie Latin," p. 297: *Nos contradictions ne sont pas ce qu'il y a de moins vrai en nous.*

3 *Letters on a Regicide Peace.*

that a Rabelaisian satire upon the English Reformed Church of a century ago would have been viewed with a quite unfriendly eye by the author of *Aids to Reflection.* French bishops may now revel in *Tartufe* or *Les Précieuses,* without being more tolerant to contemporary satirists than was that Archbishop of Paris who forbade the burial of Molière in consecrated ground. Admiring Norwegians have erected a statue to Henrik Ibsen, outside the theatre from which he was once driven by patriotic resentment, but it is not certain that they would themselves be any less indignant towards an Ibsen of to-day. Englishmen who are most appreciative of the departed Jonathan Swift are often very much irritated by the living Mr. Bernard Shaw.

Those who like to trace the literary affinities will find in Anatole France a great deal to remind them of Voltaire, whose defence of Calas was so like the defence of Dreyfus, whose burlesque of the myths was so suggestive of the corresponding passage in *L'Ile des Pingouins,* and whose *Candide* may have given many a hint for *La Rôtisserie.* But another influence is far closer. Always and everywhere one is reminded of the acknowledged idol of our author's youth, the venerable savant who welcomed all opinions and reverenced none, with the words *vous avez raison, Monsieur,* ever upon his lips, while an ironic gleam shone in his eye, and a glow of dialectic festivity spread over his features. Ernest Renan was not only the pattern for Sylvestre Bonnard, but in a very real sense for Bonnard's creator.

The same likeness appears in Paul Vence of *Le Lys Rouge.* No one who recalls the *Dialogues Philosophiques* can miss the family resemblance with *Le Livre de Mon Ami.* The portrait of Gallio in *L'Étui de Nacre* has not only the authentic touch of Renan's pencil, but even reproduces Renan's historical mistake about a relation between Gallio and Seneca. Examples can be multiplied almost at will, and one is not surprised that Anatole France should have spoken of his literary chief as *le plus sage des hommes.*

If we are in search less of a teacher whom he consciously followed than of a temperament to which his own was unconsciously akin, perhaps a different name will occur to us. We may think of that calm, reflective, half-tolerant and half-cynical *grand seigneur*, who three hundred and fifty years ago retired from the world's bustle, to spend "under the care of the learned maidens" whatever span of life might yet be allotted to him. As we read *Le Jardin d'Epicure*, that pensive figure seems to shine through the page; and though the words are the words of Anatole France, it is the very spirit of Montaigne that seems to speak. There is the same *amor fati*, the same studied quiet amid mankind's strife, the same gentle irony towards idealists, the same doubt whether anything can be much altered. We almost see again the placid critic of all human concerns, heedless alike of the bloodshed in a St. Bartholomew massacre and the cannonading of a Spanish Armada, shut up in the tower of his château with the three bay windows which every tourist knows so well, that he might amass more and more illustrations of the "wonderful, vain, diverse and wavering subjects" presented to scrutiny in the life of our race, that he might browse with equal interest among the treasures of literature both sacred and pagan, and that he might amuse his later years by covering beam and rafter with the inscriptions which stirred his fancy: the aphoristic wit of Martial, the fierce denials of Lucretius, the glowing poetry of the Psalms, the elegant lyrics of Horace, and the doleful vaticination of Ecclesiastes. Anatole France was, in many ways, the Montaigne of our time. We are tempted to say of him, as Andrew Lang said of Montaigne, that he is a man's writer, not a woman's—a tired man's, not a fresh man's. "We all come to him late indeed, but at last, and rest in his panelled library."

It is one of the shrewder among many interesting suggestions that we should look to the ancient world for his closest analogue. If we must choose among the Greeks he loved so well, by far the nearest to him in spirit was Lucian of Samosata. A reincarnationist might plausibly enough contend that it was Anatole France in an earlier embodiment who wrote *Dialogues of the Dead* or *Hermotimus*, or *The Auction of Lives*. The zealot in *Thaïs* might stand as a later Peregrinus. Those satires were among the gems of ancient literature that Anatole France knew best, and he has even imitated their form in some pieces of his own.[4]

With what a chuckle must he have read of the sale of philosophers, in which one great system-builder after another brought a poor price, but the Cynic missionary of Lucian's own time went lowest of all! And how fervently would he have added his Amen to the decision that the one thinker worth ferrying across the Styx was he who, amid all his speculative illusions, had not lost the gift of mocking laughter![5] He would join in imagination with that company in the *Charon* which climbed a high Thessalian peak to watch the comedy of men struggling below, in the vain rivalries of earth, for prizes that turned to dust in their hands. He must have reflected, with that sardonic crowd, upon the folly of those who think they are hewing their own way to fame, whilst from the vantage-ground of the peak could be seen the tireless Fates spinning for each his predetermined thread of Destiny.[6] And he must have felt how true was that picture

[4] e. g., *In the Elysian Fields*, or *New Dialogues of the Dead.*

[5] *Vit. Auct*, II; *Traj*, 24; *Dial. Mort.*, x. 9.

[6] *Charon*, 17.

of Hermotimus—grown old in the philosophic quest after a mirage—to whom at the end it seemed that hardly a step had been taken towards the goal, and yet for whom it was some satisfaction to have looked in compassionate scorn upon men still so eager in their futile dreams.[7] It is the very temperament of Anatole France, revealing—exactly after his own mind—how in satire, as in all else, there is nothing new under the sun.

But it was Roman poets rather than Greek satirists that he loved to quote, and among these, though he quotes him but seldom, it is the spirit of Lucretius that he most frequently recalls. The whole tenor of Anatole France's popular addresses might well have been taken, point for point, from *De Rerum Natura*. Man's wretchedness as arising from slavish attachment to imaginary deities whose favour he must solicit or whose wrath he must placate, the childish alarm about a world to come, the hideous barbarities perpetrated by men upon one another under the fancied direction of supernatural powers, the emancipation to be sought in a true cosmic doctrine of the universe as purely mechanical, the tranquillity which would be the reward of those who knew their present lot as what it is and could look forward to the peace of the great Sleep: herein is the Francian no less than the Lucretian gospel.

Like Lucretius, too, he was apparently interested in the science of his time by no means for its own sake, but chiefly as an instrument to undermine "superstition." For psychology, for social philosophy, for the work of a Bergson, a Taine, a Gabriel Tarde, in later life at least he cared nothing at all. Sometimes indeed he would speak of making the French workman to participate in the growing intellectual

[7] *Hermotimus*, c. 5.

riches of the world. But more frequently it was for a very special and ulterior purpose that this extending of higher education was urged. One would gather from many an address by Anatole France that his own desire in educating the *ouvrier* was to spread contempt for the priesthood, hatred of the capitalist, and revolt against the government. Such he held to be the necessary and most desirable result of acquainting the masses with astronomy, with history, with economics. But for himself there was little inspiration in the motto *Felix qui potuit rerum cognoscere causas.* He was too firmly convinced that the real causes are for ever beyond man's ken, and he often reiterated his belief that their discovery—fortunately impossible—would destroy the last chance that man could any longer find it tolerable to live. Echoing the fine scorn of Euripides, he declared the laborious and enthusiastic investigator to be merely substituting the dream of the learned for the dream of the vulgar. "What", he exclaimed, "is it that Professor So-and-so sees at the bottom of his microscope? Appearances. Nothing but appearances." [8] Whether Euripides would have been equally scornful if he had lived in the later nineteenth century, one may doubt. And one remembers with a shock of surprise just who it was that Anatole France must have had in mind when he spoke of the futile manipulator of a microscope.

There is a tale, doubtless mythical, but at least *ben trovato.* He had risen from his desk, after completing another mordant article in the Lucretian vein, in which he showed once more how men who have been face to face with Nature's more intricate secrets in a laboratory are freed for all time from the domination of a religious creed: *Tantum religio potuit suadere malorum.*[9] In the grey dusk of the evening,

[8] *Le Livre de Mon Ami,* p. 206.

[9] Cf. *De Rerum Natura,* I, v. 101.

as he strolled along the Quai Voltaire after this ringing blow against the superstitious, he collided with a short stout man apparently in haste on an errand. It was Louis Pasteur on his way to his Easter confession! Anatole France's reflections on the occurrence are not recorded.

II

His place is thus with the great pagans, but particularly with those pagans who wrote and spoke in his own language. The spirit of *insouciance*, showing itself in a certain lightness, a certain grace, a certain *clarté*, is very French, and among the French it is found most of all in Paris. In common usage *Parisianisme* means such a combination of qualities, which it is easier to recognize than to name. They are recognizable most plainly in those two special products of the French genius, unequalled and almost unchallenged by any other national literature: the *pensée* and the *conte*. And as a master of each, Anatole France was supreme in his time.

Who, for example, in contemporary writing has shown in like degree that "dexterous precision of the pointed phrase" [10] in which the art of La Rochefoucauld was so nearly unique? A reader of our generation, unacquainted with the celebrated *Maximes*, might well guess that Anatole France must have coined the aphorism: *nous avons tous assez de force pour supporter les maux d'autrui.* It might easily have been Coignard who said, *Le refus de la louange est un désir d'être loué deux fois.* The *Pensées de Riquet* might be mistaken for a fragment of La Bruyère,—with its satire so reminiscent of Swift, and yet relieved from gloom by just that human sympathy which makes all the difference

[10] G. L. Strachey: *Landmarks of French Literature*, p. 22.

between the *Caractères* and the *Tale of a Tub*. Or one thinks of the *Pensées* of Pascal. But in truth such analogies are without assignable limit.

Like Alphonse Daudet, too, whom he admired so much, Anatole France displayed his peculiar talent in the *conte* rather than in the *roman*. The small but perfect literary product was his special masterpiece. Someone has said that his power in that sort of writing should have made him practise no other, and there is perhaps point in the retort that in truth he never did write otherwise, except in the *Vie de Jeanne d'Arc*, the only book in which he proved himself capable of uninteresting work. For in none of his novels did he even attempt a coherent plot. No character of his fashioning is ever slowly unfolded to us through adventure, or through developing circumstance. The successive incidents seldom seem to rise each out of what went before. When he speaks of using the scissors on his proofsheets, rearranging sentences and paragraphs, putting last what he had written first, one feels that such flexibility might refer not only to the sentences and paragraphs but to whole chapters. And this, of course, means that there is no plot worthy of the name.

Yet the reader's attention is riveted—riveted, as Aristotle would have said, by ἦθος, not by μῦθος. Anatole France had a poor opinion of the drama,[11] and has said some very unconvincing things about its inferiority to other forms of literature. It is indeed plain that his own genius was anything but dramatic. *Crainquebille* in its stage presentation is corroborative evidence that he could never have written a good play. But he had that power which Mr. Belloc so admires in Carlyle's picture of the French Revolution, where as by a lightning flash is revealed some crisis in that

[11] P. Gsell: *Opinions of Anatole France*, p. 153, sq.

momentous drama "standing still." It is not a situation of events, it is rather an individual character which Anatole France thus lights up and reveals. Nor does he ever spoil the effect by labouring it. He left to the Romantics that rhetorical heightening and intensifying by which the effect was really lowered or reduced. What he gives us is indeed a "flash", but one whose revelation is unforgettable. He had a matchless gift for suggesting far more than he said. And what he says is often less suggestive than what he so obviously and conspicuously refrains from saying. In a few deft strokes he sketches the background for a conversation, or even just a soliloquy, narrates it, stops at exactly the right moment to leave the reader wondering, and the rest is filled in by the reader's own haunting reflections. It is like an iridescent stone, showing many colours as it is differently held and viewed. That this secret of his art was well known to the artist is clear from the title he gave to one of his books: *Mother of Pearl.*

Thus chapter after chapter, whose sequence might with equal propriety have been reversed, suffers no loss by lack of plot. Each is by itself a sort of independent *conte.* In an interesting passage of critical analysis, Anatole France has pointed out that the short story calls for a finer skill than the extended novel. Upon the work of Victor Hugo, so vast, so diffuse, so ungainly, he looked with something of the disgust of a Greek soldier for the undisciplined bulk of an Oriental host. He thought it an untrimmed thing, raw, crude, mechanical. All that was in it could have been put so much more briefly, and in consequence more artistically. Just as, other things being equal, the short sentence was best, so—he said—was the short story, and the imaginative writer should be the last to give too copious help to a reader's imagination. The *conte,* "suffices for every need", and a well-turned tale was a feast for connoisseurs,—the very elixir, the quintessence, the precious ointment of fiction.

For the literature of his day Anatole France was a reviver of antique form, the herald of another Renaissance. Not less genuinely than the Italian artists and scholars of four hundred years before, did he seek to bring back to his countrymen the savour of ancient thought. Back from *la sombre époque chrétienne* to *le parfum de la belle antiquité*! One notices this first in the reappearance of Græco-Roman moods, so near to those of an Epicurean philosopher in the Rome of the early Caesars—speculative, fatalistic, half jocund and half melancholy, viewing the cults and dogmas and institutions of the past in a temper of amused detachment. But one notices it too in the powerful and sustained influence which Anatole France exerted over a field far more his own than the field of thought. What keeps most of his speculative work alive is the medium of style in which it was conveyed, for it is not seldom the beauty of the setting which alone suggests that it holds a diamond. Not all indeed of his fellow-workmen of classic times would have approved this paramount place which he gave to form. It was one of the many wise warnings of Plutarch that, like guests at a banquet whose appetite must be allayed before they can notice the exquisite finish of the plates, the reader should have his mind well satisfied with ideas before he can consider the elegance of their exposition.[12] But by reason of this literary charm one may be certain that a great part of Anatole France's work will endure. There are indifferent pictures that are bought for the sake of their exquisite frames; but the picture can be taken out of the frame, while style cannot be separated from content. And it was on classical models

[12] Plutarch, *De rect. rat. aud.*

that our author shaped his diction. With Renan, he thought constantly of that "*chef-d'œuvre* of the Latin genius"—the French language, which he loved so well and perfected with such tireless solicitude.

He was indeed as acutely conscious as even the most fervid Romantic of the abyss into which the copying of ancient patterns had fallen when the pseudo-classicists of half a century before had tried to copy what they could only burlesque. No one could have despised more heartily that slavish following of "rules", that limiting of the poet to the use of such words as were traditionally certified to be *noble* rather than *bas*,—in short, that imposition of an artistic orthodoxy, both in verse and in prose, which made the French plays of a hundred years ago so ludicrous an episode in the progress of a great literature. What exasperated him most of all was the thought that herein was supposed to be "classical" taste; for, as Oscar Wilde would have said, he had "handled Greek things",[13] and he knew them. He felt about the Romanticism out of which in his youth his countrymen had just escaped, and about the Realism into which they were drifting, that here was a grim nemesis for such stupid mistakes about antiquity. And he would himself recall those ways of antiquity as they had indeed been. He would do for prose what André Chénier had done in his too short life for verse, showing how the paragraph no less than the *églogue* may be perfected with the perfection of a Greek vase or of a Roman inscription of the Golden Age. Such unsurpassable pieces as those in the collection entitled *Clio* are our evidence that he could do it.

III

It is more difficult to judge how much of lasting value will

[13] O. Wilde: *De Profundis.*

be found in Anatole France's work as a mirror of the times in which he lived. He once said that for those who would understand the transition from the old *régime* to the new, Balzac has done more in *La Comédie Humaine* than all the systematic historians combined. And he had the sceptic's usual distrust of history. He felt, with M. Louis Bordeau, that the recital of past events always implies a capricious selecting of what is "important", and that different men—often so much in the dark about the relative importance of events in their own day—must be very discordant judges of the perspective of the past. Anatole France would surely have welcomed that recent warning by Signor Benedetto Croce [14] that even the most sincere historian is thus an unintentional distorter of the events he tries to narrate, and that there is point in the sixteenth century inscription still to be read on an old byway in Naples, praying God to deliver us from "the lies of honest men." On this ground he turned often for the real sources of knowledge about the past to the surviving folklore, traditions, songs and ballads of old France. The works of the historians were not, he thought, wholly discredited by being likened to the stories of Mother Goose. For those stories were at least a reflection of the real mood of their composers. And though perhaps in the future the only "historical" documents would be statistical tables, there was room for doubt about them too. Caprice could enter into a Blue Book. "It is not only the Muses who lie."

This is a point that has often been urged, for example, by Carlyle in his papers *On History* and *On History Again*, or in his interesting argument that the true key to the progress of any people is to be found in the series of its poets. But that Anatole France's own pictures of French life can ever have an equal significance with those of Balzac is

[14] In *History, Its Theory and Practice,* Translation by D. Ainslie, p. 34.

not to be expected. For Balzac was at least drawing his countrymen as one of themselves, whilst Anatole France was drawing them almost as a cultured pagan of classical antiquity, who had chanced to be born in Paris in 1844, and who viewed the development of affairs in the mood of one whose own soul was in a civilization long vanished or in countries far removed.

He loved, indeed, the scenery, the antiquities, all the storied past of his native land. There are few more picturesque or more moving descriptions of rural France than are to be read in the third part of *Pierre Nozière*. The writer knew those nooks and corners of Valois, of Brittany, of Touraine, as Mr. Thomas Hardy knows his Wessex, and he loved those spots not just for the smiling verdure of the fields or the thrill of a rockbound coast, but for all the memories they brought back. He thought of the towers, the steeples, the crenellated battlements, as so many jewels which the sons of France in days gone by had set in her "robe of stone." In the landscape he could discern "the faces of our forefathers." Generation after generation, he exclaimed, had come and gone, but each had left its abiding mark, so that places still radiant with the loveliness of youth were at the same time ancient reliquaries of the French people.

But did he know the French people of his own time—not merely the insurgents of a Paris *université populaire*, the pioneers of Communist printing-presses, the mocking men of letters? Did he know the country population as they could be known by one who was not so remote from their more intimate thoughts and hopes and fears? Did he know even the average Parisian man of business? One feels that this *libre penseur* could not give a quite genuine account of a life he was so far from sharing, and that his satiric pieces will have to be taken with a very large allowance of the proverbial salt before they can be sifted into history. The interpreter was not sympathetic. He knew, for example, the Bretons, but not as Renan knew them. A phrase in the hands of a philologue, he once said, is like a flower in the hands of a botanist. And what of French piety as depicted by Anatole France? It is like the piety of the Attic age as depicted by Euripides. The coming historian will not, one may suppose, take this satirist's word for it that the priests of the closing nineteenth century were mainly impostors, that the business men were mainly profiteers, or that the politicians were mainly sycophants. And the historian's doubt may well, by reaction, go too far. He will perhaps think of not a few of these types in *Histoire Contemporaine* as our author himself thought of the traditional revolutionary types which "had never any existence except in the novels of Marmontel." And if he thinks thus, the coming historian will be wrong. For we, of this generation, know how Anatole France was often describing the actual persons he had seen.

IV

It has become common to speak of his "dilettantism." His literary kinsfolk were indeed no "men of action." From long experience of their kind, the world does not expect a littérateur to lead in the more strenuous issues of life. As Prothero says in *The Research Magnificent*, intellectuals as a rule are flimsy and uncertain people, not only critical and fastidious, but weak-handed.

Anatole France himself knew full well the defects which must accompany such mental qualities as his. He pointed out, for example, that Benjamin Constant's ideas were both too numerous and too nimble, shaping themselves in the brain not like an army into solid battalions, but rather like dancers in a ballet, whose groups are being continuously composed and recomposed.[15] Our novelist, though often asked to enter political life, would never become a candidate for the Chamber, and indeed it would have been hard to think of him as gesticulating from the Tribune. One remembers how Renan was not equally prudent, and how the electors, on the very eve of the Franco-Prussian War, rejected the greatest literary man in France for another whose name has barely survived. They may have been quite right. The candidate whose name has barely survived had the advantage of a real programme to present—a programme with at least more appeal than the vague pledge of Renan that he would support "Bonapartism liberalized". Something seems to warn the average voter against sending an *érudit* to legislate for him. In a playful mood Anatole France once said that he could never be an effective politician, because in the Chamber it was necessary to vote on one side or the other, while he belonged at heart to the Abbey of Thelema in which there was limitless scope for individuality. To the editor of *Le Temps* he gave this warning: "Never entrust the political article to one of our Thelemites. He would fill it with a gentle melancholy which would discourage your worthy readers." [16] There is indeed many a true word spoken in jest.

Yet he had power as a social and political propagandist. It lay in a certain blend of qualities not often found together, qualities in each of which taken by itself he was surpassed by not a few others, but which in unison were often overwhelming. He was no platform speaker; and when under the stress of public excitement he forced himself to speak in public, those sparkling phrases lost most of their charm as

[15] *La Vie Littéraire,* I, p. 63.

[16] *La Vie Littéraire,* First Series, Preface.

they were read in unimpressive tones from a manuscript. By turns he has been extolled as a man of immense learning, as a subtle and penetrating philosopher, as a pioneer and apostle of social progress. But, judged by really exacting standards, he was none of these things. His erudition, vast as it seemed to the popular mind, was far below that of other men whom one could name, and of whom the popular mind takes no account. To the expert philosopher he appears as constantly dealing in the commonest of philosophic commonplaces, avoiding the real sting of a problem, and making the gay paradox to do duty for reasoned argument. In the sphere of international policy, he had so many and such conflicting views in succession that one could never predict what programme he would urge next from the programme he had urged before.

Wherein, then, lay his strength? It consisted in this, that with remarkable but by no means prodigious learning, he could expound with such lucidity where the *érudit* could but confuse. In the arid debates of the schools he could discern and unfold those issues which, long settled as they might be for the scholar, had a relevance to life which the scholar had never drawn. And underlying all the contradictions of his varying public policy there was a spirit of humane enthusiasm that is so often absent from the apostle of a changeless plan.

It is generally idle to seek for some single phrase in which the characteristic view of any great writer may be expressed, for this does not lend itself—as Dr. P. T. Forsyth said of the secret of the universe—to "compression into a formula which the undergraduate can easily remember." But it is often suggestive to attempt this. One recalls, for example, how it was said of Balzac that he had just one definite moral to impart; the moral, namely, that "the importance of money can never be overestimated." That thought, whatever it may be worth, does seem to persist like a sort of undertone in all the rich and varied music of *La Comédie Humaine*. Is there a like undertone in the work of Anatole France? Those who speak of his dilettantism will at once reply that it is the motto *nil admirari*. But that would be unfair, because it would be so inadequate. Underlying all he has written, and furnishing in a measure the key by which so many discordant utterances may be brought together, is what Mr. May has called "a compassionate idealism by which he is constantly animated and which sounded so peremptorily in his ear." [17] It was as such compassion was successively stirred by very different kinds of social injustice, coming from very different quarters, that he attacked all these in turn. For he could not attack them all at once, and thus was often forced to seem the champion of one cause in which he but partially believed, because he was aiming to destroy another in which his disbelief was complete.

But it is not thus that attacks on any sort of social injustice are in the end most effective. The satirist seldom succeeds as a reformer, and he is likely to fail just in proportion as he is a talented satirist. The enterprise of *universités populaires* is almost extinct, and its great advocate lived to laugh at his own advocacy. The idea of an "international proletariat" passed from his mind like a bad dream. Twenty-two years after the Separation Law from which he expected so much, it is obvious that most of his predictions about it have been falsified. Meanwhile other leaders, with no gift like his—leaders whom he mocked as poor incompetents—have left their mark deep upon the country's destiny. And the mutual recriminations have been at least diverting. When Anatole France declared of M. Paul

[17] J. L. May: *Anatole France, the Man and his Work*, p. 21.

Desjardins that to him fine literature was as the Beast in the *Apocalypse*, and that he thought of a well-turned phrase as a public peril, the answer was quick and pungent. Not less strong in scriptural analogy, M. Desjardins said that if he must find a comparison for Anatole France, it would be with the barren fig-tree of Holy Writ.

V

The opening chapter of Lord Morley's *Voltaire* is entitled "The Ideal Man for the Time." Would such a title be at all appropriate to describe Anatole France?

The time of which Lord Morley spoke was one which required a disturbance of lazy dogmatism, a challenging of tradition, a vigorous polemic against those who would fetter new knowledge under the shackles of the past. Anatole France had a talent like Voltaire's, probably greater in degree, as most readers will judge from comparison of such a book as *Thaïs* with such a book as *Micromegas*. But this gift was not equally seasonable in the middle of the eighteenth century and in the first quarter of the twentieth.

For it is by no means the fault of this Age, as it was the fault of Voltaire's Age, to be uncritical of what has been long established, to be wedded to ancient formulas, to be over-timid about social experiment. It is not what Plato called "the torpedo shock" that is needed particularly in western Europe to-day. Men have rather reached the stage at which contempt for tradition has become the veriest commonplace, a taste for the new as such has been turned into a form of cant which only the more courageous can disregard, and the real innovator upon fashionable conventions of the moment would be he who should emphasize what is worth preserving in the inheritance of what went before.

The "ideal man" for our time is not he who will mock old myths, expose a blundering and muddled morality, inspire an ardent confidence in the individual reason, or sketch the coming triumphs of a wisdom that is well within everyone's grasp. As one reads *Vers les Temps Meilleurs*, it is of Shelley, of Godwin, of the doctrinaire "perfect-ibilians" that one thinks, with a sigh of sadness at the thought that their like should appear again after one hundred years of disillusionment. And the case is not much mended when one recalls how Anatole France in other moods had laughed that creed to scorn.

The men of the future will thus have to think of him, by no means as of one who, like Voltaire, confronted the *Zeitgeist* with a resolute and daring courage. There are too many of the darker features of French literature in his time for which Anatole France was not a critic, but rather a sponsor and a symbol. And with the passing of these, when their ephemeral popularity has gone, much of his work may pass too. One hears many a prediction about the place he will hold in the judgment of "posterity." With much formal acknowledgment that the decision is premature, critics are deciding, in the sure confidence of those who will not be there when posterity may prove them wrong. There are some definite tokens, however, which seem to indicate how he now stands in the esteem of the public, two years after his death. In other countries his fame since 1924 has grown fast, and the efforts of the translator have introduced him to an ever-widening circle of readers on both sides of the Atlantic Ocean. But in his own land he has suffered an unmistakable eclipse. Within twelve months of his death, admirers were complaining that he made so little appeal to the younger generation of Frenchmen. M. Georges Girard, speaking with the authority of a great Paris librarian, has regretted very much *l'indifférence dont on fait preuve actuellement à l'égard d'Anatole France.* It was observed that even on the occasion of his funeral there was a relatively small attendance of literary men, and that the appreciative speeches were made for the most part by politicians. A recent investigation of the books which circulate most widely among young readers revealed the fact that Anatole France is seldom in request at the library counter. As Miss Julia Wedgwood once remarked, there is an effervescence which accompanies the pungent draught of new literature, and, like other kinds of effervescence, it is followed by a flatness.[18]

No doubt he would have felt little disappointment that in these days of *vers libres* he should have little vogue with those youthful poets and poetasters on whom he coined many a biting epigram. He knew that they were having their day, a day very different from his—like the young artist Jeanne Lefuel, of whom he said that her work had a certain grace, but that her metrical defects had shocked him. He added, however, "Those defects would pass unnoticed just now; we live in a different age."[19] The peculiar service which Anatole France rendered to the literature of his country was of the kind which eager and restless youth calls reaction, just as the men of the Revival of Learning must have seemed reactionaries to many a contemner of the pagan past. And it is remembered with some satisfaction by his friends that a period of neglect has commonly followed upon the fame of other great French writers just after their death, but that in the end they came again to their own.

Nothing, however, is less predictable than the fate of

[18] Julia Wedgwood: *Nineteenth Century Teachers,* p. 22.

[19] *La Vie en Fleur,* chap. xxix.

men of letters at the hands of critics yet to come. Anatole France used to point out how doubtful we should be about the verdict of posterity, when we observe that we are ourselves "posterity" in regard to a long procession of the *grands écrivains* of the past. Had we not lost three-quarters of the works of classical antiquity, and allowed the remaining one-quarter to become almost unrecognizably corrupt? Was not Varius reputed in his day to be the equal of Vergil? Yet Varius had perished, while Aelian was a fool, but had managed to survive. Dante and Shakespeare were long held in contempt. Goethe had regarded Ronsard as the greatest of French poets, but the nineteenth century had despised him:

> Far from being infallible, there is every likelihood that posterity may make a mistake. It is ignorant, and it is indifferent. I am gazing this moment at the posterity of Corneille and Voltaire as it passes along the Quai Malaquais. It walks along, cheered by the April sun. It passes, with a veil over its nose or a cigar between its lips, and I can assure you that it cares infinitely little about Voltaire or Corneille.[20]

How much, in days to come, will posterity care for this typical representative of twentieth century *Parisianisme?* That will depend, in great measure, upon the fate of *Parisianisme* itself. For the moment, especially at the place of its birth, that literary *genre* is under a cloud, even as in countries where it is yet novel it can still create a sensation. To a later period it may appear as an idle or a noxious flippancy. But, if one may hazard a guess, its charm will return in a period later still, when reaction against its follies has ceased to make impossible a just estimate of its merits. At least for the historically-minded it can never fail to be

[20] *La Vie Littéraire,* I, pp. 112, 113.

of profound interest as a phase in literary evolution. And even after the ideas or projects he commended have been classed with other products of "long discarded, long superseded looms of human thought", Anatole France must hold an exalted place for those who can appreciate the ingenuities of a fertile imagination or the subtler witchery of words.

BIBLIOGRAPHY OF ANATOLE FRANCE'S CHIEF WORKS

(This list does not profess to be complete. It includes only such books as have been discussed, or at least mentioned, in the foregoing pages, and is added for the convenience of the reader who may wish to know the date of each volume that is cited.)

1876—*Les Noces Corinthiennes*
1879—*Jocaste*
Le Chat Maigre
1881—*Le Crime de Sylvestre Bonnard*
1882—*Les Désirs de Jean Servien*
1885—*Le Livre de Mon Ami*
1888–1892—*La Vie Littéraire* (Four Volumes)
1890—*Balthasar*
Thaïs
1892—*L'Étui de Nacre*
1893—*La Rôtisserie de la Reine Pédauque*
Les Opinions de M. Jérôme Coignard
1894—*Le Lys Rouge*
Le Jardin d'Epicure
1895—*Le Puits de Sainte-Claire*
1897—*Le Mannequin d'Osier*
L'Orme du Mail
1899—*L'Anneau d'Améthyste*
Pierre Nozière
1900—*Clio*
1901—*Monsieur Bergeret à Paris*
1902—*L'Affaire Crainquebille*
Opinions Sociales
1903—*Histoire Comique*
1905—*L'Église et la République*
Sur la Pierre Blanche
1906—*Vers les Temps Meilleurs*
1908—*L'Ile des Pingouins*

1909—*La Vie de Jeanne d'Arc*
Les Contes de Jacques Tournebroche
Les Sept Femmes de Barbe-Bleue
1910—*Aux Étudiants: Discours*
1912—*Les Dieux ont Soif*
1913—*Le Génie Latin*
1914—*La Révolte des Anges*
1915—*Sur la Voie Glorieuse*
1920—*Le Petit Pierre*
1922—*La Vie en Fleur*

INDEX

(For further indication of subjects discussed in preceding pages the the reader is referred to the analytical Table of Contents)